13.10.15

Pure Mathematics 4

CAMBRIDGE Advanced Level Mathematics

Pure Mathematics 4

Hugh Neill and
Douglas Quadling

Series editor Hugh Neill

CAMBRIDGE
UNIVERSITY PRESS

PUBLISHED BY THE PRESS SYNDICATE OF THE UNIVERSITY OF CAMBRIDGE
The Pitt Building, Trumpington Street, Cambridge, United Kingdom

CAMBRIDGE UNIVERSITY PRESS
The Edinburgh Building, Cambridge CB2 2RU, UK
40 West 20th Street, New York, NY 10011-4211, USA
10 Stamford Road, Oakleigh, VIC 3166, Australia
Ruiz de Alarcón 13, 28014 Madrid, Spain
Dock House, The Waterfront, Cape Town 8001, South Africa

http://www.cambridge.org

First published 2001

Printed in the United Kingdom at the University Press, Cambridge

Typefaces Times, Helvetica   *Systems* Microsoft® Word, MathType™

A catalogue record for this book is available from the British Library

ISBN 0 521 78371 2 paperback

Cover image: Images Colour Library

The authors and publisher would like to thank the Nuffield Foundation for providing the
artwork which appears in adapted form on page 30.

Contents

Introduction

Cambridge Advanced Level Mathematics has been written especially for the OCR modular examination. It consists of one book or half-book corresponding to each module. This book is the fourth Pure Mathematics module, P4.

The books are divided into chapters roughly corresponding to syllabus headings. Some sections include work which goes beyond the examination specification. These sections are marked with an asterisk (*) in the section heading.

Occasionally within the text paragraphs appear in *this type style*. These paragraphs are usually outside the main stream of the mathematical argument, but may help to give insight, or suggest extra work or different approaches.

References are made throughout the text to previous work in modules P1, P2 and P3. It is expected that students still have access to these books in the classroom, even if they do not have a copy for their personal use.

Numerical work is presented in a form intended to discourage premature approximation. In ongoing calculations inexact numbers appear in decimal form like 3.456..., signifying that the number is held in a calculator to more places than are given. Numbers are not rounded at this stage; the full display could be either 3.456 123 or 3.456 789. Final answers are then stated with some indication that they are approximate, for example '1.23 correct to 3 significant figures'.

There are plenty of exercises, and each chapter contains a Miscellaneous exercise which includes some questions of examination standard. Some questions which go beyond examination requirements are marked by an asterisk. In the middle and at the end of the book there is a set of Revision exercises and there are two practice examination papers. The authors thank Lawrence Jarrett, the OCR examiner who contributed to these exercises, and also Peter Thomas, who read the book very carefully and made many extremely useful and constructive comments.

The authors thank OCR and Cambridge University Press for their help in producing this book. However, the responsibility for the text, and for any errors, remains with the authors.

1 Rational functions

This chapter takes partial fractions on from P3 Chapter 7. When you have completed it, you should

- be able to put a rational function into partial fractions when one of the factors is a quadratic which does not factorise
- be able to put a rational function into partial fractions when the degree of the numerator is not less than the degree of the denominator.

1.1 Partial fractions

In P3 Chapter 7, you learned how to split rational functions of the forms

$$\frac{ax+b}{(px+q)(rx+s)} \quad \text{and} \quad \frac{ax^2+bx+c}{(px+q)(rx+s)^2}$$

into partial fractions.

Neither of these types includes a form such as $\dfrac{6x}{(x-1)(x^2+2x+3)}$, where the quadratic

factor x^2+2x+3 in the denominator does not factorise.

In this case, you would certainly expect to write

$$\frac{6x}{(x-1)(x^2+2x+3)} \equiv \frac{A}{x-1} + \frac{\text{something}}{x^2+2x+3}.$$

But what is the 'something'? Multiply by $x-1$, and put $x=1$ in the subsequent identity.

$$\frac{6x}{(x^2+2x+3)} \equiv A + \frac{(\text{something})(x-1)}{x^2+2x+3} \quad \text{with } x=1 \text{ gives } A=1.$$

Therefore $\dfrac{6x}{(x-1)(x^2+2x+3)} \equiv \dfrac{1}{x-1} + \dfrac{\text{something}}{x^2+2x+3}.$

You can now find what the 'something' is by subtraction, since

$$\frac{\text{something}}{x^2+2x+3} \equiv \frac{6x}{(x-1)(x^2+2x+3)} - \frac{1}{x-1} \equiv \frac{6x-(x^2+2x+3)}{(x-1)(x^2+2x+3)}$$

$$\equiv \frac{-x^2+4x-3}{(x-1)(x^2+2x+3)} \equiv \frac{-(x-1)(x-3)}{(x-1)(x^2+2x+3)} \equiv \frac{-x+3}{x^2+2x+3}.$$

The 'something' has the form $Bx+C$.

The method shown in this example will be called Method 1, with the change that $Bx+C$ will be used in place of 'something'.

Here are two other methods which you can use.

If you write $\dfrac{6x}{(x-1)(x^2+2x+3)} \equiv \dfrac{A}{x-1} + \dfrac{Bx+C}{x^2+2x+3}$ initially, you can combine the partial fractions to get a numerator which is a quadratic, so you can equate the coefficients of x^0, x^1 and x^2 to get three equations, and solve them for A, B and C. This is Method 2.

Or you can multiply by $x-1$ and put $x=1$ as before to get $A=1$, and then equate coefficients to find B and C. This is Method 3.

The two examples which follow show these three methods of getting the partial fractions. Use whichever method you find easiest.

Method 1 has the advantage that it is self-checking. If the fraction just before the final result does not cancel, you have made a mistake. If it cancels, there is probably no mistake.

Method 2 is in many ways the most straightforward, but involves solving three equations for A, B and C.

Notice that in Method 3 the coefficients of x^2 and x^0 are used to get the values of B and C. This is because they give the simplest equations. You will usually find that the highest and lowest powers give the simplest equations in these situations. However, you should be aware that equating the coefficients of x^0 has the same result as putting $x=0$; you get no extra information.

Example 1.1.1

Split $\dfrac{5x-4}{(x+2)(x^2+3)}$ into partial fractions.

    Method 1   Write $\dfrac{5x-4}{(x+2)(x^2+3)} \equiv \dfrac{A}{x+2} + \dfrac{Bx+C}{x^2+3}$.

    Multiply by $x+2$ to get $\dfrac{5x-4}{(x^2+3)} \equiv A + \dfrac{(Bx+C)(x+2)}{x^2+3}$, and put $x=-2$. Then

$$\frac{5\times(-2)-4}{(-2)^2+3} = A, \text{ so } A = -2.$$

    Then $\dfrac{Bx+C}{x^2+3} \equiv \dfrac{5x-4}{(x+2)(x^2+3)} - \dfrac{-2}{x+2}$

$$\equiv \frac{5x-4-(-2)(x^2+3)}{(x+2)(x^2+3)}$$

$$\equiv \frac{2x^2+5x+2}{(x+2)(x^2+3)} \equiv \frac{(x+2)(2x+1)}{(x+2)(x^2+3)} \equiv \frac{2x+1}{x^2+3}.$$

So $\dfrac{5x-4}{(x+2)(x^2+3)} \equiv \dfrac{-2}{x+2} + \dfrac{2x+1}{x^2+3}$.

Method 2   Write $\dfrac{5x-4}{(x+2)(x^2+3)} \equiv \dfrac{A}{x+2} + \dfrac{Bx+C}{x^2+3}$.

Multiply by $(x+2)(x^2+3)$ to get $5x-4 \equiv A(x^2+3) + (Bx+C)(x+2)$,

which you can write as

$$5x-4 \equiv (A+B)x^2 + (2B+C)x + 3A + 2C.$$

The three equations which you get by equating coefficients of x^0, x^1 and x^2 are

$$3A+2C=-4, \quad 2B+C=5 \quad \text{and} \quad A+B=0.$$

Solving these equations gives $A=-2$, $B=2$ and $C=1$, so

$$\frac{5x-4}{(x+2)(x^2+3)} \equiv \frac{-2}{x+2} + \frac{2x+1}{x^2+3}.$$

Method 3   Write $\dfrac{5x-4}{(x+2)(x^2+3)} \equiv \dfrac{A}{x+2} + \dfrac{Bx+C}{x^2+3}$.

Multiply by $x+2$ to get $\dfrac{5x-4}{x^2+3} \equiv A + \dfrac{(Bx+C)(x+2)}{x^2+3}$, and put $x=-2$. Then

$\dfrac{5\times(-2)-4}{(-2)^2+3} = A$, so $A=-2$.

Combining the fractions in $\dfrac{5x-4}{(x+2)(x^2+3)} \equiv \dfrac{-2}{x+2} + \dfrac{Bx+C}{x^2+3}$ and equating the

numerators gives

$$5x-4 \equiv -2(x^2+3) + (Bx+C)(x+2),$$

which you can write as

$$5x-4 \equiv (-2+B)x^2 + (2Bx+C)x - 6 + 2C.$$

Equating the coefficients of x^2 gives $-2+B=0$, so $B=2$.

Equating the coefficients of x^0 gives $-4=-6+2C$, so $C=1$.

Checking the x-coefficient: on the left side 5; on the right $2B+C=2\times2+1=5$.

Therefore $\dfrac{5x-4}{(x+2)(x^2+3)} \equiv \dfrac{-2}{x+2} + \dfrac{2x+1}{x^2+3}$.

Example 1.1.2

Find $\displaystyle\int_2^3 \frac{x+1}{(x-1)(x^2+1)}\,dx$.

To integrate you need to put $\dfrac{x+1}{(x-1)(x^2+1)}$ into partial fractions.

Method 1   Write $\dfrac{x+1}{(x-1)(x^2+1)} \equiv \dfrac{A}{x-1} + \dfrac{Bx+C}{x^2+1}$.

Multiplying by $x-1$ and putting $x=1$ gives $A=1$.

Calculating $\dfrac{x+1}{(x-1)(x^2+1)} - \dfrac{1}{x-1}$ to find the other fraction on the right gives

$$\frac{x+1}{(x-1)(x^2+1)} - \frac{1}{x-1} \equiv \frac{x+1-(x^2+1)}{(x-1)(x^2+1)} \equiv \frac{-(x^2-x)}{(x-1)(x^2+1)}$$

$$\equiv \frac{-x(x-1)}{(x-1)(x^2+1)} \equiv -\frac{x}{x^2+1}.$$

Therefore $\dfrac{x+1}{(x-1)(x^2+1)} \equiv \dfrac{1}{x-1} - \dfrac{x}{x^2+1}$. Then

$$\int_2^3 \frac{x+1}{(x-1)(x^2+1)}\,dx = \int_2^3 \left(\frac{1}{x-1} - \frac{x}{x^2+1}\right)dx = \left[\ln(x-1) - \tfrac{1}{2}\ln(x^2+1)\right]_2^3$$

$$= \left(\ln 2 - \tfrac{1}{2}\ln 10\right) - \left(\ln 1 - \tfrac{1}{2}\ln 5\right) = \ln 2 - \tfrac{1}{2}(\ln 10 - \ln 5)$$

$$= \ln 2 - \tfrac{1}{2}(\ln 2) = \tfrac{1}{2}\ln 2.$$

Example 1.1.3

Calculate $\displaystyle\int_{-2}^2 \frac{x^2+x}{(x-4)(x^2+4)}\,dx$.

Putting $\dfrac{x^2+x}{(x-4)(x^2+4)}$ into partial fractions gives $\dfrac{x^2+x}{(x-4)(x^2+4)} = \dfrac{1}{x-4} + \dfrac{1}{x^2+4}$.

So $\displaystyle\int_{-2}^2 \frac{x^2+x}{(x-4)(x^2+4)}\,dx = \int_{-2}^2 \left(\frac{1}{x-4} + \frac{1}{x^2+4}\right)dx$

$$= \int_{-2}^2 \frac{1}{x-4}\,dx + \int_{-2}^2 \frac{1}{x^2+4}\,dx.$$

The first of these integrals is $\left[\ln|x-4|\right]_{-2}^2 = \ln 2 - \ln 6 = \ln\tfrac{1}{3} = -\ln 3$.

The second integral is carried out by the substitution $x = 2\tan u$ (P3 Section 10.2).

$$\int_{-2}^{2} \frac{1}{x^2+4}\,dx = \int_{\tan^{-1}(-1)}^{\tan^{-1}1} \frac{1}{4\sec^2 u} \times 2\sec^2 u\,du = \tfrac{1}{2}[u]_{-\frac{1}{4}\pi}^{\frac{1}{4}\pi} = \tfrac{1}{4}\pi.$$

Thus $\displaystyle\int_{-2}^{2} \frac{x^2+x}{(x-4)(x^2+4)}\,dx = \tfrac{1}{4}\pi - \ln 3.$

Exercise 1A

1 Express each of the following in partial fractions.

(a) $\dfrac{x^2+x}{(x-1)(x^2+1)}$

(b) $\dfrac{2x+1}{(x+1)(x^2+2x+2)}$

(c) $\dfrac{2x^2+x-3}{(x+3)(x^2+3)}$

(d) $\dfrac{2x^2+15x}{(2x-3)(x^2+x+3)}$

(e) $\dfrac{1+2x^2}{(2+3x)(3+3x+2x^2)}$

(f) $\dfrac{17+10x}{(1+4x)(2+x+x^2)}$

(g) $\dfrac{9x+4}{(x-2)(x^2+3x+1)}$

(h) $\dfrac{9-x-4x^2}{(2x-3)(2x^2-3)}$

(i) $\dfrac{17x+3}{(3x-2)(4x^2+3)}$

(j) $\dfrac{7x-13}{(2x+1)(x^2-x+2)}$

(k) $\dfrac{x^2+25x+12}{(5x-7)(2x^2-2x+5)}$

(l) $\dfrac{11x-2x^2\ \ 60}{8x^3+27}$

2 Express each of the following in partial fractions.

(a) $\dfrac{5x^2+3x-3}{(2x-1)(x^2+3x-2)}$

(b) $\dfrac{26x^2-15}{(4x-3)(2x^2+x-2)}$

(c) $\dfrac{4x^2-x+3}{(x-1)(x^2+x+1)}$

(d) $\dfrac{12x^2-15x+10}{(3x-2)(3x^2-x+2)}$

(e) $\dfrac{9-16x}{(2-x)(4x^2+3x+1)}$

(f) $\dfrac{3-4x-x^2}{1+x^3}$

3 Find the values of the following definite integrals.

(a) $\displaystyle\int_{0}^{1} \frac{1-2x-x^2}{(1+x)(1+x^2)}\,dx$

(b) $\displaystyle\int_{1}^{2} \frac{2+3x^2}{x(x^2+2)}\,dx$

(c) $\displaystyle\int_{1}^{3} \frac{4x+9}{(2x-1)(x^2+x+2)}\,dx$

(d) $\displaystyle\int_{0}^{1} \frac{18x^2+10x+7}{(1+3x)(2x^2+x+2)}\,dx$

1.2 Improper fractions

So far all the rational functions you have seen have been 'proper' fractions. That is, the degree of the numerator has been less than the degree of the denominator.

Rational functions such as $\dfrac{x^2-3x+5}{(x+1)(x-2)}$ and $\dfrac{x^3}{x^2+1}$, in which the degree of the numerator is greater than or equal to the degree of the denominator, are called **improper fractions**.

Improper fractions are often not the most convenient form to work with; it is frequently better to express them in a different way.

For example, you cannot find $\int \dfrac{6x}{x-1}\,dx$ with the integrand in its present form, but it is quite straightforward to integrate the same expression as $\int \left(6+\dfrac{6}{x-1}\right)dx$. You get

$$\int \left(6+\frac{6}{x-1}\right)dx = 6x + 6\ln|x-1| + k.$$

Similarly, if you wish to sketch the graph of $y = \dfrac{6x}{x-1}$, although you can see immediately that the graph passes through the origin, other features are much clearer in the form $y = 6 + \dfrac{6}{x-1}$. This idea will be taken further in Chapter 4.

You may find it helpful to think about an analogy between improper fractions in arithmetic and improper fractions in algebra. Sometimes in arithmetic it is more useful to think of the number $\frac{25}{6}$ in that form; at other times it is better in the form $4\frac{1}{6}$. The same is true in algebra, and you need to be able to go from one form to the other.

In P2 Section 1.4, you learned how to divide one polynomial by another polynomial to get a quotient and a remainder.

For example, when you divide the polynomial $a(x)$ by the polynomial $b(x)$ you will get a quotient $q(x)$ and a remainder $r(x)$ defined by

$$a(x) \equiv b(x)q(x) + r(x)$$

where the degree of the remainder $r(x)$ is less than the degree of the divisor $b(x)$.

If you divide this equation by $b(x)$, you get

$$\frac{a(x)}{b(x)} \equiv \frac{b(x)q(x) + r(x)}{b(x)} \equiv q(x) + \frac{r(x)}{b(x)}.$$

Therefore, if you divide $x^2 - 3x + 5$ by $(x+1)(x-2)$ to get a number A and a remainder of the form $Px + Q$, it is equivalent to saying that

$$\frac{x^2 - 3x + 5}{(x+1)(x-2)} \equiv A + \frac{Px + Q}{(x+1)(x-2)}.$$

This form will be called **divided out form**.

The analogous process in arithmetic is to say that 25 divided by 6 is 4 with remainder 1; that is, $25 = 4 \times 6 + 1$, or $\frac{25}{6} = 4 + \frac{1}{6} = 4\frac{1}{6}$.

Example 1.2.1

Express $\dfrac{x^2 - 3x + 5}{(x+1)(x-2)}$ in the form $A + \dfrac{Px+Q}{(x+1)(x-2)}$, by finding A, P and Q.

Writing $\dfrac{x^2 - 3x + 5}{(x+1)(x-2)} \equiv A + \dfrac{Px+Q}{(x+1)(x-2)}$ and multiplying both sides by

$(x+1)(x-2)$ gives $x^2 - 3x + 5 \equiv A(x+1)(x-2) + Px + Q$.

Equating the coefficients of x^2 gives $A = 1$.

At this stage you can either continue to equate coefficients of other powers or

calculate $\dfrac{x^2 - 3x + 5}{(x+1)(x-2)} - 1$ to find $\dfrac{Px+Q}{(x+1)(x-2)}$.

Taking the second alternative,

$$\frac{x^2 - 3x + 5}{(x+1)(x-2)} - 1 \equiv \frac{x^2 - 3x + 5 - (x+1)(x-2)}{(x+1)(x-2)}$$

$$\equiv \frac{x^2 - 3x + 5 - (x^2 - x - 2)}{(x+1)(x-2)} \equiv \frac{-2x + 7}{(x+1)(x-2)}.$$

Therefore $A = 1$, $P = -2$ and $Q = 7$.

You can see from the form $\dfrac{x^2 - 3x + 5}{(x+1)(x-2)} \equiv 1 + \dfrac{-2x + 7}{(x+1)(x-2)}$ that, for large values of x,

the term on the right gets very small, so $\dfrac{x^2 - 3x + 5}{(x+1)(x-2)}$ gets very close to 1. This point is

taken further in Chapter 4.

1.3 Improper fractions and partial fractions

You can now put together the work on improper fractions in Section 1.2 with the work on partial fractions in Section 1.1 and P3 Chapter 7.

For example, if you take the result from Example 1.2.1,

$$\frac{x^2 - 3x + 5}{(x+1)(x-2)} \equiv 1 + \frac{-2x + 7}{(x+1)(x-2)},$$

you can go further by putting the right side into partial fraction form using the standard method and getting

$$\frac{x^2 - 3x + 5}{(x+1)(x-2)} \equiv 1 - \frac{3}{x+1} + \frac{1}{x-2}.$$

Example 1.3.1

Split $\dfrac{2x^2 + 4x - 3}{(x+1)(2x-3)}$ into partial fractions.

There are a number of methods you can use. You could go immediately into a partial fraction form and find the coefficients either by equating coefficients or by other methods. Or you could put it into divided out form first, and then use one of the standard methods for the remaining partial fractions.

Method A   This method goes straight into partial fraction form, but does not use the equating coefficient technique.

Write $\dfrac{2x^2 + 4x - 3}{(x+1)(2x-3)}$ in the form $\dfrac{2x^2 + 4x - 3}{(x+1)(2x-3)} \equiv A + \dfrac{B}{x+1} + \dfrac{C}{2x-3}$.

Multiplying by $x+1$ gives $\dfrac{2x^2 + 4x - 3}{2x-3} \equiv A(x+1) + B + \dfrac{C(x+1)}{2x-3}$.

Putting $x = -1$ gives $\dfrac{2 \times (-1)^2 + 4 \times (-1) - 3}{2 \times (-1) - 3} = B$, so $B = 1$.

Multiplying instead by $2x - 3$ gives $\dfrac{2x^2 + 4x - 3}{x+1} \equiv A(2x-3) + \dfrac{B(2x-3)}{x+1} + C$.

Putting $x = \frac{3}{2}$ gives $\dfrac{2 \times \left(\frac{3}{2}\right)^2 + 4 \times \left(\frac{3}{2}\right) - 3}{\left(\frac{3}{2} + 1\right)} = C$, so $C = 3$.

Therefore $\dfrac{2x^2 + 4x - 3}{(x+1)(2x-3)} \equiv A + \dfrac{1}{x+1} + \dfrac{3}{2x-3}$.

Putting $x = 0$ gives $A = 1$.

Therefore $\dfrac{2x^2 + 4x - 3}{(x+1)(2x-3)} \equiv 1 + \dfrac{1}{x+1} + \dfrac{3}{2x-3}$.

Method B   If you divide out first, you start with the form

$\dfrac{2x^2 + 4x - 3}{(x+1)(2x-3)} \equiv A + \dfrac{Px + Q}{(x+1)(2x-3)}$. By multiplying by $(x+1)(2x-3)$ and equating the coefficients of x^2, you find that $A = 1$.

Thus $\dfrac{2x^2 + 4x - 3}{(x+1)(2x-3)} \equiv 1 + \dfrac{Px + Q}{(x+1)(2x-3)}$ so $\dfrac{2x^2 + 4x - 3}{(x+1)(2x-3)} - 1 \equiv \dfrac{Px + Q}{(x+1)(2x-3)}$.

Simplifying the left side

$$\dfrac{2x^2 + 4x - 3 - (x+1)(2x-3)}{(x+1)(2x-3)} \equiv \dfrac{2x^2 + 4x - 3 - \left(2x^2 - x - 3\right)}{(x+1)(2x-3)} \equiv \dfrac{5x}{(x+1)(2x-3)}.$$

Any of the standard methods for partial fractions now shows that

$$\frac{5x}{(x+1)(2x-3)} \equiv \frac{1}{x+1} + \frac{3}{2x-3}, \text{ so } \frac{2x^2+4x-3}{(x+1)(2x-3)} \equiv 1 + \frac{1}{x+1} + \frac{3}{2x-3}.$$

Use whichever method suits you best. Equating coefficients and solving the resulting equations always works, but it is not always the quickest method.

In Example 1.3.1, the numerator $2x^2+4x-3$ was a polynomial of the same degree as the denominator $(x+1)(2x-3)$, but the numerator could be a polynomial of higher degree than the denominator.

If the polynomial in the numerator of a fraction is of higher degree than the denominator, you need to find the difference in degree. That is, if you divide the numerator by the denominator to get a quotient and a remainder, what will the degree of your quotient be? The answer will tell you what polynomial to write in the divided out form.

Example 1.3.2

Split $\dfrac{3x^4 - 3x^3 - 17x^2 - x - 1}{(x-3)(x+2)}$ into partial fractions.

In this case, the degree of the numerator is 4 and the degree of the denominator is 2. This shows that the degree of the quotient polynomial when you divide the numerator by the denominator is $4 - 2 = 2$. Therefore write $\dfrac{3x^4 - 3x^3 - 17x^2 - x - 1}{(x-3)(x+2)}$ in the form

$$\frac{3x^4 - 3x^3 - 17x^2 - x - 1}{(x-3)(x+2)} \equiv Ax^2 + Bx + C + \frac{D}{x-3} + \frac{E}{x+2},$$

where the polynomial $Ax^2 + Bx + C$ has the degree $4 - 2 = 2$.

The process of multiplying by $x-3$, and putting $x = 3$ in the resulting identity, as in Example 1.2.1, gives $D = 1$. Similarly, multiplying by $x+2$, and then putting $x = -2$ in the resulting identity, as in Example 1.2.1, gives $E = -1$. Therefore

$$\frac{3x^4 - 3x^3 - 17x^2 - x - 1}{(x-3)(x+2)} \equiv Ax^2 + Bx + C + \frac{1}{x-3} - \frac{1}{x+2}.$$

It is best now to multiply both sides of the identity by $(x-3)(x+2)$ and to equate coefficients, choosing carefully which powers of x to use to minimise the work.

$$3x^4 - 3x^3 - 17x^2 - x - 1 \equiv \left(Ax^2 + Bx + C\right)(x-3)(x+2) + (x+2) - (x-3)$$

Equating the coefficients of x^4: $3 = A$.

Equating the coefficients of x^0: $-1 = -6C + 2 + 3$, so $C = 1$.

Equating the coefficients of x^1: $-1 = -6B - C + 1 - 1$, so $B = 0$.

Therefore $\dfrac{3x^4 - 3x^3 - 17x^2 - x - 1}{(x-3)(x+2)} \equiv 3x^2 + 1 + \dfrac{1}{x-3} - \dfrac{1}{x+2}$.

Example 1.3.3

Find $\displaystyle\int \dfrac{x^3 - 3x - 4}{x^3 - 1}\,dx$.

You cannot integrate this directly, so put it into divided out form to get

$\displaystyle\int \dfrac{x^3 - 3x - 4}{x^3 - 1}\,dx = \int \left(1 + \dfrac{-3x-3}{x^3-1}\right)dx$. (It is worth doing this first before going

into partial fractions, because you might be lucky and be able to integrate the term on the right easily.) In this case you cannot directly integrate the term on the right, so put it into partial fractions, using the fact that $x^3 - 1 \equiv (x-1)(x^2 + x + 1)$. Then

$$\dfrac{-3x-3}{x^3-1} \equiv \dfrac{-3x-3}{(x-1)(x^2+x+1)} \equiv \dfrac{A}{x-1} + \dfrac{Bx+C}{x^2+x+1}.$$

Multiplying by $x-1$, and putting $x=1$ in the resulting identity, gives $A = -2$.

Therefore $\dfrac{Bx+C}{x^2+x+1} \equiv \dfrac{-3x-3}{(x-1)(x^2+x+1)} - \dfrac{-2}{x-1} \equiv \dfrac{-3x-3+2(x^2+x+1)}{(x-1)(x^2+x+1)}$

$$\equiv \dfrac{2x^2-x-1}{(x-1)(x^2+x+1)} \equiv \dfrac{(x-1)(2x+1)}{(x-1)(x^2+x+1)} \equiv \dfrac{2x+1}{x^2+x+1}.$$

Thus $\displaystyle\int \dfrac{x^3-3x-4}{x^3-1}\,dx = \int \left(1 - \dfrac{2}{x-1} + \dfrac{2x+1}{x^2+x+1}\right)dx$

$$= x - 2\ln|x-1| + \ln(x^2+x+1) + k.$$

You do not need a modulus sign for $x^2 + x + 1$ since $x^2 + x + 1 = \left(x + \tfrac{1}{2}\right)^2 + \tfrac{3}{4}$ and is therefore always positive.

Exercise 1B

1 Express the following improper fractions in partial fraction form.

(a) $\dfrac{2x^3 + x + 1}{(x+1)(x-1)}$

(b) $\dfrac{x^2 + 1}{(x+3)(x-2)}$

(c) $\dfrac{7 - 5x + 2x^2}{(3-x)(1-2x)}$

(d) $\dfrac{6x^2 + 11x + 3}{(x+2)(2x-1)}$

(e) $\dfrac{4x^3 + 6x + 1}{(x+1)(2x-1)}$

(f) $\dfrac{x(17 + 30x + 9x^2)}{(3+x)(1+3x)}$

(g) $\dfrac{2x^4 + 5x^3 - 2x - 2}{(x+2)(2x+1)}$

(h) $\dfrac{4x^4 + 8x^3 - 11x^2 - 36}{(x+3)(2x-3)}$

(i) $\dfrac{3x^4}{x^3 + 1}$

2 Find the values of the following definite integrals.

(a) $\displaystyle\int_2^3 \frac{x^3 + x^2 + x - 1}{x(x^2 - 1)}\,dx$

(b) $\displaystyle\int_1^2 \frac{2 + 2x + 2x^2 + x^3}{x^2(1+x)}\,dx$

(c) $\displaystyle\int_0^1 \frac{6x^3 - 7x^2 - 11}{(2x-3)(x^2+1)}\,dx$

(d) $\displaystyle\int_0^1 \frac{2x^4 + 3x^3 - 10x^2 - 5x + 2}{(x+1)(x^2 - x - 1)}\,dx$

Miscellaneous exercise 1

1 Express the following in partial fractions.

(a) $\displaystyle\frac{1+x}{x^2(1-x)}$

(b) $\displaystyle\frac{6 + x - x^4}{(x+2)(x^2+2)}$

2 (a) Given that
$$\frac{2}{(x-1)^2(x^2+1)} \equiv \frac{A}{x-1} + \frac{B}{(x-1)^2} + \frac{Cx}{x^2+1},$$
find the values of the constants A, B and C.

(b) Show that $\displaystyle\int_2^3 \frac{2}{(x-1)^2(x^2+1)}\,dx = a + b\ln 2$, where a and b are constants whose values you should find. (OCR)

3 (a) Find the values of A, B and C for which $\displaystyle\frac{x^2 - 2}{(x-2)^2} \equiv A + \frac{B}{x-2} + \frac{C}{(x-2)^2}$.

(b) The region bounded by the curve with equation $y = \dfrac{x^2 - 2}{(x-2)^2}$, the x-axis and the lines $x = 3$ and $x = 4$ is denoted by R. Show that R has area $(2 + 4\ln 2)$ square units. (OCR)

4 (a) Express $\displaystyle\frac{2}{(x-1)(x-3)}$ in partial fractions, and use the result to express

$\displaystyle\frac{4}{(x-1)^2(x-3)^2}$ in partial fractions.

The finite region bounded by the curve with equation $y = \dfrac{2}{(x-1)(x-3)}$ and the lines $x = 4$

and $y = \frac{1}{4}$ is denoted by R.

(b) Show that the area of R is $\ln\frac{3}{2} - \frac{1}{4}$.

(c) Calculate the volume of the solid formed when R is rotated through 2π radians about the x-axis. (OCR)

5 Evaluate $\displaystyle\int_0^1 \frac{x^2 + 6x - 4}{(x+2)(x^2+2)}\,dx$.

6 Calculate the exact value of $\displaystyle\int_0^{\frac{1}{2}} \frac{1+x+x^2}{(1-x)^2}\,dx$.

7 Calculate the exact value of $\displaystyle\int_0^1 \frac{x^2+x+1}{(2x+1)(x+1)^2}\,dx$.

8 (a) Find the value of a such that a translation in the direction of the x-axis transforms the curve with equation $y = \dfrac{x^2+ax-1}{x^3}$ into the curve with equation $y = \dfrac{x^2-2}{(x-1)^3}$.

  (b) Hence find the exact value of $\displaystyle\int_2^3 \frac{x^2-2}{(x-1)^3}\,dx$.   (OCR)

2 Summing series

This chapter is about finding formulae for the sums of series. When you have completed it, you should

- understand and be able to use sigma notation
- be able to sum series where the rth term involves some or all of r, r^2 and r^3
- be able to use a method based on differences to sum certain kinds of series
- be able to tell in simple cases when a series converges, and, if it does, to find the sum to infinity.

2.1 Sigma notation

You met sequences and series in this course in P2 Chapter 3. You saw there that u_1, u_2, ... is called a sequence, and if you need to add the terms to get $u_1 + u_2 + ... + u_n$, the sequence changes its name and is called a series.

A series is completely determined if you know a formula for u_r, the general term, and where the series starts and finishes.

The sum $u_1 + u_2 + ... + u_n$ is then written as

$$\sum_{r=1}^{n} u_r = u_1 + u_2 + ... + u_n.$$

This notation is called **sigma notation**, and is illustrated in more detail in Fig. 2.1. The letter Σ is the Greek capital letter S.

- The symbol Σ is an instruction to add.
- Following the Σ symbol is an expression for the general term of a series.
- Below the Σ symbol is the value of r corresponding to the starting term.
- Above the Σ symbol is the value of r corresponding to the last term.

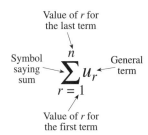

Fig. 2.1

The expression $\sum_{r=1}^{n} u_r$ is read as 'sigma from 1 to n of u_r'.

Example 2.1.1

Express as addition sums (a) $\displaystyle\sum_{r=1}^{3} r^2$, (b) $\displaystyle\sum_{r=4}^{7}(2r-1)^3$, (c) $\displaystyle\sum_{r=0}^{4} 1$.

(a) The rth term is r^2 and, as the first term has $r = 1$, the first term is 1^2. For the second term, put $r = 2$, so the second term is 2^2. The last term is the term for which $r = 3$, so the last term is 3^2. The Σ symbol means add, so

$$\sum_{r=1}^{3} r^2 = 1^2 + 2^2 + 3^2.$$

(b) The first term is $(2 \times 4 - 1)^3 = 7^3$, corresponding to $r = 4$. The second term, corresponding to $r = 5$, is $(2 \times 5 - 1)^3 = 9^3$. Continuing in this way,

$$\sum_{r=4}^{7} (2r-1)^3 = 7^3 + 9^3 + 11^3 + 13^3.$$

(c) In this case, the rth term is 1, independent of the value of r, so

$$\sum_{r=0}^{4} 1 = 1 + 1 + 1 + 1 + 1.$$

Notice that, in part (c), there are 5 terms. In general the number of terms in the series $\sum_{r=n}^{N} u_r$ is $N - n + 1$.

There is more than one way to describe a series using sigma notation. For example,

$$\sum_{r=0}^{2} (r+1)^2 = (0+1)^2 + (1+1)^2 + (2+1)^2 = 1^2 + 2^2 + 3^2,$$

which is the same as $\sum_{r=1}^{3} r^2$ in Example 2.1.1(a).

Sometimes you can break up a complicated series into simpler series. For example, you can write the sum $\sum_{r=1}^{200} (2r+1)$ in the form

$$\sum_{r=1}^{200} (2r+1) = (2 \times 1 + 1) + (2 \times 2 + 1) + (2 \times 3 + 1) + \ldots + (2 \times 200 + 1)$$

$$= (2 \times 1 + 2 \times 2 + 2 \times 3 + \ldots + 2 \times 200) + \overbrace{1 + 1 + 1 + \ldots + 1}^{200 \text{ of these}}$$

$$= 2 \times (1 + 2 + 3 + \ldots + 200) + \overbrace{1 + 1 + 1 + \ldots + 1}^{200 \text{ of these}}$$

$$= 2 \sum_{r=1}^{200} r + \sum_{r=1}^{200} 1.$$

You can now go on and sum the series, using the formula for the nth triangle number in P2 Section 3.3, since the sum $\sum_{r=1}^{200} r$ is the same as t_{200}, which is given by

$$t_{200} = \tfrac{1}{2} \times 200 \times 201 = 20\,100.$$

Therefore

$$\sum_{r=1}^{200} (2r+1) = 2 \sum_{r=1}^{200} r + \sum_{r=1}^{200} 1 = 2 \times 20\,100 + 200 = 40\,400.$$

In the example, two important rules about sigma notation were used.

The first rule is called the **addition rule** for sums:

$$\sum_{r=1}^{n}(u_r + v_r) = (u_1 + v_1) + (u_2 + v_2) + \ldots + (u_n + v_n)$$

$$= (u_1 + u_2 + \ldots + u_n) + (v_1 + v_2 + \ldots + v_n)$$

$$= \sum_{r=1}^{n}u_r + \sum_{r=1}^{n}v_r.$$

The second rule deals with the effect of multiplying each term by a constant k. It is called the **multiple rule** for sums:

$$\sum_{r=1}^{n}(ku_r) = (ku_1 + ku_2 + \ldots + ku_n) = k(u_1 + u_2 + \ldots + u_n)$$

$$= k\sum_{r=1}^{n}u_r.$$

Addition rule	$\displaystyle\sum_{r=1}^{n}(u_r + v_r) = \sum_{r=1}^{n}u_r + \sum_{r=1}^{n}v_r.$
Multiple rule	For any number k, $\displaystyle\sum_{r=1}^{n}(ku_r) = k\sum_{r=1}^{n}u_r.$

Example 2.1.2

Show that $\displaystyle\sum_{r=1}^{n}(2r+1)^2 = 4\sum_{r=1}^{n}r^2 + 4\sum_{r=1}^{n}r + \sum_{r=1}^{n}1.$

Using the addition and multiple rules,

$$\sum_{r=1}^{n}(2r+1)^2 = \sum_{r=1}^{n}\left(4r^2 + 4r + 1\right) = \sum_{r=1}^{n}4r^2 + \sum_{r=1}^{n}4r + \sum_{r=1}^{n}1$$

$$= 4\sum_{r=1}^{n}r^2 + 4\sum_{r=1}^{n}r + \sum_{r=1}^{n}1.$$

There is another important fact to notice about sigma notation. The final result is nothing to do with r. For example,

$$\sum_{r=0}^{2}\left(3 + 2r + r^2\right) = 3 + \left(3 + 2\times1 + 1^2\right) + \left(3 + 2\times2 + 2^2\right) = 3 + 6 + 11 = 20.$$

So it doesn't matter what letter you use. Thus $\displaystyle\sum_{r=0}^{2}\left(3 + 2r + r^2\right)$ is precisely the same sum as $\displaystyle\sum_{i=0}^{2}\left(3 + 2i + i^2\right)$. For this reason r is called a **dummy variable**. Another example of a dummy variable which you have met already is the x in $\displaystyle\int_a^b f(x)\,dx$. The result of this calculation only involves a and b.

When there is no possibility of confusion, you can omit the '$r=$' below the sigma symbol. Thus $\sum_{r=0}^{2}\left(3+2r+r^2\right) = \sum_{0}^{2}\left(3+2r+r^2\right)$. However, the '$r=$' will not be omitted in the Pure Mathematics modules of this course.

Exercise 2A

1 Express each of the following as addition sums.

(a) $\displaystyle\sum_{r=2}^{3} r^3$

(b) $\displaystyle\sum_{r=3}^{5} 2$

(c) $\displaystyle\sum_{r=1}^{4} \frac{1}{r}$

(d) $\displaystyle\sum_{r=1}^{4} r^2$

(e) $\displaystyle\sum_{r=2}^{5} (2r+1)$

(f) $\displaystyle\sum_{r=0}^{2} u_r$

2 Write each of the following sums using sigma notation. (Note that your answers could differ from those given.)

(a) $2+3+4$

(b) $1+4+9+16$

(c) $2+4+6+8+10$

(d) $\frac{1}{2}+\frac{1}{4}+\frac{1}{6}$

(e) $3+5+7+9$

(f) $2+5+8+11+14$

3 Write each of the following expressions as a sum, giving the first three terms and the last term of each of them. For example, $\displaystyle\sum_{r=2}^{n} 2r = 4+6+8+\ldots+2n$.

(a) $\displaystyle\sum_{r=0}^{n} r$

(b) $\displaystyle\sum_{r=2}^{n-1} r^2$

(c) $\displaystyle\sum_{r=4}^{n-4} 3$

(d) $\displaystyle\sum_{r=1}^{2n} \frac{1}{r}$

(e) $\displaystyle\sum_{r=0}^{2n-1} r^3$

(f) $\displaystyle\sum_{r=0}^{n-2} u_{r+1}$

4 Say whether each of the following statements is true or false. Be prepared to justify your answer.

(a) $\displaystyle\sum_{r=1}^{2n} r^3 = \sum_{r=0}^{2n-1} (r+1)^3$

(b) $\displaystyle\sum_{r=1}^{n} 1 = \frac{1}{2}n(n+1)$

(c) $\displaystyle\sum_{r=1}^{n} r^2 = \left(\sum_{r=1}^{n} r\right)^2$

(d) $\displaystyle\sum_{r=1}^{2n} r^3 = \sum_{r=0}^{2n} r^3$

(e) $\displaystyle\sum_{r=1}^{n} \left(2+r^2\right) = 2 + \sum_{r=1}^{n} r^2$

(f) $\displaystyle\sum_{i=1}^{2n} i^2 = \sum_{j=0}^{2n-1} (j+1)^2$

5 Calculate the value of each of the following sums.

(a) $\displaystyle\sum_{r=0}^{2} (-1)^r r$

(b) $\displaystyle\sum_{r=0}^{2} (-1)^{r-1} r$

(c) $\displaystyle\sum_{r=0}^{2} (-1)^{r+1} r$

(d) $\displaystyle\sum_{r=1}^{6} (-1)^r r^2$

(e) $\displaystyle\sum_{r=3}^{5} (-1)^{r+1} r^{-1}$

(f) $\displaystyle\sum_{r=3}^{5} (-1)^r$

6 Write each of the following in sigma notation.

(a) $1-2+3-4+\ldots+101$

(b) $-2^2+4^2-6^2+\ldots-50^2$

(c) $1-\frac{1}{2}+\frac{1}{3}-\ldots+\frac{1}{49}$

7 Write each of the following in sigma notation.

(a) $\left(1+\frac{1}{1}\right)+\left(2+\frac{1}{2}\right)+\left(3+\frac{1}{3}\right)+...+\left(100+\frac{1}{100}\right)$

(b) $1+\binom{n}{1}x+\binom{n}{2}x^2+...+\binom{n}{n}x^n$

(c) $1+2x+3x^2+4x^3+...+(n+1)x^n$

(d) $1-2x+3x^2-4x^3+...-2nx^{2n-1}$

2.2 Sum of squares of the first n natural numbers

You know from P2 Section 3.3 that the sum of the series $\sum_{r=1}^{n} r = 1+2+...+n$ is $\frac{1}{2}n(n+1)$,

and that $\sum_{r=1}^{n} 1 = n$.

In this section and the next the sums of the series

$$1^2+2^2+3^2+...+n^2 \text{ and } 1^3+2^3+3^3+...+n^3$$

will be calculated.

You can see that $\sum_{r=1}^{n} 1 = n$, which you can write as $\sum_{r=1}^{n} r^0 = n$, and you know that

$\sum_{r=1}^{n} r = \frac{1}{2}n(n+1)$. But what about similar formulae for $\sum_{r=1}^{n} r^2 = 1^2+2^2+...+n^2$ and

$\sum_{r=1}^{n} r^3 = 1^3+2^3+...+n^3$?

From the formula $\sum_{r=1}^{n} r^0 = n$, you can see that

$$\sum_{r=1}^{n} r^0 = n \times \text{a polynomial of degree 0 in } n,$$

and from the formula $\sum_{r=1}^{n} r = \frac{1}{2}n(n+1)$ that

$$\sum_{r=1}^{n} r = n \times \text{a polynomial of degree 1 in } n.$$

This suggests that $\sum_{r=1}^{n} r^2 = n \times \text{a polynomial of degree 2 in } n$.

So try making the assumption that $\sum_{r=1}^{n} r^2$ can be written in the form

$$\sum_{r=1}^{n} r^2 = n\left(A + Bn + Cn^2\right)$$

where A, B and C are constants, and see if you can find A, B and C.

This is the same as assuming that $\sum_{r=1}^{n} r^2 = An + Bn^2 + Cn^3$.

Putting $n = 1, 2$, and 3 in turn, you find that

$$\left.\begin{array}{rl}
1^2 & = A \times 1 + B \times 1^2 + C \times 1^3 \\
1^2 + 2^2 & = A \times 2 + B \times 2^2 + C \times 2^3 \\
1^2 + 2^2 + 3^2 & = A \times 3 + B \times 3^2 + C \times 3^3
\end{array}\right\}.$$

Eliminating A, B and C in turn gives the following sets of equations.

$$\left.\begin{array}{rl}
A + \;\; B + \;\;\; C & = \;\; 1 \\
2A + \;\; 4B + \;\; 8C & = \;\; 5 \\
3A + \;\; 9B + 27C & = 14
\end{array}\right\} \quad
\left.\begin{array}{rl}
A + \;\; B + \;\;\; C & = \;\; 1 \\
2B + \;\; 6C & = \;\; 3 \\
6B + 24C & = 11
\end{array}\right\} \quad
\left.\begin{array}{rl}
A + \;\; B + \;\;\; C & = \;\; 1 \\
2B + \;\; 6C & = \;\; 3 \\
6C & = \;\; 2
\end{array}\right\}$$

You can now see that $C = \frac{1}{3}$; substituting this into the equation for B and C gives $B = \frac{1}{2}$. Similarly, $A = \frac{1}{6}$.

This process suggests that $\sum_{r=1}^{n} r^2 = \frac{1}{6}n + \frac{1}{2}n^2 + \frac{1}{3}n^3$. Expressing this as a single fraction, you find that

$$\sum_{r=1}^{n} r^2 = \frac{1}{6}n + \frac{1}{2}n^2 + \frac{1}{3}n^3 = \frac{n + 3n^2 + 2n^3}{6}$$

$$= \frac{1}{6}n\left(2n^2 + 3n + 1\right) = \frac{1}{6}n(n+1)(2n+1).$$

Note that this derivation is not a proof. All it shows is that, if $\sum_{r=1}^{n} r^2$ is a cubic polynomial, then $\sum_{r=1}^{n} r^2 = \frac{1}{6}n(n+1)(2n+1)$. However, it is encouraging that $1^2 + 2^2 + 3^2 + 4^2 + 5^2 = 55$ and $\frac{1}{6} \times 5(5+1)(2 \times 5 + 1) = \frac{1}{6} \times 5 \times 6 \times 11 = 55$. The result is in fact true, but you will not see a proof until Section 2.4.

Example 2.2.1
Find the sum $1^2 + 2^2 + \ldots + 144^2$.

Putting $n = 144$ in $\sum_{r=1}^{n} r^2 = \frac{1}{6}n(n+1)(2n+1)$, you find that

$$\sum_{r=1}^{144} r^2 = \frac{1}{6} \times 144 \times 145 \times 289 = 1\,005\,720.$$

Example 2.2.2

Find the sum of the series $1 \times 2 + 2 \times 3 + 3 \times 4 + \ldots + n(n+1)$.

The rth term of this series is $r(r+1)$. Then the series is

$$\sum_{r=1}^{n} r(r+1) = \sum_{r=1}^{n}\left(r^2 + r\right)$$

$$= \sum_{r=1}^{n} r^2 + \sum_{r=1}^{n} r \qquad \text{(using the addition rule).}$$

Now you can use the formulae for $\displaystyle\sum_{r=1}^{n} r^2$ and $\displaystyle\sum_{r=1}^{n} r$, so

$$\sum_{r=1}^{n} r^2 + \sum_{r=1}^{n} r = \tfrac{1}{6}n(n+1)(2n+1) + \tfrac{1}{2}n(n+1)$$

$$= n(n+1) \times \tfrac{1}{6}(2n+1+3) = \tfrac{1}{6}n(n+1)(2n+4)$$

$$= \tfrac{1}{3}n(n+1)(n+2).$$

Therefore $1 \times 2 + 2 \times 3 + 3 \times 4 + \ldots + n(n+1) = \tfrac{1}{3}n(n+1)(n+2)$.

It is worth checking this for a small value of n. Putting $n = 2$, the left side is $1 \times 2 + 2 \times 3 = 8$. *The right side is* $\tfrac{1}{3} \times 2 \times (2+1) \times (3+1) = 8$.

You can use this method in a variety of ways. Here are two more examples.

Example 2.2.3

Find the sum $(n+1)^2 + (n+2)^2 + \ldots + (2n)^2$.

Method 1   This is $\left(1^2 + 2^2 + \quad + (2n)^2\right) - \left(1^2 + 2^2 + \ldots + n^2\right)$.

Using the formula for $\displaystyle\sum_{r=1}^{n} r^2$,

$$\left(1^2 + 2^2 + \ldots + (2n)^2\right) - \left(1^2 + 2^2 + \ldots + n^2\right)$$

$$= \sum_{r=1}^{2n} r^2 - \sum_{r=1}^{n} r^2$$

$$= \tfrac{1}{6}(2n)((2n)+1)(2(2n)+1) - \tfrac{1}{6}n(n+1)(2n+1)$$

$$= \tfrac{1}{6}(2n)(2n+1)(4n+1) - \tfrac{1}{6}n(n+1)(2n+1)$$

$$= \tfrac{1}{6}(n(2n+1))(2(4n+1) - (n+1))$$

$$= \tfrac{1}{6}n(2n+1)(7n+1).$$

Method 2   This method, which is not so efficient, expresses the rth term in the form $(n+r)^2$.

Then the series $(n+1)^2 + (n+2)^2 + \ldots + (2n)^2$ can be written in the form

$$(n+1)^2 + (n+2)^2 + \ldots + (2n)^2 = \sum_{r=1}^{n}(n+r)^2$$

$$= \sum_{r=1}^{n}\left(n^2 + 2nr + r^2\right)$$

$$= \sum_{r=1}^{n}n^2 + \sum_{r=1}^{n}2nr + \sum_{r=1}^{n}r^2 \qquad \text{(addition rule)}$$

$$= n^2\sum_{r=1}^{n}1 + 2n\sum_{r=1}^{n}r + \sum_{r=1}^{n}r^2 \qquad \text{(multiple rule)}$$

$$= n^2 \times n + 2n \times \tfrac{1}{2}n(n+1) + \tfrac{1}{6}n(n+1)(2n+1)$$

$$= n\left(n^2 + n(n+1) + \tfrac{1}{6}(n+1)(2n+1)\right)$$

$$= \tfrac{1}{6}n\left(6n^2 + 6n(n+1) + (n+1)(2n+1)\right)$$

$$= \tfrac{1}{6}n\left(14n^2 + 9n + 1\right) = \tfrac{1}{6}n(2n+1)(7n+1).$$

In the working, it is important to notice that you can take n out of the summation because it is a constant, but you cannot do the same for the summation variable r .

Example 2.2.4
Find the sum of the series $1^2 - 2^2 + 3^2 - 4^2 + \ldots + (2n-1)^2 - (2n)^2$.

Method 1   Using an 'add and subtract' method gives

$$1^2 - 2^2 + 3^2 - 4^2 + \ldots + (2n-1)^2 - (2n)^2$$

$$= 1^2 + 2^2 + 3^2 + 4^2 + \ldots + (2n-1)^2 + (2n)^2$$

$$\qquad - 2\left(2^2 + 4^2 + \ldots + (2n)^2\right)$$

$$= 1^2 + 2^2 + \ldots + (2n)^2 - 2 \times 2^2\left(1^2 + 2^2 + \ldots + n^2\right)$$

$$= \sum_{r=1}^{2n}r^2 - 8\sum_{r=1}^{n}r^2$$

$$= \tfrac{1}{6}(2n)((2n)+1)(2(2n)+1) - 8 \times \tfrac{1}{6}n(n+1)(2n+1)$$

$$= \tfrac{1}{3}n(2n+1)(4n+1) - \tfrac{4}{3}n(n+1)(2n+1)$$

$$= \tfrac{1}{3}n(2n+1)((4n+1) - 4(n+1))$$

$$= \tfrac{1}{3}n(2n+1) \times (-3) = -n(2n+1).$$

Method 2   Looking at the terms in pairs, the general term is
$(2r-1)^2 - (2r)^2 = -4r+1$. Thus the series is

$$\sum_{r=1}^{n}(-4r+1) = -4 \times \tfrac{1}{2}n(n+1) + n = -2n(n+1) + n$$

$$= n(-2n - 2 + 1) = -n(2n+1).$$

You can check this result by putting $n = 1$ or $n = 2$.

2.3 Sum of cubes of the first n natural numbers

You could try a method similar to the one for finding $\sum_{r=1}^{n} r^2$ to find a formula for $\sum_{r=1}^{n} r^3$.

You could say that you expect it to be a polynomial of degree 4 in n, and then attempt to find the coefficients. Happily you are spared this approach by a lucky accident. If you examine the corresponding values of $\sum_{r=1}^{n} r^3$ and $\sum_{r=1}^{n} r$ you find a surprising relationship.

$$\sum_{r=1}^{1} r^3 = 1^3 = 1 \qquad\qquad \sum_{r=1}^{1} r = 1$$

$$\sum_{r=1}^{2} r^3 = 1^3 + 2^3 = 9 \qquad\qquad \sum_{r=1}^{2} r = 1 + 2 = 3$$

$$\sum_{r=1}^{3} r^3 = 1^3 + 2^3 + 3^3 = 36 \qquad\qquad \sum_{r=1}^{3} r = 1 + 2 + 3 = 6$$

$$\sum_{r=1}^{4} r^3 = 1^3 + 2^3 + 3^3 + 4^3 = 100 \qquad\qquad \sum_{r=1}^{4} r = 1 + 2 + 3 + 4 = 10$$

This suggests that $\sum_{r=1}^{n} r^3 = \left(\sum_{r=1}^{n} r \right)^2$.

If you check this for $n = 5$, you find that $\sum_{r=1}^{n} r = 15$ and $\sum_{r=1}^{5} r^3 = 225$, so the relation

$$\sum_{r=1}^{n} r^3 = \left(\sum_{r=1}^{n} r \right)^2 \text{ holds for } n = 1, \dots, 5. \text{ It actually holds for all } n, \text{ so } \sum_{r=1}^{n} r^3 = \tfrac{1}{4} n^2 (n+1)^2.$$

The sums of the early powers of the natural numbers are

$$\sum_{r=1}^{n} 1 = \overbrace{1 + 1 + \dots + 1}^{n \text{ of these}} = n,$$

$$\sum_{r=1}^{n} r = 1 + 2 + \dots + n = \tfrac{1}{2} n(n+1),$$

$$\sum_{r=1}^{n} r^2 = 1^2 + 2^2 + \dots + n^2 = \tfrac{1}{6} n(n+1)(2n+1),$$

$$\sum_{r=1}^{n} r^3 = 1^3 + 2^3 + \dots + n^3 = \tfrac{1}{4} n^2 (n+1)^2.$$

Note that the result $\sum_{r=1}^{n} r^3 = \tfrac{1}{4} n^2 (n+1)^2$ has not been proved. A proof is asked for in

Miscellaneous exercise 2 Question 10, and a different proof is given in Example 3.3.1.

Example 2.3.1

Find a formula for $1 \times 2 \times 4 + 2 \times 3 \times 5 + \ldots + n(n+1)(n+3)$.

The rth term is $r(r+1)(r+3)$, so the sum of the series is $\displaystyle\sum_{r=1}^{n} r(r+1)(r+3)$.

As $r(r+1)(r+3) = r^3 + 4r^2 + 3r$, the required sum is

$$\sum_{r=1}^{n} r(r+1)(r+3) = \sum_{r=1}^{n} \left(r^3 + 4r^2 + 3r \right) = \sum_{r=1}^{n} r^3 + 4\sum_{r=1}^{n} r^2 + 3\sum_{r=1}^{n} r$$

$$= \tfrac{1}{4} n^2 (n+1)^2 + 4 \times \tfrac{1}{6} n(n+1)(2n+1) + 3 \times \tfrac{1}{2} n(n+1)$$

$$= \tfrac{1}{12} n(n+1)\big(3n(n+1) + 8(2n+1) + 18\big)$$

$$= \tfrac{1}{12} n(n+1)\big(3n^2 + 19n + 26\big).$$

As a check, put $n = 1$. The left side is $1 \times 2 \times 4 = 8$, and the right side is $\tfrac{1}{12} \times 1 \times 2 \times (3 + 19 + 26) = 8$.

Example 2.3.2

Calculate $1^3 - 2^3 + 3^3 - 4^3 + \ldots$

(a) when the last term is even, and

(b) when the last term is odd.

(a) Suppose the last term is even. Then

$$1^3 - 2^3 + \ldots - n^3 = 1^3 + 2^3 + \ldots + n^3 - 2\big(2^3 + 4^3 + \ldots + n^3\big)$$

$$= \sum_{r=1}^{n} r^3 - 2 \times 2^3 \left(1^3 + 2^3 + \ldots + \left(\tfrac{1}{2} n\right)^3 \right)$$

$$= \sum_{r=1}^{n} r^3 - 16 \sum_{r=1}^{\frac{1}{2}n} r^3$$

$$= \tfrac{1}{4} n^2 (n+1)^2 - 16 \times \tfrac{1}{4} \left(\tfrac{1}{2} n\right)^2 \left(\left(\tfrac{1}{2} n\right) + 1\right)^2$$

$$= \tfrac{1}{4} n^2 (n+1)^2 - \tfrac{1}{4} n^2 (n+2)^2$$

$$= \tfrac{1}{4} n^2 (-2n - 3) = -\tfrac{1}{4} n^2 (2n+3).$$

(b) Now suppose that n is odd. Then

$$1^3 - 2^3 + \ldots + n^3 = 1^3 + 2^3 + \ldots + n^3 - 2\big(2^3 + 4^3 + \ldots + (n-1)^3\big)$$

$$= \sum_{r=1}^{n} r^3 - 2 \times 2^3 \left(1^3 + 2^3 + \ldots + \left(\tfrac{1}{2}(n-1)\right)^3 \right)$$

$$= \sum_{r=1}^{n} r^3 - 16 \sum_{r=1}^{\frac{1}{2}(n-1)} r^3$$

$$= \tfrac{1}{4} n^2 (n+1)^2 - 16 \times \tfrac{1}{4} \left(\tfrac{1}{2}(n-1)\right)^2 \left(\left(\tfrac{1}{2}(n-1)\right) + 1\right)^2$$

$$= \tfrac{1}{4} n^2 (n+1)^2 - \tfrac{1}{4} (n-1)^2 (n+1)^2 = \tfrac{1}{4} (n+1)^2 (2n-1).$$

Exercise 2B

1 Use the formulae for $\sum_{r=1}^{n} 1$, $\sum_{r=1}^{n} r$, $\sum_{r=1}^{n} r^2$ and $\sum_{r=1}^{n} r^3$ to find the following sums.

(a) $1^2 + 2^2 + \ldots + 100^2$

(b) $2 \times 3 + 3 \times 4 + \ldots + 99 \times 100$

(c) $(1 + 1^2) + (2 + 2^2) + \ldots + (20 + 20^2)$

(d) $1 \times 2 \times 3 + 2 \times 3 \times 4 + \ldots + 98 \times 99 \times 100$

2 Use the formulae for $\sum_{r=1}^{n} 1$, $\sum_{r=1}^{n} r$, $\sum_{r=1}^{n} r^2$ and $\sum_{r=1}^{n} r^3$ to find the following sums.

(a) $\sum_{r=0}^{n} (r + 1)$ 　　(b) $\sum_{r=1}^{n} (2r + 1)$ 　　(c) $\sum_{r=1}^{n} r^2(r - 1)$ 　　(d) $\sum_{r=1}^{2n} (2r - 1)$

3 Write down the formulae for $\sum_{r=1}^{n} 1$ and $\sum_{r=1}^{n} r$. Use these formulae to write down the sum of

the arithmetic series $a, a + d, a + 2d, \ldots, a + (n-1)d$.

Verify that your answer agrees with the formula given in P2 Section 3.6.

4 Find the sum of

(a) the squares of the integers less than 100 which are divisible by 3,

(b) the squares of the integers less than 100 which are not divisible by 3.

5 Find the sum of the series $1 \times 2^2 + 2 \times 3^2 + \ldots + n(n + 1)^2$.

6 Find the sum of n terms of the series

$$(p - 1)(p + 1) + (p - 2)(p + 2) + (p - 3)(p + 3) + \ldots.$$

7 Find the sums of the series

(a) $1 \times n + 2 \times (n - 1) + \ldots + n \times 1$, 　　(b) $1 \times n^2 + 2 \times (n - 1)^2 + \ldots + n \times 1^2$.

8 Calculate the following sums.

(a) $\sum_{r=1}^{100} r(r + 2)(r + 3)$ 　　(b) $\sum_{r=1}^{100} r(r^2 - 1)$ 　　(c) $\sum_{r=1}^{100} r(r + 3)(r + 6)$

9 Find the sum to n terms of the series $1^3 - 2^3 + 3^3 - 4^3 + \ldots$.

10 Find the sum to n terms of the series $1^4 - 2^4 + 3^4 - 4^4 + \ldots$.

2.4 A method based on differences

In this section you will see a method which can be useful for summing series. Suppose for

the moment that you know the formulae for $\sum_{r=1}^{n} 1$ and $\sum_{r=1}^{n} r$, and that you want one for $\sum_{r=1}^{n} r^2$.

Consider the equation $(r+1)^3 - r^3 = 3r^2 + 3r + 1$. If you swap the sides and write it for values of r starting from 1 and going up to n, you get

$$
\begin{array}{ccccccccc}
3 \times 1^2 & + & 3 \times 1 & + & 1 & = & 2^3 & - & 1^3 \\
3 \times 2^2 & + & 3 \times 2 & + & 1 & = & 3^3 & - & 2^3 \\
3 \times 3^2 & + & 3 \times 3 & + & 1 & = & 4^3 & - & 3^3 \\
\vdots & & \vdots & & \vdots & & \vdots & & \vdots \\
3(n-1)^2 & + & 3(n-1) & + & 1 & = & n^3 & - & (n-1)^3 \\
3n^2 & + & 3n & + & 1 & = & (n+1)^3 & - & n^3
\end{array}
$$

Now add down the columns. The left side is $3\sum_{r=1}^{n} r^2 + 3\sum_{r=1}^{n} r + \sum_{r=1}^{n} 1$. On the right side, most of the terms cancel, leaving $(n+1)^3 - 1^3 = (n+1)^3 - 1$. Therefore

$$3\sum_{r=1}^{n} r^2 + 3\sum_{r=1}^{n} r + \sum_{r=1}^{n} 1 = (n+1)^3 - 1.$$

If you transfer $\sum_{r=1}^{n} 1$ and $3\sum_{r=1}^{n} r$ to the right side of the equation, and substitute for them,

$$
\begin{aligned}
3\sum_{r=1}^{n} r^2 &= (n+1)^3 - 1 - 3\sum_{r=1}^{n} r - \sum_{r=1}^{n} 1 \\
&= (n+1)^3 - 1 - \tfrac{3}{2}n(n+1) - n \\
&= (n+1)^3 - \tfrac{3}{2}n(n+1) - (1+n) \\
&= (n+1)\left((n+1)^2 - \tfrac{3}{2}n - 1\right) \\
&= (n+1)\left(n^2 + 2n + 1 - \tfrac{3}{2}n - 1\right) \\
&= (n+1)\left(n^2 + \tfrac{1}{2}n\right) = \tfrac{1}{2}n(n+1)(2n+1).
\end{aligned}
$$

Therefore, on dividing by 3, $\sum_{r=1}^{n} r^2 = \tfrac{1}{6}n(n+1)(2n+1)$.

It is helpful to look more carefully at this process, which relies on the original equation that enables the right side to cancel when you add the terms.

Suppose a function $g(r)$, defined for $r \in \mathbb{N}$, can be written in the form $f(r+1) - f(r)$ where $f(r)$ is a function also defined for $r \in \mathbb{N}$. Then you can write

$$
\begin{array}{ccccc}
g(1) & = & f(2) & - & f(1) \\
g(2) & = & f(3) & - & f(2) \\
g(3) & = & f(4) & - & f(3) \\
\vdots & & \vdots & & \vdots \\
g(n-1) & = & f(n) & - & f(n-1) \\
g(n) & = & f(n+1) & - & f(n)
\end{array}
$$

and adding down the columns gives

$$\sum_{r=1}^{n} g(r) = f(n+1) - f(1).$$

Thus, this gives you a method for summing the series $\sum_{r=1}^{n} g(r)$.

Difference method

If $g(r) = f(r+1) - f(r)$ for $r \in \mathbb{N}$, then

$$\sum_{r=1}^{n} g(r) = f(n+1) - f(1).$$

Example 2.4.1

Express $\dfrac{1}{r(r+1)}$ in partial fractions. Hence show that $\displaystyle\sum_{r=1}^{n} \dfrac{1}{r(r+1)} = \dfrac{n}{n+1}$.

Write $\dfrac{1}{r(r+1)}$ in partial fractions as $\dfrac{1}{r(r+1)} \equiv \dfrac{1}{r} - \dfrac{1}{r+1}$.

The expression $\dfrac{1}{r(r+1)} = \dfrac{1}{r} - \dfrac{1}{r+1}$ is of the form $g(r) = f(r+1) - f(r)$ with

$g(r) = \dfrac{1}{r(r+1)}$ and $f(r) = -\dfrac{1}{r}$. Therefore, summing, $\displaystyle\sum_{r=1}^{n} g(r) = f(n+1) - f(1)$; that

is,

$$\sum_{r=1}^{n} \frac{1}{r(r+1)} = -\frac{1}{n+1} - \left(-\frac{1}{1}\right) = 1 - \frac{1}{n+1} = \frac{(n+1)-1}{n+1} = \frac{n}{n+1}.$$

Example 2.4.2

Express $\dfrac{3-r}{r(r+1)(r+3)}$ in partial fractions. Hence find an expression for

$\displaystyle\sum_{r=1}^{n} \dfrac{3-r}{r(r+1)(r+3)}$ for $n \geqslant 3$.

Using one of the standard methods for partial fractions (see P3 Section 7.4),

$$\frac{3-r}{r(r+1)(r+3)} \equiv \frac{1}{r} - \frac{2}{r+1} + \frac{1}{r+3}.$$

Writing out the terms of the series using this formula, you find the following.

$$\frac{2}{1\times2\times4} = \frac{1}{1} - \frac{2}{2} + \cancel{\frac{1}{4}}$$

$$\frac{1}{2\times3\times5} = \frac{1}{2} - \frac{2}{3} + \cancel{\frac{1}{5}}$$

$$\frac{0}{3\times4\times6} = \frac{1}{3} - \cancel{\frac{2}{4}} + \cancel{\frac{1}{6}}$$

$$\frac{-1}{4\times5\times7} = \cancel{\frac{1}{4}} - \cancel{\frac{2}{5}} + \cancel{\frac{1}{7}}$$

$$\vdots \qquad \vdots \qquad \vdots \qquad \vdots$$

$$\frac{3-(n-3)}{(n-3)(n-2)n} = \cancel{\frac{1}{n-3}} - \cancel{\frac{2}{n-2}} + \cancel{\frac{1}{n}}$$

$$\frac{3-(n-2)}{(n-2)(n-1)(n+1)} = \cancel{\frac{1}{n-2}} - \cancel{\frac{2}{n-1}} + \frac{1}{n+1}$$

$$\frac{3-(n-1)}{(n-1)n(n+2)} = \cancel{\frac{1}{n-1}} - \cancel{\frac{2}{n}} + \frac{1}{n+2}$$

$$\frac{3-n}{n(n+1)(n+3)} = \cancel{\frac{1}{n}} - \frac{2}{n+1} + \frac{1}{n+3}$$

When you add the terms notice that almost every positive term on the right side is balanced by a corresponding negative term, and that only terms at the beginning and end remain. You need a little care in keeping track of it all.

$$\sum_{r=1}^{n} \frac{3-r}{r(r+1)(r+3)} = \frac{1}{1} - \frac{2}{2} + \frac{1}{2} - \frac{2}{3} + \frac{1}{3} + \frac{1}{n+3} - \frac{2}{n+1} + \frac{1}{n+2} + \frac{1}{n+1}$$

$$= \frac{1}{6} + \frac{1}{n+3} + \frac{1}{n+2} - \frac{1}{n+1} = \frac{1}{6} + \frac{n^2+2n-1}{(n+1)(n+2)(n+3)}.$$

You can see from the pattern of terms crossed out in the diagram that the sum is valid for $n \geqslant 3$.

2.5 Convergence of series

Now that you have some series for which you can find the sum, it is natural to ask, does the series converge as n increases? You have seen this situation before.

In P2 Section 10.3, the sum of the geometric series

$$1 + r + r^2 + \ldots + r^n$$

was shown to tend to a limit if $|r| < 1$. The geometric series is said to be 'convergent'.

The key to the convergence of the geometric series is the behaviour of its sum function

$$S_n = \frac{a(r^n - 1)}{r-1}.$$

This idea can be generalised.

Let $S_n = \sum_{r=1}^{n} u_n$. Then if, as $n \to \infty$, S_n approaches a limit, the

series $\sum_{r=1}^{n} u_n$ **converges**. The limit is written as $\sum_{r=1}^{\infty} u_n$.

If this limit is S, then S is said to be the **sum** of the series $\sum_{r=1}^{\infty} u_n$.

Example 2.5.1

Show that the series of triangle numbers $1 + 3 + 6 + 10 + \ldots$ does not converge.

Since the general term t_r of the triangle numbers is given by $t_r = \frac{1}{2}r(r+1)$, the

sum function for the triangle numbers is $S_n = \sum_{r=1}^{n} \frac{1}{2}r(r+1)$. Then, using the result

of Example 2.2.2,

$$S_n = \frac{1}{6}n(n+1)(n+2).$$

Since $S_n = \frac{1}{6}n(n+1)(n+2) > \frac{1}{6}n^3$ and $\frac{1}{6}n^3$ can be made as large as you please by taking n to be large enough, the series of triangle numbers does not converge.

Example 2.5.2

Show that the series $\dfrac{1}{1 \times 2} + \dfrac{1}{2 \times 3} + \ldots + \dfrac{1}{n(n+1)}$ converges to 1 as n tends to infinity.

From Example 2.4.1, the sum function is $S_n = \dfrac{n}{n+1}$.

If you express S_n in divided out form, you get

$$S_n = \frac{n}{n+1} = 1 - \frac{1}{n+1}.$$

You can see that, if you make n large, $S_n \to 1$. Therefore the series converges to 1.

Another way to see that $S_n \to 1$ is to write $S_n = \dfrac{n}{n+1} = \dfrac{1}{1 + \dfrac{1}{n}}$. As n gets large, $\dfrac{1}{n} \to 0$,

so $S_n \to 1$.

The method of dividing the numerator and denominator by n is an example of a useful technique for showing that functions of this type approach a limit. For example, if you

wish to show that $\dfrac{(n+1)(n+2)(n+3)}{n^3}$ has the limit 1 as $n \to \infty$, then write

$\dfrac{(n+1)(n+2)(n+3)}{n^3} = \left(1 + \dfrac{1}{n}\right)\left(1 + \dfrac{2}{n}\right)\left(1 + \dfrac{3}{n}\right)$, and the limit becomes much clearer. The

process of writing down the limit in this way relies on some important results about limits, which are stated here without proof. You may assume these results.

If $\lim_{n \to \infty} u_n = u$ and $\lim_{n \to \infty} v_n = v$, then $\lim_{n \to \infty} (u_n \pm v_n) = u \pm v$,

$\lim_{n \to \infty} (u_n v_n) = uv$, and, provided $v \neq 0$, $\lim_{n \to \infty} \left(\dfrac{u_n}{v_n} \right) = \dfrac{u}{v}$.

In many cases it is not easy to tell whether or not a series converges, because you can only find the sum function for a very limited number of series. Other, more advanced methods are then required.

Exercise 2C

1 (a) Write down the rth term of the series $\dfrac{2}{1 \times 3} + \dfrac{2}{3 \times 5} + \dfrac{2}{5 \times 7} + \dots$, and express it in partial fractions.

   (b) Find the sum of n terms of the series $\dfrac{2}{1 \times 3} + \dfrac{2}{3 \times 5} + \dfrac{2}{5 \times 7} + \dots$.

2 Put $\dfrac{1}{(r-2)r}$ into partial fractions, and use your result to show that

$\displaystyle\sum_{r=3}^{n} \dfrac{1}{(r-2)r} = \dfrac{3}{2} - \dfrac{1}{n-1} - \dfrac{1}{n}$. Find the limit as $n \to \infty$ of $\displaystyle\sum_{r=3}^{n} \dfrac{1}{(r-2)r}$.

3 (a) Prove that if $f(r) = r!$, then $f(r+1) - f(r) = r \times r!$.

   (b) Sum the series $1 \times 1! + 2 \times 2! + 3 \times 3! + \dots + n \times n!$.

4 Simplify $\frac{1}{4} r(r+1)(r+2)(r+3) - \frac{1}{4}(r-1)r(r+1)(r+2)$, and use your result to find

$\displaystyle\sum_{r=1}^{n} r(r+1)(r+2)$.

5 Simplify $(2r+1)^5 - (2r-1)^5$, and use your result to derive a formula for $\displaystyle\sum_{r=1}^{n} r^4$.

6 Express $\dfrac{r}{(r-1)(r+1)}$ in partial fractions, and use your result to sum the series

$S_n = \dfrac{2}{1 \times 3} - \dfrac{4}{3 \times 5} - \dots + \dfrac{(-1)^n 2n}{(2n-1)(2n+1)}$. Calculate $\lim_{n \to \infty} S_n$.

Miscellaneous exercise 2

1 Express $\dfrac{1}{r^2 - 1}$ in the form $\dfrac{A}{r-1} + \dfrac{B}{r+1}$, for constants A and B.

Show that $\displaystyle\sum_{r=2}^{n} \dfrac{1}{r^2 - 1} = \dfrac{3}{4} - \dfrac{2n+1}{2n(n+1)}$.

(OCR)

2 (a) Use the formulae for $\sum\limits_{k=1}^{n} k$ and $\sum\limits_{k=1}^{n} k^2$ to show that $\sum\limits_{k=1}^{n} (2k-1)^2 = \lambda n\left(4n^2-1\right)$ where λ is a constant to be determined.

   (b) Find the sum of the squares of all the odd numbers between 100 and 200. (OCR)

3 The rth term of a finite series is u_r, and the sum of n terms is denoted by S_n, so $S_n = \sum\limits_{r=1}^{n} u_r$. If $S_n = 2n^2 + 3n$, express u_r as a function of r and also find $\sum\limits_{r=n}^{2n} u_r$. (OCR)

4 Show that $n(n+1)(n+2)-(n-1)n(n+1) = 3n(n+1)$. Hence, or otherwise, find a formula for $S_n = \sum\limits_{r=1}^{n} r(r+1)$. Use this result to prove that $\sum\limits_{r=1}^{n} r^2 = \frac{1}{6}n(n+1)(2n+1)$. Hence, or otherwise, find a formula for the sum to n terms of
$$4^2 + 7^2 + 10^2 + 13^2 + \ldots.$$
(OCR)

5 Prove that the sum of the series $(1\times3)+(2\times4)+(3\times5)+\ldots+n(n+2)$ is $\frac{1}{6}n(n+1)(2n+7)$. (OCR)

6 Prove that $\dfrac{1}{1\times2\times3} + \dfrac{1}{2\times3\times4} + \ldots + \dfrac{1}{n(n+1)(n+2)} = \dfrac{1}{4} - \dfrac{1}{2(n+1)(n+2)}$. (OCR)

7 If $S_n = 1\times n + 2(n-1) + 3(n-2) + \ldots + (n-1)\times2 + n\times1$, where n is a positive integer, prove that $S_{n+1} - S_n = \frac{1}{2}(n+1)(n+2)$.

   Prove that $S_n = \frac{1}{6}n(n+1)(n+2)$. (OCR, adapted)

8 Find the sum of the series $\sum\limits_{n=1}^{100} n\left(n^2+2\right)$. (OCR)

9 (a) Express $\dfrac{1}{n^3-n}$ in partial fractions.

   (b) Find the sum of the series $\sum\limits_{n=2}^{N} \dfrac{1}{n^3-n}$.

   (c) Deduce that the series
   $$\frac{1}{6} + \frac{1}{24} + \frac{1}{60} + \ldots + \frac{1}{n^3-n} + \ldots$$
   is convergent, and find its sum to infinity. (OCR, adapted)

10 Simplify $(2r+1)^4 - (2r-1)^4$.

   By considering $\sum\limits_{r=1}^{n} \left((2r+1)^4 - (2r-1)^4\right)$, prove that $\sum\limits_{r=1}^{n} r^3 = \frac{1}{4}n^2(n+1)^2$.

3 Mathematical induction

This chapter introduces a powerful method of proof called mathematical induction which is used to prove statements which involve positive integers. When you have completed the chapter, you should

- understand and be able to use the method of mathematical induction
- understand the terms 'proposition', 'basis case', and 'inductive step'
- be able to guess results, in simple cases, and prove them by mathematical induction.

3.1 The principle of mathematical induction

In P2 Chapter 8 you were introduced to the logic of mathematics and some methods of proof. In this chapter you will meet a quite different method of proof which can be applied to a number of widely differing situations.

The idea behind it is very straightforward. Imagine an infinite set of dominoes, each standing on its end, and placed close enough to the next domino so that if it falls over, it also knocks over the next domino. See Fig. 3.1.

Push the first domino over. The second domino falls over, and pushes the third domino over, and so on. Eventually all the dominoes fall over!

Fig. 3.1

Suppose now that you have a set S of positive integers. You are given that if any positive integer k belongs to S then $k+1$ also belongs to S. You are also given that 1 belongs to S. What can you say about the set S?

The answer is that, since $1 \in S$, $2 \in S$. And since $2 \in S$, $3 \in S$. And so on, until eventually every positive integer belongs to S. That is, S is the set of positive integers.

Notice the analogy between the integers and the dominoes. The statement

$$1 \in S$$

corresponds to the fact that the first domino is pushed over.

And the statement

$$\text{if } k \in S \text{ then } (k+1) \in S$$

corresponds to the statement that if one domino falls over so does the next.

The two statements, '$1 \in S$' and 'if $k \in S$ then $(k+1) \in S$' together imply that S is the set of positive integers, which corresponds to the conclusion that all the dominoes fall over.

The discussion before the last paragraph can be summarised in the following way, and is called the **principle of mathematical induction**.

> The **principle of mathematical induction** states
>
> that if S is a set of positive integers, and
>
> $$\text{if } 1 \in S \quad \text{and} \quad k \in S \Rightarrow (k+1) \in S,$$
>
> then S is the set of all positive integers.

You cannot *prove* the principle of mathematical induction. The statement in the shaded box is essentially an assumption about the positive integers, that is a fundamental property of the positive integers.

Notice also that both suppositions are necessary if all the dominoes are to fall over in the way described. If the first domino is not pushed over, none of them will fall over. And if the connecting link between any pair of dominoes is broken, the falling process will stop, and not all the dominoes will fall over.

Showing that $1 \in S$ is called the **basis case**.

The linking mechanism between k and $k+1$, that is $k \in S \Rightarrow (k+1) \in S$, is called the **inductive step**.

3.2   Using the principle of mathematical induction

Mathematical induction is used to establish the truth of propositions about positive integers. A proposition in this context is a statement about a number n, which stands for a positive integer.

Here are some examples of propositions.

$$\sum_{r=1}^{n} r^3 = \tfrac{1}{4} n^2 (n+1)^2.$$

$$\frac{\mathrm{d}}{\mathrm{d}x}\left(x^n\right) = nx^{n-1}.$$

$$2^n > n$$

The sum of the angles in a convex n-sided polygon is $180(n-2)$ degrees.

$7^{2n-1} + 3^{2n}$ is divisible by 8.

In a set of n positive integers there is a smallest member (or two or more of them).

To emphasise that the proposition is about positive integers, it is often denoted by $\mathrm{P}(n)$, which you can think of as a proposition about n.

Notice that the second and third propositions still make sense (and are in fact true) if n stands for any number, not necessarily an integer. But the proof by induction only holds for the case when n is a positive integer.

Example 3.2.1
Prove that $1 + 3 + \ldots + (2n - 1) = n^2$ is true for all integers $n \geqslant 1$.

Proposition   Let $P(n)$ be the proposition that

$$1 + 3 + \ldots + (2n - 1) = n^2.$$

Let T be the set of positive integers for which $P(n)$ is true.

The proof will involve showing that T has the properties $1 \in T$ and $k \in T \Rightarrow (k + 1) \in T$, and so, from the principle of mathematical induction in the shaded box, T will be the set of positive integers, showing that $P(n)$ is true for all positive integers.

Notice that to say that T is the set of positive integers for which $P(n)$ is true does not imply that the proposition is actually true. For all we know at the moment, T may have no members.

Basis case   To show that $1 \in T$, that is the proposition is true for $n = 1$, substitute $n = 1$ in the proposition. When $n = 1$ the left side is 1; when $n = 1$ the right side is $1^2 = 1$. Therefore $P(1)$ is true, so $1 \in T$.

Inductive step   *You have to establish that $k \in T \Rightarrow (k + 1) \in T$.*

Suppose that $k \in T$, that is $P(k)$ is true. This means that

$$1 + 3 + \ldots + (2k - 1) = k^2.$$

You now have to prove that $k \in T \Rightarrow (k + 1) \in T$; that is, if $P(k)$ is true, then $P(k + 1)$ is true. This is the same as proving that if the statement $1 + 3 + \ldots + (2k - 1) = k^2$ is true, then $1 + 3 + \ldots + (2k - 1) + (2k + 1) = (k + 1)^2$ is true.

Starting with the left side, $1 + 3 + \ldots + (2k - 1) + (2k + 1)$,

$$
\begin{aligned}
1 + 3 + \ldots + (2k - 1) + (2k + 1) &= (1 + 3 + \ldots + (2k - 1)) + (2k + 1) \\
&= k^2 + (2k + 1) \quad \text{(because $P(k)$ is true)} \\
&= k^2 + 2k + 1 \\
&= (k + 1)^2.
\end{aligned}
$$

Therefore, if $k \in T$, then $k + 1 \in T$,   or $k \in T \Rightarrow (k + 1) \in T$.

Completion   Therefore, using the principle of mathematical induction, T is the set of positive integers. So $P(n)$ is true for all positive integers; that is, $1 + 3 + \ldots + (2n - 1) = n^2$ is true for all positive integers.

Notice where in the inductive step the supposition that $1 + 3 + \ldots + (2k - 1) = k^2$ is true was used. Some people find this the most difficult part of proof by mathematical induction.

In practice, this detailed form of writing out an induction proof is streamlined by leaving out detail. This is taken up in the next section.

3.3 Examples of proof by induction

This section consists almost wholly of examples to show the wide variety of situations in which you can use proof by mathematical induction.

Every proof by mathematical induction consists of four parts:
- a statement of the proposition
- a proof of the basis case
- a proof of the inductive step
- the completion of the proof.

The first example is like Example 3.2.1, and is the proof of the formula for the sum of the cubes of the first n positive integers, $\sum_{r=1}^{n} r^3 = \frac{1}{4} n^2 (n+1)^2$, which was derived, but not proved, in Section 2.3.

Example 3.3.1

Prove that $\sum_{r=1}^{n} r^3 = \frac{1}{4} n^2 (n+1)^2$ is true for all positive integers n.

Proposition   Let $P(n)$ be the proposition that $\sum_{r=1}^{n} r^3 = \frac{1}{4} n^2 (n+1)^2$.

Basis case   When $n=1$ the left side is $1^3 = 1$; when $n=1$ the right side is $\frac{1}{4} \times 1^2 \times (1+1)^2 = \frac{1}{4} \times 1 \times 2^2 = 1$. Therefore $P(1)$ is true.

Inductive step   Suppose that $P(k)$ is true. Then $\sum_{r=1}^{k} r^3 = \frac{1}{4} k^2 (k+1)^2$.

$$\sum_{r=1}^{k+1} r^3 = \left(1^3 + 2^3 + \ldots + k^3\right) + (k+1)^3 = \sum_{r=1}^{k} r^3 + (k+1)^3$$

$$= \frac{1}{4} k^2 (k+1)^2 + (k+1)^3 = \frac{1}{4}(k+1)^2 \left(k^2 + 4(k+1)\right)$$

$$= \frac{1}{4}(k+1)^2 \left(k^2 + 4k + 4\right) = \frac{1}{4}(k+1)^2 (k+2)^2.$$

This is $P(n)$ with $n = k+1$. Therefore, if $P(k)$ is true, then $P(k+1)$ is true.

Completion   Using the principle of mathematical induction, $P(n)$ is true for all positive integers, so $\sum_{r=1}^{n} r^3 = \frac{1}{4} n^2 (n+1)^2$ is true for all positive integers n.

Example 3.3.2

Prove that for all positive integers n, $\dfrac{\mathrm{d}}{\mathrm{d}x}\left(x^n\right) = nx^{n-1}$.

Proposition   Let $P(n)$ be the proposition that $\dfrac{\mathrm{d}}{\mathrm{d}x}\left(x^n\right) = nx^{n-1}$.

Basis case   When $n = 1$ the left side is $\dfrac{d}{dx}\left(x^1\right) = \dfrac{d}{dx}(x) = 1$; when $n = 1$ the right side is $1x^{1-1} = 1x^0 = 1$. Therefore $P(1)$ is true.

Inductive step   Suppose that $P(k)$ is true. Then $\dfrac{d}{dx}\left(x^k\right) = kx^{k-1}$.

$$\frac{d}{dx}\left(x^{k+1}\right) = \frac{d}{dx}\left(x^k \times x\right)$$
$$= \frac{d}{dx}\left(x^k\right) \times x + x^k \times \frac{d}{dx}(x) \quad \text{(by the product rule, P3 Section 8.1)}$$
$$= kx^{k-1} \times x + x^k \times 1$$
$$= kx^k + x^k$$
$$= (k+1)x^k.$$

This is $P(n)$ with $n = k+1$. Therefore, if $P(k)$ is true, then $P(k+1)$ is true.

Completion   Using the principle of mathematical induction, $P(n)$ is true for all positive integers, so $\dfrac{d}{dx}\left(x^n\right) = nx^{n-1}$ is true for all positive integers n.

Example 3.3.3
Prove that $2^n > n$ for all positive integers n.

Proposition   Let $P(n)$ be the proposition that $2^n > n$.

Basis case   When $n = 1$ the left side is $2^1 = 2$; when $n = 1$ the right side is 1. As $2 > 1$, $P(1)$ is true.

Inductive step   Suppose that $P(k)$ is true. Then $2^k > k$.

$$2^{k+1} = 2 \times 2^k$$
$$> 2 \times k$$
$$= k + k$$
$$\geqslant k + 1 \quad \text{(since } k \geqslant 1\text{)}.$$

Therefore, if $P(k)$ is true, then $P(k+1)$ is true.

Completion   Using the principle of mathematical induction, $P(n)$ is true for all positive integers, so $2^n > n$ for all positive integers n.

Example 3.3.4
Prove that the sum of the angles in a convex n-sided polygon is $180(n-2)$ degrees.

Note that the statement to be proved does not place any conditions on n, but the idea is meaningless unless $n \geqslant 3$. So take the basis case to be $n = 3$, and use mathematical induction to prove the statement for $n \geqslant 3$.

Proposition   For $n \geqslant 3$, let $P(n)$ be the proposition that the sum of the angles in a convex n-sided polygon is $180(n-2)$ degrees.

Basis case   The basis case is $n = 3$. When $n = 3$, the polygon is a triangle and the sum of the angles is 180 degrees; when $n = 3$, $180(n-2) = 180$. So $P(3)$ is true.

Inductive step   Suppose that $P(k)$ is true, where $k \geqslant 3$. Then the angle sum of a k-sided polygon is $180(k-2)$ degrees. Now consider the convex $(k+1)$-sided polygon, $A_1 A_2 \ldots A_{k-1} A_k A_{k+1}$ (see Fig. 3.2). As the polygon is convex, you can join A_k to A_1 to form a convex k-sided polygon, together with a triangle.

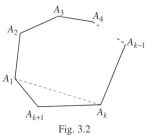

Fig. 3.2

Therefore the sum of the angles is the sum of the angles in a convex k-sided polygon, together with a triangle, that is $\big(180(k-2)+180\big)$ degrees, or $180((k+1)-2)$ degrees.

Therefore, if $P(k)$ is true, then $P(k+1)$ is true.

Completion   Using the principle of mathematical induction, $P(n)$ is true for all positive integers $\geqslant 3$, so the sum of the angles in a convex n-sided polygon is $180(n-2)$ degrees.

Example 3.3.5
Prove that for all positive integers n, $7^{2n-1} + 3^{2n}$ is divisible by 8.

Proposition   Let $P(n)$ be the proposition that $7^{2n-1} + 3^{2n}$ is divisible by 8.

Basis case   When $n = 1$, $7^{2n-1} + 3^{2n} = 7^1 + 3^2 = 7 + 9 = 16$, which is divisible by 8. Therefore $P(1)$ is true.

Inductive step   Begin by looking at $f(k+1) - f(k)$ where $f(k) = 7^{2k-1} + 3^{2k}$.

$$f(k+1) - f(k) = \left(7^{2k+1} + 3^{2(k+1)}\right) - \left(7^{2k-1} + 3^{2k}\right)$$
$$= \left(7^2 \times 7^{2k-1} - 7^{2k-1}\right) + \left(3^2 \times 3^{2k} - 3^{2k}\right)$$
$$= \left(7^2 - 1\right) \times 7^{2k-1} + \left(3^2 - 1\right) \times 3^{2k}$$
$$= 48 \times 7^{2k-1} + 8 \times 3^{2k}.$$

So, taking $f(k)$ to the right side of the equation,

$$\left(7^{2k+1} + 3^{2(k+1)}\right) = \left(7^{2k-1} + 3^{2k}\right) + 8\left(6 \times 7^{2k-1} + 3^{2k}\right).$$

Now suppose that $P(k)$ is true. Then as both expressions in brackets on the right are divisible by 8, the expression on the left is also divisible by 8; that is, $P(k+1)$ is true.

Therefore if $P(k)$ is true, then $P(k+1)$ is true.

Completion   Using the principle of mathematical induction, $P(n)$ is true for all positive integers, so $7^{2n-1} + 3^{2n}$ is divisible by 8 for all positive integers n.

Example 3.3.6

Prove that any set of positive integers has a smallest member (or two or more of them).

> **Proposition** Let $P(n)$ be the proposition that in a set of n positive integers there is a smallest member.

> **Basis case** When $n = 1$, the set consists of just one number. Therefore $P(1)$ is true.

> **Inductive step** Suppose that $P(k)$ is true. Then every set of k positive integers has a least member. Now consider a set of $k + 1$ positive integers, and divide it into a set of k positive integers, and one integer. The set of k positive integers has a least member r, by hypothesis. Suppose the single integer is s. Then the smaller of r and s will be a least member for the set of $k + 1$ positive integers.

> Therefore if $P(k)$ is true, then $P(k + 1)$ is true.

> **Completion** Using the principle of mathematical induction, $P(n)$ is true for all positive integers, so in any set of positive integers there is a smallest member.

This result, which appears obvious, will be used in module P6.

Exercise 3A

1 In Example 3.2.1, the formula for the sum of the first n odd numbers was proved. Guess a formula for the sum of the first n even numbers, by adding 1 to each odd number.

   (a) Write down a statement of the proposition to be proved.

   (b) Complete the proof by induction.

2 Use the method of mathematical induction to prove that, for all positive integers n,
$$1^2 + 2^2 + \ldots + n^2 = \tfrac{1}{6}n(n+1)(2n+1).$$

3 Use the method of mathematical induction to prove that, for all positive integers n,
$$1 \times 4 + 2 \times 5 + 3 \times 6 + \ldots + n(n+3) = \tfrac{1}{3}n(n+1)(n+5).$$

4 Use the principle of mathematical induction to prove that, for all positive integers n,
$$1 \times 2 + 2 \times 3 + \ldots + n(n+1) = \tfrac{1}{3}n(n+1)(n+2).$$

5 Use the principle of mathematical induction to prove that, for integers $n > 2$,
$$\sum_{r=2}^{n}(r-1)r = \tfrac{1}{3}n(n^2 - 1).$$

6 Use the principle of mathematical induction to prove that, for all positive integers n,
$$\frac{d^n}{dx^n}\sin x = \sin\left(x + \tfrac{1}{2}n\pi\right).$$

7 Find and prove a result similar to that of Question 6 for $\dfrac{d^n}{dx^n}\cos x$.

8 Prove that if $u_{n+2} = 3u_{n+1} - 2u_n$ for all positive integers n, and $u_1 = 1$, $u_2 = 3$, then $u_n = 2^n - 1$.

9 Prove that if $u_{n+2} = 5u_{n+1} - 6u_n$ for all positive integers n, and $u_0 = u_1 = -1$, then $u_n = 3^n - 2^{n+1}$.

10 Consider the sequence $u_{n+1} = u_n + (2n+1)$, with $u_1 = 1$. Calculate the values of u_2, u_3 and u_4, and use your results to guess at the form of u_n. Prove your guess by mathematical induction.

11 Prove by mathematical induction that $\displaystyle\sum_{r=1}^{n} 2r > n^2$.

12 Find numerically the first few values of the sum $\displaystyle\sum_{r=1}^{n} \frac{1}{\sqrt{r}}$, and compare your results with $\sqrt{n}$. Make a conjecture, and prove it by mathematical induction.

13 A sequence is defined by $a_{n+1} = \sqrt{2 + a_n}$ and $a_1 = 3$. Prove by mathematical induction that $a_n > 2$ for all positive integers.

14 Prove that the sum of the digits of a number divisible by 9 is itself divisible by 9. (Hint: let $P(n)$ be the proposition that the sum of the digits of $9n$ is divisible by 9.)

15 Prove that $(1+x)^n > 1 + nx$ for all $x > 0$ and for integers $n > 1$.

16 The nth member a_n of a sequence is defined by $a_n = 5^n + 12n - 1$. By considering $a_{n+1} - 5a_n$ prove that a_n is divisible by 16.

17 If n is a positive integer and $n < t < n+1$, show that $\dfrac{1}{n+1} < \dfrac{1}{t}$.

Deduce that

$$\int_n^{n+1} \frac{1}{n+1}\, dt < \int_n^{n+1} \frac{1}{t}\, dt, \quad \text{and hence that} \quad \frac{1}{n+1} < \ln\left(1 + \frac{1}{n}\right).$$

Use this result to prove by induction that $\dfrac{1}{2} + \dfrac{1}{3} + \dfrac{1}{4} + \ldots + \dfrac{1}{n} < \ln n$ for $n \geq 2$.

3.4 The inductive method

In Section 2.3, a formula for the sum of the cubes of the first n positive integers was guessed as $\displaystyle\sum_{r=1}^{n} r^3 = \tfrac{1}{4} n^2 (n+1)^2$. This result was then proved in Example 3.3.1.

This is an example of the inductive method: compute, conjecture, prove. You perform some calculations, conjecture a general result, and then prove it by induction.

Here are some more examples of the inductive method.

Example 3.4.1

By calculating some specific values for the sum $\sum_{r=1}^{n} \dfrac{1}{r(r+1)}$, conjecture a result and prove it by mathematical induction.

Here are the first few values.

$$\frac{1}{1\times2} = \frac{1}{2},$$

$$\frac{1}{1\times2} + \frac{1}{2\times3} = \frac{1}{2} + \frac{1}{6} = \frac{3+1}{6} = \frac{4}{6} = \frac{2}{3},$$

$$\frac{1}{1\times2} + \frac{1}{2\times3} + \frac{1}{3\times4} = \frac{1}{2} + \frac{1}{6} + \frac{1}{12} = \frac{6+2+1}{12} = \frac{9}{12} = \frac{3}{4}.$$

It is tempting to conjecture that $\sum_{r=1}^{n} \dfrac{1}{r(r+1)} = \dfrac{n}{n+1}$ for all positive integers n.

Proposition   Let P(n) be the proposition that $\sum_{r=1}^{n} \dfrac{1}{r(r+1)} = \dfrac{n}{n+1}$.

Basis case   The basis case has been proved in the numerical examples. Therefore P(1) is true.

Inductive step   Suppose that P(k) is true. Then $\sum_{r=1}^{k} \dfrac{1}{r(r+1)} = \dfrac{k}{k+1}$.

$$\sum_{r=1}^{k+1} \frac{1}{r(r+1)} = \sum_{r=1}^{k} \frac{1}{r(r+1)} + \frac{1}{(k+1)(k+2)}$$

$$= \frac{k}{k+1} + \frac{1}{(k+1)(k+2)}$$

$$= \frac{k(k+2)+1}{(k+1)(k+2)}$$

$$= \frac{k^2 + 2k + 1}{(k+1)(k+2)}$$

$$= \frac{(k+1)^2}{(k+1)(k+2)} = \frac{k+1}{k+2}.$$

Therefore, if P(k) is true, then P($k+1$) is true.

Completion   Using the principle of mathematical induction, P(n) is true for all positive integers, so $\sum_{r=1}^{n} \dfrac{1}{r(r+1)} = \dfrac{n}{n+1}$ for all positive integers n.

Example 3.4.2

Find and prove a formula for $\dfrac{d^n}{dx^n}\left(xe^x\right)$.

Looking at the first few values gives:

$$\frac{d}{dx}(xe^x) = 1 \times e^x + x \times e^x = (x+1)e^x,$$

$$\frac{d^2}{dx^2}(xe^x) = \frac{d}{dx}((x+1)e^x) = 1 \times e^x + (x+1) \times e^x = (x+2)e^x,$$

$$\frac{d^3}{dx^3}(xe^x) = \frac{d}{dx}((x+2)e^x) = 1 \times e^x + (x+2) \times e^x = (x+3)e^x.$$

The conjecture is $\dfrac{d^n}{dx^n}(xe^x) = (x+n)e^x$ for all positive integers n.

Proposition   Let $P(n)$ be the proposition that $\dfrac{d^n}{dx^n}(xe^x) = (x+n)e^x$.

Basis case   In this example, you can take $n = 0$ as the basis case. When $n = 0$, you need to interpret $\dfrac{d^n}{dx^n}(xe^x)$ as differentiating zero times, so the result is xe^x. But the formula gives, when $n = 0$, $(x+0)e^x = xe^x$. So $P(0)$ is true.

Inductive step   Suppose that $P(k)$ is true. Then $\dfrac{d^k}{dx^k}(xe^x) = (x+k)e^x$.

$$\begin{aligned}
\frac{d^{k+1}}{dx^{k+1}}(xe^x) &= \frac{d}{dx}\left(\frac{d^k}{dx^k}(xe^x)\right)\\[2mm]
&= \frac{d}{dx}((x+k)e^x)\\[2mm]
&= 1 \times e^x + (x+k) \times e^x\\[2mm]
&= (x+k+1)e^x.
\end{aligned}$$

Therefore, if $P(k)$ is true, then $P(k+1)$ is true.

Completion   Using the principle of mathematical induction, $P(n)$ is true for all positive integers, so $\dfrac{d^n}{dx^n}(xe^x) = (x+n)e^x$ for all positive integers n.

You may wonder whether there is any way of proving results about real numbers using the principle of induction. The answer is 'no'. The problem with real numbers is that there is no next number in the same way that there is with integers. In fact, the analogy with a row of dominoes at the beginning of the chapter has no parallel in dealing with real numbers.

Exercise 3B

1 By calculating $\sum_{r=1}^{n}(3r(r+1)+1)$ for the first few values of n, make a conjecture about the value of the sum, and prove it by mathematical induction.

2 Make a conjecture about the sum of the series
$$1\times1!+2\times2!+3\times3!+\ldots+n\times n!$$
and prove it by mathematical induction.

3 Calculate the sums of three consecutive cubes in a number of cases, and make a conjecture about a factor of the sum of three consecutive cubes. Prove your conjecture.

4 Make a conjecture about a number which divides $3^{2n+1}+2^{4n+2}$, and prove it.

5 The diagram shows four straight lines in a plane. They are said to be in general position, because no three meet at the same point and no two of them are parallel.

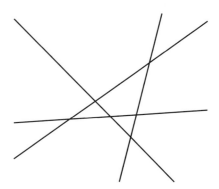

(a) Make a table showing the number of regions into which the plane is divided when there are 1, 2, 3, 4 and 5 lines.

(b) Make a conjecture about the quadratic expression which takes these values. (Hint: try subtracting 1 from each of them.)

(c) Prove your conjecture by induction. The inductive step will require you to add a new line in general position.

Miscellaneous exercise 3

1 Let $f(n)=3f(n-1)+8$, with $f(1)=11$. Prove by induction that $f(n)=5\times3^n-4$.

2 Prove by induction that the sum of the series $(1\times3)+(2\times4)+(3\times5)+\ldots+n(n+2)$ is $\frac{1}{6}n(n+1)(2n+7)$ (OCR)

3 Prove by induction that $\dfrac{1}{1\times2\times3}+\dfrac{1}{2\times3\times4}+\ldots+\dfrac{1}{n(n+1)(n+2)}=\dfrac{1}{4}-\dfrac{1}{2(n+1)(n+2)}$.

(OCR)

4 If $S_n=1\times n+2(n-1)+3(n-2)+\ldots+(n-1)\times2+n\times1$, where n is a positive integer, prove that $S_{n+1}-S_n=\frac{1}{2}(n+1)(n+2)$.
Use induction to prove that $S_n=\frac{1}{6}n(n+1)(n+2)$.   (OCR)

5   Prove the identity $\cos \alpha \cos 2\alpha \cos 4\alpha \ldots \cos 2^n \alpha \equiv \dfrac{\sin 2^{n+1} \alpha}{2^{n+1} \sin \alpha}$, where α is not an integer multiple of π.

6   Prove that $\dfrac{1}{a(a+1)} + \dfrac{1}{(a+1)(a+2)} + \ldots + \dfrac{1}{(a+n-1)(a+n)} = \dfrac{n}{a(a+n)}$.

7   Prove by mathematical induction that, for all positive integers n,
$$\frac{1}{2} + \frac{1}{4} + \frac{1}{8} + \frac{1}{16} + \ldots + \frac{1}{2^n} = 1 - \frac{1}{2^n}.$$
(OCR)

8   Prove that $13^n + 6^{n-1}$ is divisible by 7.

9   Prove that, if n is a positive integer, $5^{2n} + 12^{n-1}$ is divisible by 13.

10   Prove that, if n is a positive integer, $5^{2n+2} - 24n - 25$ is divisible by 576.   (OCR)

11   Show that, if you were trying to prove the false proposition
$$1 + 2 + 3 + \ldots + n = \tfrac{1}{2}(n-1)(n+2),$$
the inductive step works perfectly but the basis case does not.

12   (a)   An arithmetic progression is such that the sum of the first 12 terms is 270 and the sum of the first 17 terms is 510. Find the first term and the common difference.

   (b)   A geometric progression is such that the sum of the first two terms is 1 and the sum of the first four terms is 5. Given that all the terms are positive, find the first term and the common ratio.

   (c)   A new series is formed as follows. The kth term of the new series is the product of the kth term of the arithmetic progression in (a) and the kth term of the geometric progression in (b). Show that the kth term of the new series is $(k+1)2^{k-1}$.

   Prove by induction that $\displaystyle\sum_{k=1}^{n} (k+1)2^{k-1} = n2^n$.   (OCR)

13   If $x^3 = x+1$, prove by induction that $x^{3n} = a_n x + b_n + c_n x^{-1}$,
where $a_1 = 1$, $b_1 = 1$, $c_1 = 1$ and $a_n = a_{n-1} + b_{n-1}$, $b_n = a_{n-1} + b_{n-1} + c_{n-1}$, $c_n = a_{n-1} + c_{n-1}$
for $n = 2, 3, \ldots$.   (OCR)

14   An emerging currency has two kinds of bank note, one for 5 schenkels and one for 9 schenkels. Prove that every account greater than 31 schenkels can be paid without change by using the 5 schenkel and 9 schenkel notes.

4 Graphs of rational functions

This chapter is about sketching graphs of rational functions without using a calculator. When you have completed it, you should

- be able to sketch graphs of rational functions in which the denominator is linear
- know the meaning of the term 'asymptote' and be able to find vertical, horizontal and oblique asymptotes
- be able to sketch graphs of rational functions in which the denominator is linear or quadratic
- be able to use an algebraic method to determine 'forbidden' regions of some rational functions.

4.1 Functions with linear denominators

In previous modules you learnt how to sketch graphs of various forms: straight lines and circles, and trigonometric, exponential and logarithmic functions. In this chapter this sequence of graphs is taken forward to include rational functions.

The form $y = \dfrac{k}{x-a}$

The key to sketching the graph $y = \dfrac{k}{x-a}$, where k and a are constants, is knowing the shape of the graph $y = \dfrac{1}{x}$. From P1 Section 8.5, the graph of $y = \dfrac{1}{x-a}$ is the graph of $y = \dfrac{1}{x}$ translated by a in the positive x-direction. The graph of $y = \dfrac{k}{x-a}$ is a stretch of factor k in the y-direction of the graph of $y = \dfrac{1}{x-a}$.

Fig. 4.1 shows graphs of $y = \dfrac{1}{x}$ and $y = \dfrac{2}{x+1}$ to illustrate these remarks.

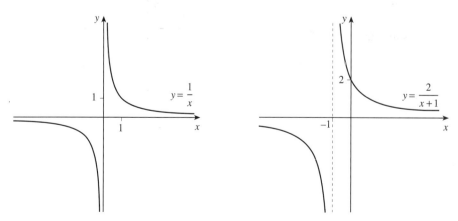

Fig. 4.1

For many purposes a sketch, rather than a carefully drawn graph, is all that is required. If so, you do not need to put in an enormous amount of detail. You should mark important points, and show the general behaviour of the graph, but it is not necessary to plot the graph on graph paper, or to do a pseudo-plot on lined paper using the distance between the lines as a unit for an approximate square.

Notice the vertical lines $x = 0$ on the graph of $y = \dfrac{1}{x}$ and $x = -1$ on the graph of $y = \dfrac{2}{x+1}$. These lines are examples of vertical **asymptotes**. In fact, all vertical asymptotes are lines of the form $x = \text{constant},$ where the constant is the value of x excluded from the domain of the function whose graph you are drawing. Thus $y = \dfrac{1}{x}$ is not defined for $x = 0$, and $x = 0$ is an asymptote; similarly, $y = \dfrac{2}{x+1}$ is not defined when $x = -1$, and $x = -1$ is an asymptote.

In the previous paragraph, the word 'vertical' was used to mean 'parallel to the y-axis'. It is convenient, although strictly incorrect, to do this, and to use the word 'horizontal' to mean 'parallel to the x-axis'.

The graphs of $y = \dfrac{1}{x}$ and $y = \dfrac{2}{x+1}$ also have the same horizontal asymptote as each other, namely $y = 0$. It is easy to see that when x is large, each of the graphs becomes close to $y = 0$.

Example 4.1.1

Sketch the function $f(x) = \dfrac{3}{2-x}$, and give the equation of the vertical asymptote.

Write the equation of the function in the form $f(x) = \dfrac{3}{2-x} = \dfrac{-3}{x-2}$, so that it is in the form $\dfrac{k}{x-a}$ with $k = -3$ and $a = 2$.

The graph is then the graph of $y = \dfrac{1}{x}$ translated by 2 units in the positive x-direction, and then stretched by a factor of -3 in the y-direction, which involves a reflection in the x-axis.

The vertical asymptote is the line with equation $x = 2$.

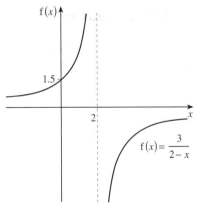

Fig. 4.2

The form $y = \dfrac{cx - d}{x - a}$

The key to sketching a graph with this form of equation, as will be the case in much of this chapter, is to start by putting the right side of equation into divided out form (or, later, into partial fraction form). The equation then takes the form $y = c + \dfrac{k}{x - a}$, which

you should recognise as being the graph of $y = \dfrac{k}{x - a}$ translated by c in the y-direction.

An example will help you to see what is happening.

Example 4.1.2

Sketch the curve with equation $y = \dfrac{2x + 1}{x + 1}$. Give the equations of the asymptotes.

Begin by writing $\dfrac{2x + 1}{x + 1} \equiv A + \dfrac{B}{x + 1}$, and finding $A = 2$ and $B = -1$. Then

$$y = 2 + \frac{-1}{x + 1}.$$

This is the graph of $y = \dfrac{1}{x + 1}$, reflected in the x-axis, and then translated by 2 units in the positive y-direction. The graph is shown in Fig. 4.3.

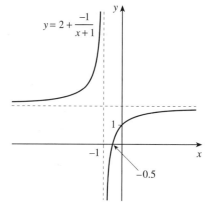

Fig. 4.3

The vertical asymptote is $x = -1$ and the horizontal asymptote is $y = 2$.

As a final check, note that $y = 0$ when $x = -0.5$, and $y = 1$ when $x = 0$.

The form $y = \dfrac{cx^2 + dx + e}{x - a}$

Once again, you should use the divided out form to turn an equation of the form $y = \dfrac{cx^2 + dx + e}{x - a}$ into the form $y = Ax + B + \dfrac{C}{x - a}$. An example will clarify how you can obtain information from expressions of this form.

Example 4.1.3

Sketch the curve with equation $y = \dfrac{x^2 - 3x + 3}{x - 2}$, and identify the asymptotes.

Write the equation of the curve in divided out form as $y = x - 1 + \dfrac{1}{x - 2}$.

You can then see that the graph has a vertical asymptote at $x = 2$.

When x is just greater than 2, y is very large and positive. When x is just less than 2, $|y|$ is very large and y is negative.

It also looks as though the graph has an oblique asymptote. You can check this by letting $x \to \infty$. The part of the equation $\dfrac{1}{x-2}$ then becomes very small and the graph approaches the straight line with equation $y = x - 1$.

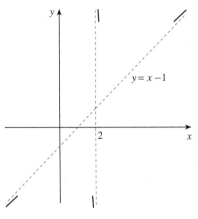

When $|x|$ is large and x is positive, y is just greater than $x - 1$; similarly, when $|x|$ is large and x is negative, y is just less than $x - 1$. These pieces are shown in Fig. 4.4.

Fig. 4.4

To check for maxima and minima, note that the domain of definition of $x - 1 + \dfrac{1}{x-2}$ is $\mathbb{R}$, $x \ne 2$. Then $\dfrac{dy}{dx} = 1 - \dfrac{1}{(x-2)^2}$.

This is defined for all x except $x = 2$, and is 0 when $(x-2)^2 = 1$, that is when $x = 3$ and $x = 1$, with corresponding y-values $y = 3$ and $y = -1$. Thus there are turning values at $(3,3)$ and $(1,-1)$. Also $\dfrac{d^2 y}{dx^2} = \dfrac{2}{(x-2)^3}$, which is positive when $x = 3$ and negative when $x = 1$, showing that $(3,3)$ is a minimum and $(1,-1)$ is a maximum.

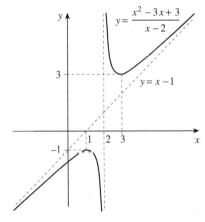

The graph is completed in Fig. 4.5. The asymptotes are $x = 2$ and $y = x - 1$.

Fig. 4.5

Exercise 4A

1 For each of the following graphs, write down the equations of the vertical and horizontal asymptotes, and draw a sketch.

(a) $y = \dfrac{2}{x}$

(b) $y = \dfrac{1}{x-1}$

(c) $y = \dfrac{3}{x+2}$

(d) $y = \dfrac{5}{2x-1}$

(e) $y = 1 + \dfrac{2}{x}$

(f) $y = 3 - \dfrac{2}{x+1}$

(g) $y = 4 + \dfrac{3}{x+2}$

(h) $y = 3 - \dfrac{5}{2x-1}$

(i) $y = \dfrac{1+x}{x}$

(j) $y = \dfrac{x-1}{x}$

(k) $y = \dfrac{2-x}{1-x}$

(l) $y = \dfrac{2+3x}{2+x}$

2   For each of the following graphs, find the equations of any vertical, horizontal and oblique asymptotes. Draw diagrams similar to Fig. 4.4, and join up the pieces to sketch the graph.

(a) $y = x + \dfrac{1}{x}$ (b) $y = x + 1 - \dfrac{1}{x}$ (c) $y = 3x - 2 - \dfrac{1}{x - 1}$

(d) $y = x - 3 + \dfrac{1}{x - 2}$ (e) $y = \dfrac{x^2 - 2}{x}$ (f) $y = \dfrac{x^2 - 2x - 1}{x - 1}$

(g) $y = \dfrac{x^2 + 3x + 1}{x + 2}$ (h) $y = \dfrac{2x^2 + x}{x + 1}$ (i) $y = \dfrac{3 + x - 2x^2}{1 + 2x}$

3   For each of the following graphs, find the coordinates of any maxima and minima, and distinguish between them.

(a) $y = x + \dfrac{4}{x}$ (b) $y = x + 1 + \dfrac{1}{1 + x}$ (c) $y = 8x + 3 + \dfrac{1}{1 + 2x}$

4   For each of the following graphs, find the equations of any asymptotes, find the coordinates of the points where the graphs cross the coordinate axes, find the coordinates of any maxima and minima, and sketch the curve.

(a) $y = x - \dfrac{1}{x}$ (b) $y = x + \dfrac{1}{x}$ (c) $y = 3 + 2x + \dfrac{1}{2x}$

(d) $y = x - 1 - \dfrac{1}{2x - 1}$ (e) $y = \dfrac{9x^2 - 5x - 3}{x - 1}$ (f) $y = \dfrac{2x^2}{2x - 1}$

4.2   Functions with quadratic denominators which factorise

If the denominator of $y = \dfrac{px^2 + qx + r}{ax^2 + bx + c}$ has factors $dx - e$ and $fx - g$, then the expression can be transformed by division and partial fractions into the form $y = A + \dfrac{B}{dx - e} + \dfrac{C}{fx - g}$, as described in Section 1.3.

You will find a summary of the methods for producing a sketch later in the section, after some examples.

Example 4.2.1

Sketch the graph of $y = \dfrac{x^2 - x - 2}{(x - 1)(x - 3)}$.

It is useful first to do some preliminary detective work with the equation in this form. By solving the equation $x^2 - x - 2 = 0$ you can see that the graph crosses the x-axis at $x = -1$ and $x = 2$.

The graph crosses the y-axis when $x = 0$, that is at $\left(0, -\frac{2}{3}\right)$.

The vertical asymptotes are $x = 3$ and $x = 1$.

When you use partial fractions and write the equation as $y = 1 + \dfrac{1}{x-1} + \dfrac{2}{x-3}$ you can see that, as $x \to \infty$, $y \to 1$, so $y = 1$ is a horizontal asymptote. What is more, when $|x|$ is large and x is positive, y is just greater than 1, so the graph approaches the asymptote $y = 1$ from the positive side. When $|x|$ is large and x is negative, y is just less than 1, so the graph approaches the asymptote $y = 1$ from the negative side.

Now look at what happens to the graph at each side of the vertical asymptotes. When x is just less than 1, the term $\dfrac{1}{x-1}$ has large modulus and is negative, but when x is just greater than 1, the term $\dfrac{1}{x-1}$ is large and positive. Around $x = 1$ the term $\dfrac{1}{x-1}$ dominates the other terms, 1 and $\dfrac{2}{x-3}$.

Similarly, when x is just less than 3, the term $\dfrac{2}{x-3}$ has large modulus and is negative, but when x is just greater than 3 the term $\dfrac{2}{x-3}$ is large and positive. Around $x = 3$ the term $\dfrac{2}{x-3}$ dominates the terms 1 and $\dfrac{1}{x-1}$.

At this stage, you can put these pieces in a diagram as shown in Fig. 4.6. (Note that different scales have been used for the x- and y-axes.)

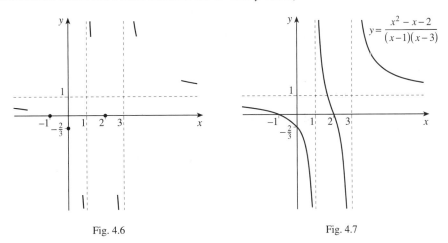

Fig. 4.6   Fig. 4.7

Now check for maxima and minima. When $y = 1 + \dfrac{1}{x-1} + \dfrac{2}{x-3}$,

$\dfrac{dy}{dx} = -\dfrac{1}{(x-1)^2} - \dfrac{2}{(x-3)^2}$. The value of $\dfrac{dy}{dx}$ is always negative, since perfect squares are always positive or zero, so there are no maxima or minima, and the gradient always slopes down from left to right. You can fill in the remainder of the graph as in Fig. 4.7.

Example 4.2.2

Sketch the graph of $y = \dfrac{x^2 - 7x + 14}{(x-1)(x-3)}$.

Attempting to solve the equation $x^2 - 7x + 14 = 0$ shows that the graph does not cross the x-axis. The graph crosses the y-axis when $x = 0$, that is at $\left(0, 4\frac{2}{3}\right)$.

The vertical asymptotes are $x = 3$ and $x = 1$.

Using partial fractions, $y = 1 - \dfrac{4}{x-1} + \dfrac{1}{x-3}$. As $x \to \infty$, $y \to 1$, so $y = 1$ is a horizontal asymptote. When x is large and positive, y is just less than 1, so the graph approaches the asymptote $y = 1$ from the negative side. When $|x|$ is large and x is negative, y is just greater than 1, so the graph approaches the asymptote $y = 1$ from the positive side.

When x is just less than 1, the term $-\dfrac{4}{x-1}$ is large and positive, but when x is just greater than 1, the term $-\dfrac{4}{x-1}$ has large modulus and is negative.

Similarly, when x is just less than 3, the term $\dfrac{1}{x-3}$ has large modulus and is negative, but when x is just greater than 3, the term $\dfrac{1}{x-3}$ is large and positive.

At this stage, you can put these pieces in a diagram as shown in Fig. 4.8.

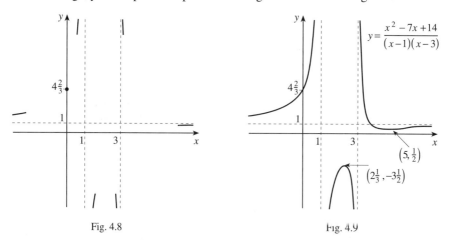

Fig. 4.8   Fig. 4.9

Before you fill in the gaps, you need information about maxima and minima. From the pieces in Fig. 4.8, it looks as though there is a maximum between 1 and 3, and a minimum greater than 3.

When $y = 1 - \dfrac{4}{x-1} + \dfrac{1}{x-3}$, $\dfrac{dy}{dx} = \dfrac{4}{(x-1)^2} - \dfrac{1}{(x-3)^2}$. For maxima and minima,

$\dfrac{dy}{dx} = 0$, so $\dfrac{4}{(x-1)^2} - \dfrac{1}{(x-3)^2} = 0$, or $\dfrac{4}{(x-1)^2} = \dfrac{1}{(x-3)^2}$. Therefore

$2(x-3) = \pm(x-1)$, giving $x = 5$ and $2\frac{1}{3}$. The corresponding y-values are $\frac{1}{2}$ and

$-3\frac{1}{2}$. Also $\dfrac{d^2y}{dx^2} = \dfrac{-8}{(x-1)^3} + \dfrac{2}{(x-3)^3}$, which is positive when $x = 5$ and negative

when $x = 2\frac{1}{3}$, showing that $\left(5, \frac{1}{2}\right)$ is a minimum and $\left(2\frac{1}{3}, -3\frac{1}{2}\right)$ a maximum. You

can fill in the details and obtain Fig. 4.9.

Here is a summary of the methods you can use. You will see that for some of the processes it is better to have the equation of the graph with a common denominator, while for others the partial fraction form is more helpful.

> Look for the places where the graph crosses the axes, and mark them.
>
> Look for vertical asymptotes, and check the behaviour of the curve on each side of the asymptote.
>
> Look for horizontal asymptotes, and investigate how the curve approaches the asymptote.
>
> Look for any oblique asymptotes.
>
> Find any maxima and minima.

Other graphs, which are not drawn here but are left as exercises, are the curves with

equations of the forms $y = \dfrac{kx}{(ax-b)^2}$ and $y = \dfrac{x}{(x-1)^2}$.

4.3 Functions with quadratic denominators which do not factorise

An important feature of graphs of functions with quadratic denominators which do not factorise is that, as there are no values for which the denominator is zero, there are no points for which the function is undefined, and there are no vertical asymptotes. The curve therefore has no breaks.

Example 4.3.1

Sketch the curve with equation $y = \dfrac{1}{x^2 + 2x + 2}$.

The denominator does not factorise, and completing the square (see P1 Section 4.3) shows that $x^2 + 2x + 2 = (x+1)^2 + 1$. It is therefore always positive, so y is always positive. The minimum value of the denominator is 1 when $x = -1$, so the value of y has a maximum of 1 when $x = -1$.

For values of x with large modulus, both positive and negative, the denominator is very large, so $y \to 0$.

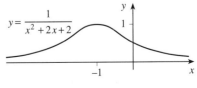

Fig. 4.10

You can fill in the details to get the graph shown in Fig. 4.10.

Example 4.3.2

Sketch the curve with equation $y = \dfrac{x}{x^2 + 1}$.

The denominator is always positive, so y is positive when x is positive and negative when x is negative. In fact, $\dfrac{x}{x^2 + 1}$ is an odd function, and so its graph is symmetrical about the origin.

For values of x with large modulus, both positive and negative, you can see by

writing the equation in the form $y = \dfrac{\dfrac{1}{x}}{1 + \dfrac{1}{x^2}}$ that $y \to 0$ as $x \to \infty$ and as $x \to -\infty$.

To look for maxima and minima, $\dfrac{dy}{dx} = \dfrac{1 - x^2}{\left(x^2 + 1\right)^2}$, so $\dfrac{dy}{dx} = 0$ when $x = \pm 1$.

The corresponding y-values are $\tfrac{1}{2}$ and $-\tfrac{1}{2}$. To verify whether these are maxima or minima it

is easiest to look at the sign of $\dfrac{dy}{dx}$. If $|x| < 1$,

$\dfrac{dy}{dx} > 0$, and if $|x| > 1$, $\dfrac{dy}{dx} < 0$. This shows that

$\left(1, \tfrac{1}{2}\right)$ is a maximum and $\left(-1, -\tfrac{1}{2}\right)$ is a minimum.

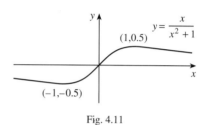

Fig. 4.11

You can fill in the details and obtain Fig. 4.11.

Example 4.3.3

Sketch the curve with equation $y = \dfrac{x^2 - 7x + 6}{x^2 + 1}$.

With the equation in the given form, you can see that the graph cuts the x-axis at $x = 1$ and $x = 6$, and the y-axis at $y = 6$.

For values of x with large modulus, both positive and negative, it is helpful to write the equation in the divided out form
$y = 1 - \dfrac{7x - 5}{x^2 + 1}$. Then you can see that $y \to 1$
as $x \to \infty$ and as $x \to -\infty$; when x is large and positive, $y < 1$, and when $|x|$ is large and x is negative, $y > 1$.

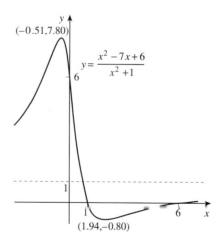

Fig. 4.12

Differentiating, $\dfrac{dy}{dx} = \dfrac{7x^2 - 10x - 7}{\left(x^2 + 1\right)^2}$, so $\dfrac{dy}{dx} = 0$ when $x \approx 1.94$ and $x \approx -0.51$,

with corresponding y-values -0.80 and 7.80. It is awkward to determine whether these are maxima or minima, but you can appeal to the continuity of the curve to complete the sketch.

Exercise 4B

1 Sketch the following graphs, giving the equations of any asymptotes and the coordinates of any maxima and minima.

(a) $y = \dfrac{1}{x(x-2)}$

(b) $y = \dfrac{x-1}{x(x-2)}$

(c) $y = \dfrac{(x-1)^2}{x(x-2)}$

(d) $y = x + \dfrac{1}{x-1}$

(e) $y = \dfrac{x^2}{(x+2)(x-2)}$

(f) $y = \dfrac{x}{(x+2)(x-2)}$

(g) $y = \dfrac{1}{x+2} + \dfrac{1}{x-2}$

(h) $y = \dfrac{1}{x^2-4}$

2 Sketch the following graphs, giving the equations of any asymptotes and the coordinates of any maxima and minima.

(a) $y = \dfrac{1}{x^2}$

(b) $y = \dfrac{x-1}{x^2}$

(c) $y = \dfrac{1}{(x-1)^2}$

(d) $y = \dfrac{x}{(x-1)^2}$

3 Sketch the following graphs, giving the equations of any asymptotes and the coordinates of any maxima and minima.

(a) $y = \dfrac{1}{x^2+1}$

(b) $y = \dfrac{x+1}{x^2+2x+2}$

(c) $y = \dfrac{-x}{x^2+1}$

(d) $y = \dfrac{1+x}{x^2+x+1}$

4 For each of the following graphs, find the equations of any asymptotes, find the coordinates of the points where the graphs cross the coordinate axes, find the coordinates of any maxima and minima, and sketch the curve.

(a) $y = \dfrac{x^2+2}{x^2+2x+3}$

(b) $y = \dfrac{x^2}{x^2-2x+1}$

(c) $y = \dfrac{x^2-1}{x^2-2x+1}$

(d) $y = \dfrac{x^2-1}{x^2+1}$

4.4 An algebraic technique

One piece of information you use in sketching graphs is the position of the maximum and minimum points. So far you have found these by differentiation, but for many rational functions there is another method which uses the theory of quadratic equations.

Look back at Fig. 4.5, which is reproduced here as Fig. 4.13, and ask the question 'for what values of x does y take a particular value k?' You could solve this graphically by drawing the horizontal line $y = k$, and finding where it cuts the graph $y = \dfrac{x^2-3x+3}{x-2}$. You can see from the figure that if $k < -1$ or $k > 3$ there are two values of x, if $-1 < k < 3$ there are no values and if $k = -1$ or $k = 3$ there is just one value.

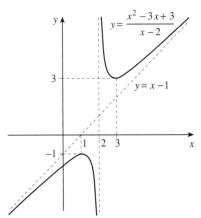

Fig. 4.13

For a general value of y the values of x are given by the equation $y(x-2) = x^2 - 3x + 3$, which can be written as a quadratic equation in x,

$$x^2 - (y+3)x + (2y+3) = 0.$$

How many values of x there are depends on the discriminant '$b^2 - 4ac$'. The discriminant in this case is $(y+3)^2 - 4 \times 1 \times (2y+3)$, which can be simplified as $y^2 - 2y - 3$, with factors $(y-3)(y+1)$.

If $y < -1$ or $y > 3$ this discriminant is positive, so there are two values of x. If $-1 < y < 3$ the discriminant is negative, so there are no values of x. This is just the result found above from Fig. 4.13.

When $y = -1$ the quadratic equation becomes $x^2 - 2x + 1 = 0$, which is $(x-1)^2 = 0$, and when $y = 3$ the equation becomes $x^2 - 6x + 9 = 0$, which is $(x-3)^2 = 0$. So the turning points are $(1, -1)$ and $(3, 3)$.

Example 4.4.1

Show that the graph $y = \dfrac{x-1}{x^2 + 3}$ can only take values in the interval $-\frac{1}{2} \leqslant y \leqslant \frac{1}{6}$.

You can rewrite this equation in the form $y(x^2 + 3) = x - 1$ and then as a quadratic equation in x,

$$yx^2 - x + (3y+1) = 0.$$

The discriminant '$b^2 - 4ac$' for the quadratic expression $yx^2 - x + (3y+1)$ is $1^2 - 4 \times y \times (3y+1)$. For the equation $yx^2 - x + (3y+1) = 0$ to have real roots, $1^2 - 4y(3y+1) \geqslant 0$.

$$1 - 12y^2 - 4y \geqslant 0 \quad \Leftrightarrow \quad 12y^2 + 4y - 1 \leqslant 0$$
$$\Leftrightarrow \quad (6y-1)(2y+1) \leqslant 0$$
$$\Leftrightarrow \quad -\tfrac{1}{2} \leqslant y \leqslant \tfrac{1}{6}.$$

Therefore the only points on the graph of $y = \dfrac{x-1}{x^2 + 3}$ are those for which $-\frac{1}{2} \leqslant y \leqslant \frac{1}{6}$.

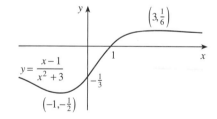

Fig. 4.14

You may wish to compare this method with that of P3 Example 8.3.2, which involves differentiating a quotient. The graph of $y = \dfrac{x-1}{x^2 + 3}$ is shown in Fig. 4.14.

Example 4.4.2

(a) Find the equations of the asymptotes of $y = \dfrac{2x^2 - 5x + 4}{x - 2}$.

(b) Find the values of y for which there are no points on the curve.

(a) The denominator is zero at $x = 2$, so $x = 2$ is a vertical asymptote.

Writing $\dfrac{2x^2 - 5x + 4}{x - 2}$ in divided out form shows that $y = 2x - 1 + \dfrac{2}{x - 2}$. You can

see that as $|x|$ gets large, the term $\dfrac{2}{x - 2}$ becomes very small, and the graph

behaves like $y = 2x - 1$. The line $y = 2x - 1$ is an oblique asymptote.

(b) Writing $y = \dfrac{2x^2 - 5x + 4}{x - 2}$ in the form $y(x - 2) = 2x^2 - 5x + 4$ and

rearranging it as a quadratic equation in x gives

$$2x^2 - (5 + y)x + (4 + 2y) = 0.$$

For a point (x, y) to exist on the graph of $y(x - 2) = 2x^2 - 5x + 4$, the

discriminant must be non-negative, that is $(5 + y)^2 - 4 \times 2 \times (4 + 2y) \geqslant 0$

$$\begin{aligned}
(5 + y)^2 - 4 \times 2 \times (4 + 2y) \geqslant 0 \quad &\Leftrightarrow \quad 25 + 10y + y^2 - 32 - 16y \geqslant 0 \\
&\Leftrightarrow \quad y^2 - 6y - 7 \geqslant 0 \\
&\Leftrightarrow \quad (y + 1)(y - 7) \geqslant 0 \\
&\Leftrightarrow \quad y \leqslant -1 \quad \text{or} \quad y \geqslant 7.
\end{aligned}$$

Therefore no part of the graph lies between $y = -1$ and $y = 7$.

Example 4.4.3

Show that the graph of $y = \dfrac{x^2 - x - 2}{(x - 1)(x - 3)}$ takes all possible values of y.

Rewriting the equation $y = \dfrac{x^2 - x - 2}{(x - 1)(x - 3)}$ as a quadratic equation in x gives

$y(x - 1)(x - 3) = x^2 - x - 2$, which can be rearranged as

$$(y - 1)x^2 + (1 - 4y)x + (3y + 2) = 0.$$

The discriminant of $(y - 1)x^2 + (1 - 4y)x + (3y + 2)$ is

$$(1 - 4y)^2 - 4 \times (y - 1) \times (3y + 2), \quad \text{which is} \quad 4y^2 - 4y + 9.$$

Notice that, by completing the square (see P1 Section 4.3),

$$4y^2 - 4y + 9 \equiv (2y - 1)^2 + 8,$$

which is always positive.

Thus the equation $(y - 1)x^2 + (1 - 4y)x + (3y + 2) = 0$ has real roots whatever the

value of y, so the graph takes all possible values of y.

This method, using the discriminant '$b^2 - 4ac$', works because the equation of the graph reduces to a quadratic equation in x.

Exercise 4C

Use the algebraic technique described in Section 4.4 for the questions in this exercise.

1 Prove that

(a) if $y = \dfrac{x^2 + x + 1}{x^2 + 1}$, then $\frac{1}{2} \leqslant y \leqslant \frac{3}{2}$,

(b) if $y = \dfrac{x^2 + 1}{x^2 + x + 1}$, then $\frac{2}{3} \leqslant y \leqslant 2$.

2 Prove that if $y = \dfrac{1 - 2x - x^2}{x^2}$, then $y \geqslant -2$.

3 Find any restrictions on the values that y can take for the following functions.

(a) $y = \dfrac{x + 1}{(x - 1)^2}$

(b) $y = \dfrac{x^2 - x}{2x - 1}$

(c) $y = \dfrac{8x - 3}{(2x - 1)(2x + 3)}$

4 Prove that if $y = \dfrac{x - k}{x^2 - 4x - k}$ can take all values as x varies, then $0 < k < 5$.

5 Find a condition on k so that $y = \dfrac{x - k}{x^2 - 4x + k}$ can take all values as x varies.

Miscellaneous exercise 4

1 Find the equations of the asymptotes of $y = x + 1 + \dfrac{1}{x + 1}$.

2 Let $f(x) = \dfrac{1}{(x - 2)(x + 2)}$. For what values of x is $f(x)$ positive? Write down the equations of the asymptotes of $y = f(x)$.

3 Find the stationary values of the function $f(x) = \dfrac{x}{x^2 + 4}$, and write down the equations of any asymptotes. Sketch the graph of $y = f(x)$, showing the asymptotes and the stationary values.

4 Find any stationary values of the function $f(x) = \dfrac{x}{x^2 - 4}$, and write down the equations of the asymptotes. Sketch the graph of $y = f(x)$, showing the asymptotes and the stationary values.

5 Find the maximum and minimum values on the curve $y = \dfrac{x}{x^2 + 3x + 4}$, and sketch the curve.

6 Find a condition on p such that $y = \dfrac{x^2 + px}{x^2 + p}$ takes all values as x varies.

7 In each part of the question, suggest a possible equation for the graph which is sketched.

(a)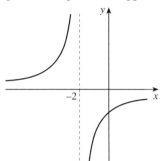

(b)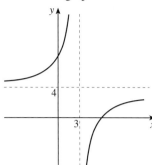

(c)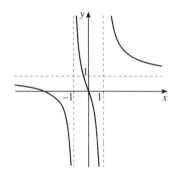

(d)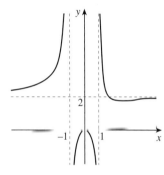

8 (a) Find the coordinates of the points at which the graph of $y = \dfrac{x^2 - 2}{(x-2)^2}$ cuts the coordinate axes.

(b) Find the equations of both the asymptotes of the curve.

(c) Find the coordinates of the turning point on the graph.

(d) Sketch the graph. (OCR, adapted)

9 Sketch the graph of $y = \dfrac{x^2 + x + 1}{(x-1)^2}$, and prove that, for all values of x, $y \geq \frac{1}{4}$.

(OCR, adapted)

10 The diagram shows a sketch of the curve with equation $y = \dfrac{3 + 6x}{(x-1)^2}$.

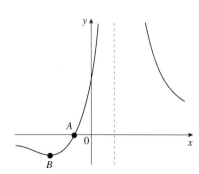

(a) Write down the coordinates of A, and state the equation of the vertical asymptote, shown as a broken line.

(b) Determine the coordinates of the minimum point B. Hence show that $\dfrac{3 + 6x}{(x-1)^2} \geq -1$. (OCR, adapted)

11 (a) Given that $k = \dfrac{(x+2)^2}{x+1}$, show that $x^2 + (4-k)x + (4-k) = 0$. Write down the condition for the roots of this quadratic equation to be real. Hence show that k cannot take values between 0 and 4.

   (b) Find the coordinates of the turning points on the curve with equation $y = \dfrac{(x+2)^2}{x+1}$.

   Sketch the curve, and mark clearly the positions of the turning points. (OCR)

12 The curve C_1 has equation $y = \dfrac{x+a}{x-a}$, where a is a positive constant.

   (a) Show that $\dfrac{dy}{dx} < 0$ at all points of C_1.

   (b) Draw a sketch of C_1.

   The curve C_2 has equation $y = \left(\dfrac{x+a}{x-a}\right)^2$.

   (c) Show by differentiation that C_2 has exactly one stationary point and find the coordinates of this point.

   (d) On a separate diagram draw a sketch of C_2.

   (e) Show by means of a graphical argument that there are values of m, which need not be specified, such that the equation
   $$m(x-a)^3 - (x+a)^2 = 0$$
   has three distinct roots. (OCR)

5 Graphs of functions involving square roots

This chapter is about the relationship between the graphs of $y = f(x)$ and $y^2 = f(x)$.
When you have completed it, you should

- know how to sketch the graph of $y^2 = f(x)$ given the graph of $y = f(x)$
- know that the graph of $y^2 = f(x)$ is symmetrical about the x-axis
- know that the graphs of $y = f(x)$ and $y^2 = f(x)$ intersect when $y = 0$ and $y = 1$
- know the gradients of both graphs are zero for the same values of x provided $y \neq 0$
- know how to predict the gradient of $y^2 = f(x)$ as it crosses the x-axis.

5.1 Graphs involving square roots

Suppose that you know the shape of the graph of $y = f(x)$. What can you deduce about
the graph $y^2 = f(x)$?

You can get the graph of $y^2 = f(x)$ quickly on your graphic calculator by recognising that if
$y^2 = f(x)$, then $y = \pm\sqrt{f(x)}$, so the graph of $y^2 = f(x)$ consists of the two graphs $y = \sqrt{f(x)}$
and $y = -\sqrt{f(x)}$. One of these lies wholly above or on the x-axis, and the other below or
on it. You can therefore draw the graph of $y^2 = f(x)$ by drawing $y = \sqrt{f(x)}$ and then
combining it with its reflection in the x-axis to produce a symmetrical graph.

Example 5.1.1
(a) Sketch the curves $y = x$ and $y^2 = x$.
(b) Use your calculator to sketch, on the same set of axes, the graphs of $y = x(4 - x)$
and $y^2 = x(4 - x)$.
What features do these graphs have in common?

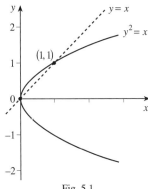

Fig. 5.1

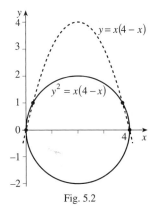

Fig. 5.2

The sketches are shown in Figs. 5.1 and 5.2. The solid graphs are the graphs of
$y^2 = x$ and $y^2 = x(4 - x)$.

In each case, the solid graph exists only when the dashed graph is above or on the
x-axis. The solid graph and the dashed graph meet where $y = 0$ and where $y = 1$.

The graph of $y^2 = x(4 - x)$ looks like a circle. If you write its equation in the form $x^2 - 4x + y^2 = 0$, or $(x - 2)^2 + y^2 = 4$, the work of P3 Chapter 3 tells you that it is a circle with centre $(2, 0)$ and radius 2.

Both of the properties mentioned in Example 5.1.1 above are general properties, and do not rely on the specific curves being drawn.

- If the value of $f(x)$ is negative in the interval $a < x < b$, then, since $y^2 \geqslant 0$, the graph of $y^2 = f(x)$ does not exist in the interval $a < x < b$.
- The graphs of $y^2 = f(x)$ and $y = f(x)$ intersect where $y^2 = y$, that is where $y = 0$ and $y = 1$. The graphs do not intersect anywhere else.

It is also worth noting that if $f(x) > 1$, then $f(x) > \sqrt{f(x)}$, and if $0 < f(x) < 1$, then $\sqrt{f(x)} > f(x)$. This means that, apart from points where $f(x) = 0$, the part of the graph of $y^2 = f(x)$ for which y is positive is always closer to the line $y = 1$ than the graph of $y = f(x)$. You can see this in Figs. 5.1 and 5.2.

5.2 Properties of gradient

In this section, the letter y always refers to the y in the equation $y^2 = f(x)$, except when $y = f(x)$ is mentioned explicitly.

If you look again at Figs. 5.1 and 5.2, you will see that when $f(x)$ is increasing, $y = \sqrt{f(x)}$ is also increasing; similarly, they decrease together. If they have stationary points, they have them at the same values of x.

Increasing and decreasing functions

You can see that a function and its square root increase and decrease together by differentiating $y^2 = f(x)$ implicitly. You then find

$$2y \frac{dy}{dx} = f'(x).$$

Consider now the points on $y^2 = f(x)$ for which y is positive, as opposed to the points for which y is zero. Then $\dfrac{dy}{dx}$ and $f'(x)$ have the same sign. Therefore, when $f'(x) > 0$, $\dfrac{dy}{dx} > 0$; similarly, when $f'(x) < 0$, $\dfrac{dy}{dx} < 0$.

Stationary values

From the equation $2y \dfrac{dy}{dx} = f'(x)$, it follows that, if $y \neq 0$ when $f'(x) = 0$, then $\dfrac{dy}{dx} = 0$.

The condition $y \neq 0$ is important: if $y = 0$ the result could be false. For example, draw the graphs of $y = x^2$ and $y^2 = x^2$ on your calculator. When $y = 0$, one of the graphs has a minimum; the other has $\dfrac{dy}{dx} = \pm 1$.

The gradient when $y = 0$

The gradient at points on the x-axis, where $f(x) = 0$, needs more detailed investigation.

In the equation $2y\dfrac{dy}{dx} = f'(x)$, if $y = 0$ then $\dfrac{dy}{dx}$ is undefined. But Figs. 5.1 and 5.2 show that it is possible for the graph of $y^2 = f(x)$ to have a tangent parallel to the y-axis. You know from P3 Section 11.2 that this occurs when $\dfrac{dx}{dy} = 0$.

To find $\dfrac{dx}{dy}$, differentiate the equation $y^2 = f(x)$ with respect to y. Then

$$2y = f'(x)\frac{dx}{dy}.$$

You can see from this that, if $f'(x) \neq 0$, then

$$y = 0 \quad \Rightarrow \quad \frac{dx}{dy} = 0,$$

so that the tangent is parallel to the y-axis. This is illustrated in Fig. 5.3.

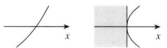

Graph of $f(x)$ crossing the x-axis, (where $f'(x) \neq 0$)   Graph of $y^2 = f(x)$

Fig. 5.3

The shaded part of the graph indicates that this is a 'forbidden region'.

But if $f'(x) = 0$ when $y = 0$, the equations $2y\dfrac{dy}{dx} = f'(x)$ and $2y = f'(x)\dfrac{dx}{dy}$ become

$$2 \times 0 \times \frac{dy}{dx} = 0 \quad \text{and} \quad 2 \times 0 = 0 \times \frac{dx}{dy}.$$

Neither equation tells you anything about the gradient of $y^2 = f(x)$. Fig. 5.4 shows that there are many cases. There is no general rule, and you must consider each function on its merits.

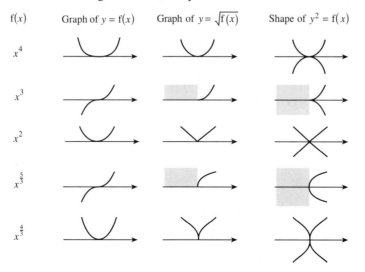

$f(x)$	Graph of $y = f(x)$	Graph of $y = \sqrt{f(x)}$	Shape of $y^2 = f(x)$

Fig. 5.4

Here are properties which should enable you to sketch the graph of $y^2 = f(x)$ given the graph of $y = f(x)$.

> If $f(x) < 0$, the graph of $y^2 = f(x)$ does not exist.
>
> The graphs of $y = f(x)$ and $y^2 = f(x)$ intersect where $y = 0$ and $y = 1$.
>
> Provided that $y > 0$, the gradients of $y = f(x)$ and $y = \sqrt{f(x)}$ have the same sign, and have stationary values at the same values of x.
>
> At points where $f(x) = 0$, provided that $f'(x) \neq 0$, the graph of $y^2 = f(x)$ crosses the x-axis in the direction parallel to the y-axis.
>
> The graph of $y^2 = f(x)$ is symmetrical about the x-axis.

Example 5.2.1

Fig. 5.5 shows a sketch of the graph of $y = f(x)$, for some function $f(x)$. On the same axes sketch the graph of $y^2 = f(x)$.

The method used is to draw $y = \sqrt{f(x)}$, and then to reflect the result in the x-axis. Each step of the text is illustrated in Fig. 5.6.

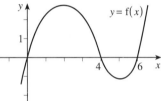

Fig. 5.5

Shade in the 'no-go regions' where $f(x) < 0$.

Draw the line $y = 1$ and mark the points where the graph of $y = f(x)$ meets the lines $y = 0$ (the x-axis), and $y = 1$. The graph of $y = \sqrt{f(x)}$ must pass through these points.

Remember that the graph of $y = \sqrt{f(x)}$ is always closer to the line $y = 1$ than the graph of $y = f(x)$ (except when $f(x) = 0$).

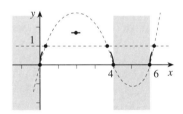

Fig. 5.6

Identify the point on $y = f(x)$ for which $y > 0$ and $f'(x) = 0$. Mark the corresponding point on $y = \sqrt{f(x)}$ which also has a gradient of zero.

At the points where the graph of $y = f(x)$ crosses the x-axis, the graph of $y^2 = f(x)$ has a vertical tangent. Note that the gradient of $y = f(x)$ is not zero at these points. You can now join the points and pieces to obtain a line for which y is positive.

Now recall that the graph of $y^2 = f(x)$ is symmetrical about the x-axis and complete the curve which is the solid curve in Fig. 5.7.

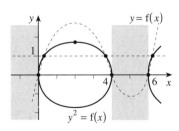

Fig. 5.7

With practice this process is quite quick.

Example 5.2.2
Draw the graph of $y = x(x-2)$; deduce from it the shape of the graph of $y^2 = x(x-2)$.

Fig. 5.8 shows the graph of $y = x(x-2)$, which is the dashed parabola.

The solid line is the graph of $y^2 = x(x-2)$. It exists only when $y = x(x-2)$ is positive.

The graphs of $y = x(x-2)$ and $y^2 = x(x-2)$ meet when $y = 0$ and $y = 1$.

The graph of $y^2 = x(x-2)$ has vertical tangents when $y = 0$, and is symmetrical about the x-axis.

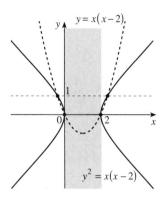

Fig. 5.8

Example 5.2.3

Fig. 5.9 shows the graph of $y = \dfrac{(x+1)(x-2)}{(x-1)(x-3)}$, which was discussed in Example 4.2.1.

Use the graph to draw a sketch of $y^2 = \dfrac{(x+1)(x-2)}{(x-1)(x-3)}$.

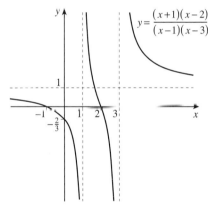

Fig. 5.9

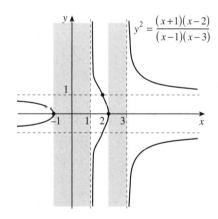

Fig. 5.10

From Fig. 5.9, $\dfrac{(x+1)(x-2)}{(x-1)(x-3)} \geqslant 0$ only in the intervals $x \leqslant -1$, $1 < x \leqslant 2$ and

$x > 3$. Therefore the graph of $y^2 = \dfrac{(x+1)(x-2)}{(x-1)(x-3)}$ exists only for these intervals.

The graphs of $y = \dfrac{(x+1)(x-2)}{(x-1)(x-3)}$ and $y^2 = \dfrac{(x+1)(x-2)}{(x-1)(x-3)}$ intersect when $y = 0$ and

when $y = 1$, that is at $(-1,0)$, $\left(1\tfrac{2}{3}, 1\right)$ and $(2,0)$.

The tangents to $y = \dfrac{(x+1)(x-2)}{(x-1)(x-3)}$ at $(-1,0)$ and $(2,0)$ are not horizontal, so, from

the result in the shaded box (page 60), the graph of $y^2 = \dfrac{(x+1)(x-2)}{(x-1)(x-3)}$ has

vertical tangents at these points.

The next example shows the kinds of things that can happen when you start with a graph which has a discontinuity in its gradient.

Example 5.2.4
Sketch the graphs of $y = 1 - |x|$ and $y^2 = 1 - |x|$.

The graph of $y = 1 - |x|$ is shown in Fig. 5.11. You can see that the 'no-go regions' for $y^2 = 1 - |x|$ are $x < -1$ and $x > 1$.

The graph of $y = 1 - |x|$ crosses the x-axis at $45°$, so the tangents to the graph at these points on $y^2 = 1 - |x|$ are both parallel to the y-axis.

The only point on the graph of $y = 1 - |x|$ which you need to treat with suspicion is the sharp corner at the point $(0,1)$. What is the gradient there?

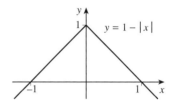

Fig. 5.11

To answer this question, it is helpful to say that the graph of $y^2 = 1 - |x|$ is the same as

$$y^2 = \begin{cases} 1 - x & \text{for } x \geqslant 0, \\ 1 + x & \text{for } x < 0. \end{cases}$$

Now consider $y^2 = 1 - x$ for $x > 0$. Differentiating $y^2 = 1 - x$ implicitly,

$$2y\frac{dy}{dx} = -1,$$

so when y is close to 1, $\dfrac{dy}{dx}$ is close to $-\dfrac{1}{2}$.

When $x < 0$, and y is close to 1, $\dfrac{dy}{dx}$ is close to $\dfrac{1}{2}$.

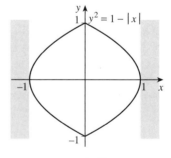

Fig. 5.12

The graph is shown in Fig. 5.12. There is a maximum at $(0,1)$ and a minimum at $(0,-1)$.

Note that these maxima and minima are not stationary points, because there is no tangent at these points.

Exercise 5

1 Sketch the graphs of

(a) $y^2 = 3x - 6$,   (b) $y^2 = 2x + 9$,   (c) $y^2 = 5 - x$,   (d) $y^2 + \frac{1}{2}x + 2 = 0$.

2 Sketch the graphs of

(a) $y^2 = x(x - 9)$,   (b) $y^2 = x^2 - 9$,   (c) $y^2 = 9 - x^2$,   (d) $y^2 = x(9 - x)$.

3 Sketch the graphs of

(a) $y^2 = x^2 + 2$,   (b) $y^2 = (x - 2)^2 + 1$,   (c) $y^2 = x^2 + 2x + 9$,   (d) $y^2 = (x + 1)^2$.

4 (a) Sketch the graph of $y = x^3 + 8$ and hence sketch the graph of $y^2 = x^3 + 8$.

(b) Sketch the graph of $y = x^3 - 1$ and hence sketch the graph of $y^2 = x^3 - 1$.

5 Sketch graphs of the following, paying particular attention to the form of the graph near the point $(3, 0)$.

(a) $y^2 = (x - 1)(x - 3)$ (b) $y^2 = (x - 1)(x - 3)^2$

(c) $y^2 = (x - 1)(x - 3)^3$ (d) $y^2 = (x - 1)(x - 3)^4$

6 Determine the coordinates of the stationary points on the curve $y = x^2(6 - x)$. Sketch the graph of $y = x^2(6 - x)$.

Also sketch the graph of $y^2 = x^2(6 - x)$; state the coordinates of the points where the tangent is parallel to the x-axis, and find the gradient of the curve at the origin.

7 Sketch the graph of $y^2 = (11 + x)(9 - x)$. Show that this is the equation of a circle and determine its radius and centre.

8 In the following equations, a and b are positive constants. Which of the following could be the equation of the curve shown?

(a) $y^2 = (x + a)(x - b)$ (b) $y^2 = (x + a)^2(x - b)$

(c) $y^2 = (x + a)(x - b)^3$ (d) $y^2 = (x + a)^3(x - b)$

(e) $y^2 = (x + a)(x - b)^2$ (f) $y^2 = (x + a)(x - b)^4$

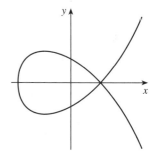

9 In the following equations, p and q are positive constants. Which of the following could be the equation of the curve shown?

(a) $y^2 = x(x + p)(x - q)$ (b) $y^2 = (x + p)(x - q)$

(c) $y^2 = x(p + x)(q - x)$ (d) $y^2 = x^2(x + p)(x - q)^2$

(e) $y^2 = x(x + p)^2(x - q)$ (f) $y^2 = x^3(p + x)(q - x)$

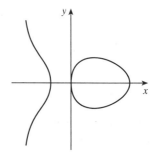

10 Find the coordinates of the points of intersection of the curves $y = x^2 - 6x + 9$ and $y^2 = x^2 - 6x + 9$ and illustrate with sketch graphs.

11 Sketch the graphs of $y = \sin x$, $y = \cos x$ and $y = \tan x$ for $0 \leqslant x \leqslant 4\pi$. Hence sketch the graphs of $y^2 = \sin x$, $y^2 = \cos x$ and $y^2 = \tan x$ for $0 \leqslant x \leqslant 4\pi$.

12 Sketch the graphs of
     (a) $y^2 = e^x$,   (b) $y^2 = e^x - 1$,   (c) $y^2 = 4e^{-3x}$,   (d) $y^2 = e^{2x} - e^2$.

13 The diagram shows the graph $y = f(x)$, which has a minimum point at $(-3, 1)$ and a maximum point at $(2, 5)$. Copy the diagram and, on the same axes, draw the graph of $y^2 = f(x)$ showing how the two graphs are related. State the coordinates of the points of $y^2 = f(x)$ at which the tangent is parallel to the x-axis.

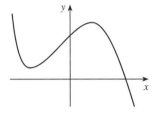

14 Sketch the graph of $y = 9 - 4x^2$ and hence sketch the graph of $y^2 = 9 - 4x^2$. (This is the equation of an ellipse; its equation is more usually written as $4x^2 + y^2 = 9$.)

15 Sketch the graph of the ellipse $4x^2 - 12x + y^2 = 7$.

16 Sketch on the same diagram the graphs of $y^2 = x^2 + 1$ and $y^2 = x^2$. (The first graph is a rectangular hyperbola and the second graph shows its asymptotes.)

17 Show that the asymptotes of the curve $y = \dfrac{x^2}{x+3}$ are $x = -3$ and $y = x - 3$.

     (a) Sketch the graph of $y = \dfrac{x^2}{x+3}$.

     (b) Sketch the curve $y^2 = \dfrac{x^2}{x+3}$, paying particular attention to the shape of the curve at the origin.

18 Sketch in separate diagrams the graphs of
     (a) $y^2 = x - 2$,   (b) $y^2 = (x-2)^2$,   (c) $y^2 = (x-2)^3$,   (d) $y^2 = (x-2)^4$.

Miscellaneous exercise 5

1 Sketch in separate diagrams the curves with equations
    (a) $y = x(1 - x^2)$,   (b) $y^2 = x(1 - x^2)$.   (OCR)

2 A sketch of the graph of $y = f(x)$ is shown in the diagram. On separate diagrams, sketch the graphs of
    (a) $y^2 = f(x)$,
    (b) $y = \sqrt{f(x)}$.   (OCR)

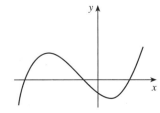

3 On separate diagrams sketch the graphs of

(a) $y = x^2(x+b)$,   (b) $y^2 = x^2(x+b)$.

where b is a positive constant. You should indicate clearly the slope of each curve near
points where $y = 0$.   (OCR)

4 Sketch on separate diagrams the curves whose equations are

(a) $y = \dfrac{x}{1+x}$,   (b) $y^2 = \dfrac{x}{1+x}$.   (OCR)

5 The graph of $y = f(x)$ has asymptotes
$x = 0$, $x = a$ and $y = 0$ and is shown in
the figure. Sketch the graphs of

(a) $y = |f(x)|$,

(b) $y^2 = f(x)$.   (OCR)

6 Sketch the graph of $y^2 = \dfrac{x+a}{x+b}$, where a and b are positive constants such that $b > a$.
                                                                              (OCR)

7 Sketch on separate diagrams the curves with equations

(a) $y = \dfrac{1}{x^2 - a^2}$,   (b) $y = \left|\dfrac{1}{x^2 - a^2}\right|$,   (c) $y^2 = \dfrac{1}{x^2 - a^2}$,

where a is a positive constant. You should state, in each case, the equation of any
asymptote(s) and the coordinates of any stationary points.   (OCR)

8 The equation of a curve is $y^2 = \dfrac{x}{1+x^2}$. Show that the y-axis is a tangent to the curve at
the origin and find the coordinates of all the turning points on the curve. Sketch the curve.
                                                                              (OCR)

9 The sketches show the graphs of $y^2 = f(x)$ and $y = |f(x)|$ for a certain function f.

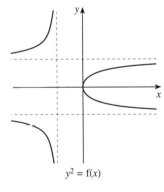

$y^2 = f(x)$

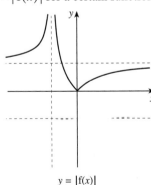

$y = |f(x)|$

(a) Sketch the graph of $y = f(x)$.   (b) Sketch the graph of $y = f(|x|)$. (OCR)

10 The notation $[x]$ means the greatest integer whose value is not greater than x. (So, for
example, $[3.7] = 3$, $[2.0] = 2$ and $[-1.85] = -2$.) Sketch the graphs of

(a) $y = [x]$,   (b) $y^2 = [x]$,   (c) $y = x - [x]$,   (d) $y^2 = x - [x]$.

Revision exercise 1

1 Use the method of mathematical induction to prove that

$$\frac{1^2}{1\times 3}+\frac{2^2}{3\times 5}+\ldots+\frac{n^2}{(2n-1)(2n+1)}=\frac{n(n+1)}{2(2n+1)}.$$

2 Find the factors of x^3+8, and hence split $\dfrac{6(x-2)}{x^3+8}$ into partial fractions.

Make a rough sketch of the curve with equation $y=\dfrac{6(x-2)}{x^3+8}$, indicating where the curve crosses the axes.

Show that $\displaystyle\int_0^1 \frac{6(x-2)}{x^3+8}\,dx=a\ln b$, where a is a negative integer and b is a positive integer.

Find the values of a and b.

Justify from your sketch the fact that the value of the integral is negative.

3 A curve has equation $y=\dfrac{4x(5-x)}{x+4}$.

(a) Find $\dfrac{dy}{dx}$. Hence find the coordinates of the two stationary points.

(b) Write down the equation of the asymptote parallel to the y-axis. Express the equation of the curve in divided out form, and hence find the equation of the oblique asymptote.

(c) Sketch the curve.

(d) On a separate diagram, sketch the curve with equation $y^2=\dfrac{4x(5-x)}{x+4}$. Give the coordinates of the four points on this curve where the tangent is parallel to the x-axis, and the two points where the tangent is parallel to the y-axis.   (MEI, adapted)

4 (a) Solve the inequality $\dfrac{1}{x(x+2)}>\dfrac{4}{5}$.

(b) Express $\dfrac{1}{r(r+2)}$ in partial fractions. Hence find the sum of the series

$$\frac{1}{1\times 3}+\frac{1}{2\times 4}+\frac{1}{3\times 5}+\ldots+\frac{1}{n(n+2)}.$$

(c) Prove by induction that $\displaystyle\sum_{r=1}^{n}\frac{(-1)^r}{r(r+2)}=\frac{(-1)^n}{2(n+1)(n+2)}-\frac{1}{4}$.   (MEI)

5 (a) Find the values of the constants A and B for which $x^3+1\equiv(x+1)(x^2+Ax+B)$.

(b) Prove by induction that $\displaystyle\sum_{r=1}^{n}r(2r^2-3r+2)=\tfrac{1}{2}n(n^3+1)$ for all positive integers n.   (OCR)

6 Prove that the sum of the first n terms of the series

$$1^2 + 2 \times 2^2 + 3^2 + 2 \times 4^2 + 5^2 + 2 \times 6^2 + \ldots$$

is $\frac{1}{2} n(n+1)^2$ when n is even. Find a similar formula for the sum when n is odd.

7 (a) Sketch the curve with equation $y = \dfrac{x}{x+1}$, giving the equations of all its asymptotes.

    (b) Sketch the curve with equation $y = \sqrt{\dfrac{x}{x+1}}$.

8 Prove by mathematical induction that

$$\left(1 - \frac{1}{2}\right)\left(1 - \frac{1}{3}\right)\left(1 - \frac{1}{4}\right)\ldots\left(1 - \frac{1}{n}\right) = \frac{1}{n}.$$

9 Sketch the graph of $y^2 = |x+2| + |x-2|$.

10 (a) Sketch the graph of $y = \dfrac{5-x}{\left(x^2 + 1\right)(x-1)}$.

    (b) Calculate the area bounded by the graph of $y = \dfrac{5-x}{\left(x^2+1\right)(x-1)}$, the line $x = 2$,

    the x-axis and the line $x = 3$, giving your answer in exact form.

11 Suppose that $a_0 = 1$, and that a_1, a_2, $\ldots$, a_n, $\ldots$ are positive numbers such that $a_{r+1}^2 > a_r a_{r+2}$ for $r = 0, 1, 2, \ldots$. Prove that

$$a_1 > a_2^{\frac{1}{2}} > a_3^{\frac{1}{3}} > a_4^{\frac{1}{4}} > \ldots > a_n^{\frac{1}{n}} > \ldots.$$

12 Find the sum $n^2 + \left((n-1)^2 - 1^2\right) + \left((n-2)^2 - 2^2\right) + \ldots + \left((n-r)^2 - r^2\right)$, when r is an integer which is less than $\frac{1}{2} n$.

How does your answer differ, if at all, if r is an integer which can be greater than or equal to $\frac{1}{2} n$?

13 The diagram shows the graph of a function $y = f(x)$.

Show on a sketch, the graph of

(a) $y = |f(x)|$,

(b) $y^2 = f(x)$,

(c) $y = \sqrt{f(x)}$.

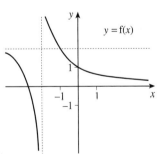

14 Let $f(r) = \dfrac{1}{k+1} r(r+1)(r+2)\ldots(r+k)$, where r and k are positive integers.

(a) Find and simplify an expression for $f(r+1) - f(r)$.

(b) Find the sum of the series

$$1 \times 2 \times 3 \times 4 + 2 \times 3 \times 4 \times 5 + \ldots + n(n+1)(n+2)(n+3).$$

6 Trigonometric functions

This chapter assembles all the important results about differentiation and integration which involve trigonometric functions and their inverses. When you have completed it, you should

- know the key derivatives and integrals, and how to obtain others from them
- be familiar with a variety of methods of finding trigonometric integrals
- be able to select and use appropriate trigonometric substitutions for evaluating integrals.

Before reading the chapter you will find it helpful to review some derivatives of trigonometric functions by working through Exercise 6A. Questions 1(a), (b), (e), (g) and (h) are specially important and are worth remembering.

Exercise 6A

1 Taking the derivatives of $\sin x$ and $\cos x$ as the starting point, prove the following results. In parts (e) to (i), give a reason for the inequality conditions.

(a) $\dfrac{d}{dx}(\tan x) = \sec^2 x$

(b) $\dfrac{d}{dx}(\sec x) = \sec x \tan x$

(c) $\dfrac{d}{dx}(\cot x) = -\operatorname{cosec}^2 x$

(d) $\dfrac{d}{dx}(\operatorname{cosec} x) = -\operatorname{cosec} x \cot x$

(e) If $0 < x < \pi$, $\dfrac{d}{dx}(\ln(\sin x)) = \cot x$

(f) If $-\tfrac{1}{2}\pi < x < \tfrac{1}{2}\pi$, $\dfrac{d}{dx}(\ln(\cos x)) = -\tan x$

(g) If $-\tfrac{1}{2}\pi < x < \tfrac{1}{2}\pi$, $\dfrac{d}{dx}(\ln(\sec x)) = \tan x$

(h) If $-\tfrac{1}{2}\pi < x < \tfrac{1}{2}\pi$, $\dfrac{d}{dx}(\ln(\sec x + \tan x)) = \sec x$

(i) If $0 < x < \pi$, $\dfrac{d}{dx}\left(\ln\left(\tan \tfrac{1}{2} x\right)\right) = \operatorname{cosec} x$

2 Rewrite the results in Question 1 in the form of indefinite integrals. For parts (e) to (i), give alternative indefinite integrals for other intervals of values of x.

3 Show that $\dfrac{d}{dx}(\sin^2 x) = \dfrac{d}{dx}(-\cos^2 x) = \dfrac{d}{dx}(-\tfrac{1}{2}\cos 2x)$. What is the connection between $\sin^2 x$, $-\cos^2 x$ and $-\tfrac{1}{2}\cos 2x$?

6.1 Integrating trigonometric functions

The derivatives of $\sin x$ and $\cos x$, together with rules such as the chain rule and the product rule, are enough to enable you to differentiate almost any expression involving trigonometric functions. But integration is less predictable.

Even such a simple integral as $\int \sqrt{\sin x}\, dx$ is impossible to find. It is not just that you don't yet know enough to be able to work it out. There is in fact no function $f(x)$ involving the functions with which you are familiar (powers, logarithm, exponential, and so on) such that

$$f'(x) = \sqrt{\sin x}\,.$$

It is not easy to tell by inspection whether it is going to be possible to integrate a particular function or not. There are, however, a few general procedures, and with experience you should recognise which (if any) are likely to work in a particular case.

(i) Using trigonometric identities

Identities, such as Pythagoras' identities and the addition formulae, can often be used to convert a trigonometric integrand into a form whose integral you already know. Some of the most useful ones were listed in P3 Section 2.4, but here are some more examples.

Example 6.1.1

Find $\int \tan^2 x\, dx$

One of the trigonometric forms of Pythagoras' theorem is $1 + \tan^2 x = \sec^2 x$, and you know the integral of $\sec^2 x$ (see Exercise 6A Question 1(a)). So

$$\int \tan^2 x\, dx = \int \left(\sec^2 x - 1\right) dx = \tan x - x + k.$$

Example 6.1.2

Evaluate $\displaystyle\int_0^{\frac{1}{2}\pi} \sqrt{1 + \sin x}\, dx$.

None of the standard identities involves $1 + \sin x$ directly; the nearest is $1 + \cos 2A = 2\cos^2 A$. But $\sin x$ can be written as $\cos\left(\frac{1}{2}\pi - x\right)$; if you write $\frac{1}{2}\pi - x$ in place of $2A$ in that identity you get

$$1 + \sin x = 1 + \cos\left(\tfrac{1}{2}\pi - x\right) = 2\cos^2\left(\tfrac{1}{4}\pi - \tfrac{1}{2}x\right), \text{ so that}$$

$$\sqrt{1 + \sin x} = \sqrt{2}\,\cos\left(\tfrac{1}{4}\pi - \tfrac{1}{2}x\right).$$

(Note that over the interval of integration $0 < x < \frac{1}{2}\pi$, $0 < \frac{1}{4}\pi - \frac{1}{2}x < \frac{1}{4}\pi$, so that $\cos\left(\frac{1}{4}\pi - \frac{1}{2}x\right)$ is the *positive* square root of $1 + \sin x$.) Then

$$\int_0^{\frac{1}{2}\pi} \sqrt{1 + \sin x}\, dx = \int_0^{\frac{1}{2}\pi} \sqrt{2}\,\cos\left(\tfrac{1}{4}\pi - \tfrac{1}{2}x\right) dx$$

$$= \left[-2\sqrt{2}\,\sin\left(\tfrac{1}{4}\pi - \tfrac{1}{2}x\right)\right]_0^{\frac{1}{2}\pi}$$

$$= -2\sqrt{2}\left(\sin 0 - \sin \tfrac{1}{4}\pi\right) = 2\sqrt{2} \times \frac{1}{\sqrt{2}} = 2.$$

An alternative way of completing the integration would be to notice that

$$\sqrt{2}\cos\left(\tfrac{1}{4}\pi - \tfrac{1}{2}x\right) = \sqrt{2}\left(\cos\tfrac{1}{4}\pi\cos\tfrac{1}{2}x + \sin\tfrac{1}{4}\pi\sin\tfrac{1}{2}x\right)$$
$$= \cos\tfrac{1}{2}x + \sin\tfrac{1}{2}x.$$

Try squaring this last expression; you should then see why

$$\left(\cos\tfrac{1}{2}x + \sin\tfrac{1}{2}x\right)^2 = 1 + \sin x.$$

(ii) Using integration by substitution

If the integrand can be put into a form such as $f(\sin x)\cos x$, $f(\cos x)\sin x$ or $f(\tan x)\sec^2 x$, then you can transform the integral by using a substitution such as $u = \sin x$, $u = \cos x$ or $u = \tan x$.

Example 6.1.3

Find (a) $\displaystyle\int \frac{\cos x}{(1+\sin x)^2}\,dx$, (b) $\displaystyle\int \cos^4 x\,\sin^3 x\,dx$, (c) $\displaystyle\int \sec^4 x\,dx$.

(a) If $u = \sin x$, then $\dfrac{du}{dx} = \cos x$, so

$$\int \frac{\cos x}{(1+\sin x)^2}\,dx = \int \frac{1}{(1+\sin x)^2}\times\frac{du}{dx}\,dx = \int \frac{1}{(1+u)^2}\,du$$

$$= -\frac{1}{1+u} + k = -\frac{1}{1+\sin x} + k.$$

(b) In the form given the integrand is not in either of the forms $f(\sin x)\cos x$ or $f(\cos x)\sin x$. But you can write it as

$$\cos^4 x\,\sin^2 x\,\sin x = \cos^4 x\left(1-\cos^2 x\right)\sin x.$$

Then, if $u = \cos x$, $\dfrac{du}{dx} = -\sin x$, so

$$\int \cos^4 x\,\sin^3 x\,dx = \int \cos^4 x\left(1-\cos^2 x\right)\times\left(-\frac{du}{dx}\right)dx$$

$$= \int -u^4\left(1-u^2\right)du$$

$$= \tfrac{1}{7}u^7 - \tfrac{1}{5}u^5 + k = \tfrac{1}{7}\cos^7 x - \tfrac{1}{5}\cos^5 x + k.$$

(c) Write $\sec^4 x$ as $\sec^2 x\,\sec^2 x = \left(1+\tan^2 x\right)\sec^2 x$. Then the substitution $u = \tan x$ gives

$$\int \sec^4 x\,dx = \int \left(1+\tan^2 x\right)\times\frac{du}{dx}\,dx = \int \left(1+u^2\right)du$$

$$= u + \tfrac{1}{3}u^3 + k = \tan x + \tfrac{1}{3}\tan^3 x + k.$$

With practice you may find that in simple examples you can do the substitution in your head and write the answer down in a single step.

(iii) Using integration by parts

Integration by parts is the standard method if the integrand is the product of a trigonometric function and some other function such as a polynomial or an exponential. You can also use it sometimes for products of two trigonometric functions.

Example 6.1.4

Find (a) $\displaystyle\int x \sec^2 x \, dx$, (b) $\displaystyle\int \cos x \ln(\cos x) \, dx$, (c) $\displaystyle\int e^{2x} \sin x \, dx$.

(a) Express the integrand as $u\dfrac{dv}{dx}$, where $u = x$ and $\dfrac{dv}{dx} = \sec^2 x$, so that $v = \tan x$.

Then

$$\int x \sec^2 x \, dx = x \tan x - \int 1 \times \tan x \, dx = x \tan x - \ln|\sec x| + k,$$

using the result in Exercise 6A Question 1(g).

(b) You don't know how to integrate $\ln(\cos x)$, so take $u = \ln(\cos x)$, $\dfrac{dv}{dx} = \cos x$, that is $v = \sin x$. Then, if $-\tfrac{1}{2}\pi < x < \tfrac{1}{2}\pi$,

$$\int \cos x \ln(\cos x) \, dx = \int \ln(\cos x) \cos x \, dx$$

$$= \ln(\cos x) \sin x - \int \frac{1}{\cos x}(-\sin x) \times \sin x \, dx$$

$$= \ln(\cos x) \sin x + \int \frac{1 - \cos^2 x}{\cos x} \, dx$$

$$= \ln(\cos x) \sin x + \int (\sec x - \cos x) \, dx$$

$$= \ln(\cos x) \sin x + \ln(\sec x + \tan x) - \sin x + k.$$

(c) Take $u = e^{2x}$, $\dfrac{dv}{dx} = \sin x$, so that $v = -\cos x$:

$$\int e^{2x} \sin x \, dx = -e^{2x} \cos x + \int 2e^{2x} \cos x \, dx$$

But $\displaystyle\int e^{2x} \cos x \, dx$ is no easier to find than $\displaystyle\int e^{2x} \sin x \, dx$!

However, if you use the same method again, taking $u = 2e^{2x}$, $\dfrac{dv}{dx} = \cos x$,

$$\int 2e^{2x} \cos x \, dx = 2e^{2x} \sin x - \int 4e^{2x} \sin x \, dx.$$

Putting the two equations together,

$$\int e^{2x} \sin x \, dx = -e^{2x} \cos x + 2e^{2x} \sin x - 4 \int e^{2x} \sin x \, dx,$$

so $$5 \int e^{2x} \sin x \, dx = -e^{2x} \cos x + 2e^{2x} \sin x,$$

$$\int e^{2x} \sin x \, dx = \tfrac{1}{5} e^{2x} (2 \sin x - \cos x).$$

6.2 A useful substitution

If $t = \tan \tfrac{1}{2} x$, the double angle formula gives

$$\tan x = \tan 2\left(\tfrac{1}{2} x\right) = \frac{2 \tan \tfrac{1}{2} x}{1 - \tan^2 \tfrac{1}{2} x} = \frac{2t}{1 - t^2}.$$

You can then use Pythagoras' identity to obtain

$$\sec^2 x = 1 + \tan^2 x = 1 + \frac{4t^2}{\left(1 - t^2\right)^2} = \frac{\left(1 - t^2\right)^2 + 4t^2}{\left(1 - t^2\right)^2}$$

$$= \frac{1 - 2t^2 + t^4 + 4t^2}{\left(1 - t^2\right)^2} = \frac{1 + 2t^2 + t^4}{\left(1 - t^2\right)^2} = \frac{\left(1 + t^2\right)^2}{\left(1 - t^2\right)^2}.$$

Remarkably this is an exact square, so that you can take square roots to obtain

$$\sec x = \pm \frac{1 + t^2}{1 - t^2}.$$

To settle the question of the sign, note that if $-\tfrac{1}{2}\pi < x < \tfrac{1}{2}\pi$, $\sec x > 0$ and $t^2 < 1$. If $-\pi < x < -\tfrac{1}{2}\pi$ or $\tfrac{1}{2}\pi < x < \pi$, $\sec x < 0$ and $t^2 > 1$. (Outside the range $-\pi < x < \pi$, both $\sec x$ and $\tan \tfrac{1}{2} x$ repeat with period 2π.) Since $1 + t^2$ is always positive, the ambiguous sign is always $+$, so that

$$\sec x = \frac{1 + t^2}{1 - t^2}$$

(except when $x = -\tfrac{1}{2}\pi$ or $\tfrac{1}{2}\pi$, where neither side is defined).

You can now express other trigonometric functions in terms of t:

$$\cos x = \frac{1}{\sec x} = \frac{1 - t^2}{1 + t^2},$$

$$\sin x = \tan x \times \cos x = \frac{2t}{1 - t^2} \times \frac{1 - t^2}{1 + t^2} = \frac{2t}{1 + t^2}.$$

There are no exceptions to these; they hold also when $x = \pm \tfrac{1}{2}\pi$.

Also $\dfrac{dt}{dx} = \frac{1}{2}\sec^2\frac{1}{2}x = \frac{1}{2}\left(1+t^2\right)$, so $\dfrac{dx}{dt} = \dfrac{1}{\frac{dt}{dx}} = \dfrac{2}{1+t^2}$.

If $t = \tan\frac{1}{2}x$,

$$\sin x = \frac{2t}{1+t^2}, \qquad \cos x = \frac{1-t^2}{1+t^2} \qquad \text{and} \qquad \frac{dx}{dt} = \frac{2}{1+t^2}.$$

This means that you can use the substitution $t = \tan\frac{1}{2}x$ to convert integrals involving trigonometric functions of x into integrals involving algebraic functions of t.

Example 6.2.1

Find $\displaystyle\int \operatorname{cosec} x\, dx$.

$$\int \frac{1}{\sin x}\,dx = \int \frac{1+t^2}{2t} \times \frac{2}{1+t^2}\,dt = \int \frac{1}{t}\,dt = \ln|t| + k = \ln\left|\tan\frac{1}{2}x\right| + k.$$

Example 6.2.2

Evaluate $\displaystyle\int_0^{\frac{1}{3}\pi} \frac{1}{4+5\cos x}\,dx$.

When $x = \frac{1}{3}\pi$, $t = \tan\frac{1}{6}\pi = \dfrac{1}{\sqrt{3}}$, so

$$\int_0^{\frac{1}{3}\pi} \frac{1}{4+5\cos x}\,dx = \int_0^{\frac{1}{\sqrt{3}}} \frac{1}{4+5\left(\dfrac{1-t^2}{1+t^2}\right)} \times \frac{2}{1+t^2}\,dt$$

$$= \int_0^{\frac{1}{\sqrt{3}}} \frac{2}{4\left(1+t^2\right)+5\left(1-t^2\right)}\,dt = \int_0^{\frac{1}{\sqrt{3}}} \frac{2}{9-t^2}\,dt.$$

You can evaluate this integral by using partial fractions:

$$\int_0^{\frac{1}{\sqrt{3}}} \frac{2}{9-t^2}\,dt = \int_0^{\frac{1}{\sqrt{3}}} \frac{1}{3}\left(\frac{1}{3+t}+\frac{1}{3-t}\right)dt$$

$$= \left[\tfrac{1}{3}\left(\ln(3+t)-\ln(3-t)\right)\right]_0^{\frac{1}{\sqrt{3}}}$$

$$= \tfrac{1}{3}\left(\ln\!\left(\left(3+\frac{1}{\sqrt{3}}\right)\middle/\left(3-\frac{1}{\sqrt{3}}\right)\right)-\ln\!\left(\frac{3}{3}\right)\right)$$

$$= \tfrac{1}{3}\ln\!\left(\frac{3\sqrt{3}+1}{3\sqrt{3}-1}\right).$$

The substitution is also sometimes useful in solving trigonometric equations.

Example 6.2.3
Find the solutions of $4\sin x + 3\cos x + 2 = 0$ in the interval $-\pi < x < \pi$.

The substitution $t = \tan\frac{1}{2}x$ converts the equation to

$$4 \times \frac{2t}{1+t^2} + 3 \times \frac{1-t^2}{1+t^2} + 2 = 0, \quad 8t + 3(1-t^2) + 2(1+t^2) = 0, \quad t^2 - 8t - 5 = 0,$$

with solution $t = 4 \pm \sqrt{21}$. This gives $\frac{1}{2}x = -0.5275\ldots$ or $1.4548\ldots$, so $x = -1.06$ or 2.91 correct to 3 significant figures.

But beware! There are some questions for which this method gives you only part of the solution. See Exercise 6B Question 10.

Exercise 6B

1 Use suitable identities to find the following integrals.

(a) $\int \cot^2 x \, dx$ 　　(b) $\int \tan^3 x \, dx$ 　　(c) $\int \tan^4 x \, dx$

2 Use substitutions to find the following integrals.

(a) $\int \cos x \sqrt{\sin x} \, dx$ 　　(b) $\int \cos^3 x \sin^2 x \, dx$ 　　(c) $\int \sin^5 x \, dx$

(d) $\int \frac{\cos^3\theta}{\sin^2\theta} d\theta$ 　　(e) $\int \frac{\cos\theta + \sin\theta}{\cos\theta - \sin\theta} d\theta$ 　　(f) $\int \frac{\sec^2 t}{1+\tan t} dt$

3 Write in their simplest forms $(\sec\theta + \tan\theta)(\sec\theta - \tan\theta)$, $(1-\sin\theta)(1+\sin\theta)$ and $(\cos\theta + \sin\theta)^2$. Use your answers to find the following integrals.

(a) $\int \frac{1}{(\sec\theta + \tan\theta)^2} d\theta$ 　　(b) $\int \frac{1}{1-\sin\theta} d\theta$ 　　(c) $\int (1+\sin 2\theta)^{\frac{3}{2}} d\theta$

4 Use integration by parts to find the following integrals.

(a) $\int x \csc^2 x \, dx$ 　　(b) $\int \sin x \ln(\sin x) dx$ for $0 < x < \pi$

(c) $\int \sec^2 x \ln(\sec x) dx$ for $0 < x < \frac{1}{2}\pi$

5 Use integration by parts to find the following integrals.

(a) $\int e^\theta \cos\theta \, d\theta$ 　　(b) $\int e^\theta \sin 2\theta \, d\theta$ 　　(c) $\int e^{\theta\cos\alpha} \cos(\theta\sin\alpha) d\theta$

6 If $f(x) = \int \frac{\cos x}{\cos x + \sin x} dx$ and $g(x) = \int \frac{\sin x}{\cos x + \sin x} dx$, find $f(x) + g(x)$ and $f(x) - g(x)$, and hence find $f(x)$ and $g(x)$. Use your answers to find the values of

(a) $\int_0^{\frac{1}{2}\pi} \frac{1}{1+\tan x} dx$, 　　(b) $\int_0^{\frac{1}{4}\pi} \frac{1-\tan x}{1+\tan x} dx$.

7 If $\tan\frac{1}{2}x = 0.5$, find the values of $\sin x$ and $\cos x$.

8 If $\sin x = 0.6$, find the possible values of $\tan \frac{1}{2} x$.

9 Use the substitution $t = \tan \frac{1}{2} x$ to find the solutions of the following equations in the interval $-\pi < x < \pi$ correct to 4 decimal places.

(a) $7 \sin x + \cos x = 5$ (b) $4 \sin x - 7 \cos x = 1$ (c) $8 \cos x - \sin x = 4$

10 Use each of the three methods (a), (b) and (c) to find the roots between 0 and 360 of the equation $5 \sin x° - 3 \cos x° = 3$.

(a) Express the left side in the form $R \sin(x - \alpha)°$.

(b) Take the term $3 \cos x°$ to the right side of the equation and use double angle formulae to express both sides as functions of $\frac{1}{2} x°$.

(c) Express $\sin x°$ and $\cos x°$ in terms of $t = \tan \frac{1}{2} x°$, and solve an algebraic equation for t.

Why does the answer given by (c) differ from those given by (a) and (b)?

11 Use the substitution $t = \tan \frac{1}{2} x$ to find the following integrals.

(a) $\displaystyle \int \frac{5}{3 \sin x + 4 \cos x} \, dx$ (b) $\displaystyle \int \sec x \, dx$ (c) $\displaystyle \int \frac{1}{7 \cos x - \sin x + 5} \, dx$

12 Find the following integrals.

(a) $\displaystyle \int x \cot^2 x \, dx$ (b) $\displaystyle \int \frac{1}{\sec t - 1} \, dt$ (c) $\displaystyle \int \frac{\cot \theta}{1 - \sin \theta} \, d\theta$

(d) $\displaystyle \int \cos x \ln(\sin x) \, dx$ (e) $\displaystyle \int \frac{\sin \theta}{\cos \theta - \sin \theta} \, d\theta$ (f) $\displaystyle \int \cot^4 x \, dx$

(g) $\displaystyle \int \frac{\sin t}{1 + \cos t} \, dt$ (h) $\displaystyle \int \frac{1}{12 \sin \theta - 5 \cos \theta} \, d\theta$ (i) $\displaystyle \int \tan u \ln(\sec u) \, du$

(j) $\displaystyle \int \frac{1}{1 + \cot x} \, dx$

13 One of the three integrals (a), (b) and (c) can be found exactly, but the others can't. Find the one which comes out exactly, and investigate the difficulties which arise when you try to find the others.

(a) $\displaystyle \int x \tan x \, dx$ (b) $\displaystyle \int x \tan^2 x \, dx$ (c) $\displaystyle \int x^2 \tan x \, dx$

6.3* Inverse trigonometric functions

The inverse trigonometric functions $\sin^{-1}$, $\cos^{-1}$ and $\tan^{-1}$ were defined in P3 Section 1.7. There are also inverse functions $\sec^{-1}$, $\csc^{-1}$ and $\cot^{-1}$, but you don't need to know about all six of them.

Take $\sec^{-1}$ as an example. To define this you have to restrict the domain of the function $\sec$ to make it one–one. Fig. 6.1 shows that this can be done in the same way as for $\cos$ (except that $\sec$ is not defined at $\frac{1}{2}\pi$), and the graphs of the inverse functions are then as shown in Fig. 6.2.

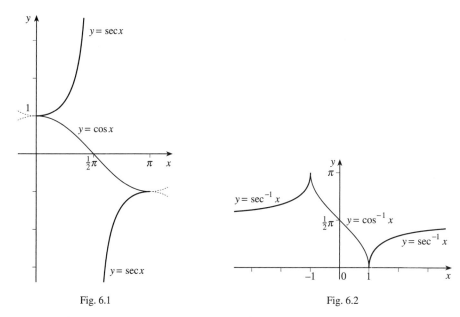

Fig. 6.1   Fig. 6.2

Notice that $\cos^{-1}$ has domain $-1 \leqslant x \leqslant 1$, and $\sec^{-1}$ has a domain combining the two intervals $x \leqslant -1$ and $x \geqslant 1$. Both have range $0 \leqslant x \leqslant \pi$, except that the range of $\sec^{-1}$ excludes $\frac{1}{2}\pi$.

But there is a closer connection between these functions, since

$$y = \sec^{-1}x \iff \sec y = x \iff \cos y = \frac{1}{x} \iff y = \cos^{-1}\left(\frac{1}{x}\right).$$

This means that, for any x in the domain of $\sec^{-1}$,

$$\sec^{-1}x = \cos^{-1}\left(\frac{1}{x}\right).$$

You can find for yourself similar relations connecting $\csc^{-1}$ with $\sin^{-1}$, and $\cot^{-1}$ with $\tan^{-1}$. If you restrict the domains of cosec and cot in the same way as for sin and tan, to the interval $-\frac{1}{2}\pi \leqslant x \leqslant \frac{1}{2}\pi$ (except that neither cosec nor cot is defined at 0), you obtain:

Reciprocal rules

$$\sec^{-1}x = \cos^{-1}\left(\frac{1}{x}\right), \qquad \csc^{-1}x = \sin^{-1}\left(\frac{1}{x}\right), \qquad \cot^{-1}x = \tan^{-1}\left(\frac{1}{x}\right).$$

Another set of relations between inverse trigonometric functions can be derived from the symmetries of the graphs. Fig. 6.3 shows the graphs of $\sin x$ from $-\frac{1}{2}\pi$ to $\frac{1}{2}\pi$ and $\cos x$ from 0 to π. If you reflect the sine graph in the y-axis and then translate the result by $\frac{1}{2}\pi$ in the x-direction you get the cosine

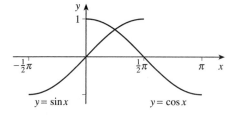

Fig. 6.3

graph. The effect on the x-coordinates is to transform x first to $-x$, then to $\frac{1}{2}\pi - x$. So, for $-\frac{1}{2}\pi \leqslant x \leqslant \frac{1}{2}\pi$ (so $0 \leqslant \frac{1}{2}\pi - x \leqslant \pi$),

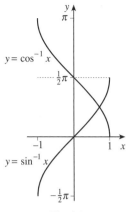

$$\cos\left(\frac{1}{2}\pi - x\right) = \sin x.$$

This can also be interpreted in terms of the inverse functions shown in Fig. 6.4. The equivalent equation is

$$\cos^{-1} x = -\sin^{-1} x + \frac{1}{2}\pi,$$
$$\text{or} \quad \cos^{-1} x + \sin^{-1} x = \frac{1}{2}\pi.$$

Fig. 6.4

This is called a 'complement rule' (since angles which add up to $\frac{1}{2}\pi$ are said to be complementary).

Using this in combination with the reciprocal rules gives

$$\sec^{-1} x + \operatorname{cosec}^{-1} x = \cos^{-1}\left(\frac{1}{x}\right) + \sin^{-1}\left(\frac{1}{x}\right) = \frac{1}{2}\pi.$$

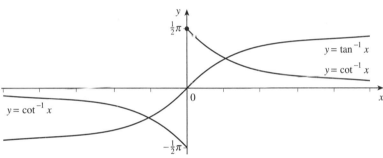

Fig. 6.5

The corresponding result for $\tan^{-1}$ and $\cot^{-1}$ is a little more complicated. You can see from the graphs in Fig. 6.5 that

$$\tan^{-1} x + \cot^{-1} x = \frac{1}{2}\pi \ \text{if} \ x \geqslant 0, \qquad \tan^{-1} x + \cot^{-1} x = -\frac{1}{2}\pi \ \text{if} \ x < 0.$$

Complement rules

$$\cos^{-1} x + \sin^{-1} x = \frac{1}{2}\pi, \qquad \sec^{-1} x + \operatorname{cosec}^{-1} x = \frac{1}{2}\pi,$$

$$\tan^{-1} x + \cot^{-1} x = \frac{1}{2}\pi \ \text{if} \ x \geqslant 0, \qquad \tan^{-1} x + \cot^{-1} x = -\frac{1}{2}\pi \ \text{if} \ x < 0.$$

One other useful identity for inverse trigonometric functions can be deduced from the addition formula for $\tan(A + B)$. Writing A as $\tan^{-1} a$, and B as $\tan^{-1} b$, so that $a = \tan A$, $b = \tan B$, the identity

$$\tan(A + B) = \frac{\tan A + \tan B}{1 - \tan A \tan B} \quad \text{becomes}$$

$$\tan\left(\tan^{-1} a + \tan^{-1} b\right) = \frac{a+b}{1-ab}.$$

This means that

$$\tan^{-1} a + \tan^{-1} b + k\pi = \tan^{-1}\left(\frac{a+b}{1-ab}\right)$$

where the number k has to be chosen so that the left side lies between $-\frac{1}{2}\pi$ and $\frac{1}{2}\pi$.

Example 6.3.1
Find the value of $\tan^{-1} 2 + \tan^{-1} 3$.

Since $\tan^{-1} 2$ and $\tan^{-1} 3$ are both between $\frac{1}{4}\pi$ and $\frac{1}{2}\pi$, their sum is between $\frac{1}{2}\pi$ and π, so k must be taken as -1.

$$\tan^{-1} 2 + \tan^{-1} 3 - \pi = \tan^{-1}\left(\frac{2+3}{1-6}\right) = \tan^{-1}(-1) = -\frac{1}{4}\pi.$$

Therefore $\tan^{-1} 2 + \tan^{-1} 3 = \pi - \frac{1}{4}\pi = \frac{3}{4}\pi.$

6.4 Differentiating the inverse functions

You only need to learn how to differentiate $\tan^{-1} x$ and $\sin^{-1} x$. The complement and reciprocal rules can then be used to find derivatives of the other inverse functions.

If $y = \tan^{-1} x$, then $x = \tan y$, so that $\dfrac{dx}{dy} = \sec^2 y$, and

$$\frac{dy}{dx} = \frac{1}{\dfrac{dx}{dy}} = \frac{1}{\sec^2 y}.$$

But you want an answer in terms of x rather than y, so $\sec^2 y$ has to be expressed in terms of x. This is simple, since $\sec^2 y = 1 + \tan^2 y = 1 + x^2$.

Therefore

$$\frac{dy}{dx} = \frac{1}{1+x^2}.$$

Similarly, if $y = \sin^{-1} x$, then $x = \sin y$, so that $\dfrac{dx}{dy} = \cos y$, and

$$\frac{dy}{dx} = \frac{1}{\dfrac{dx}{dy}} = \frac{1}{\cos y}.$$

Since $\cos^2 y = 1 - \sin^2 y$, it follows that $\cos y = \pm\sqrt{1 - \sin^2 y} = \pm\sqrt{1 - x^2}$,

$$\frac{dy}{dx} = \pm\frac{1}{\sqrt{1-x^2}}.$$

The extra complication in this case is to settle the doubt about the sign. You can do this by observing that the graph of $\sin^{-1} x$ (see Fig. 6.4) always has a positive gradient. Since $\sqrt{1-x^2}$ is positive by definition, it follows that

$$\frac{dy}{dx} = +\frac{1}{\sqrt{1-x^2}}.$$

Notice that $\dfrac{dy}{dx}$ is not defined when $x = \pm 1$, where the graph is parallel to the y-axis.

$$\frac{d}{dx}\left(\tan^{-1} x\right) = \frac{1}{1+x^2}.$$

$$\text{For } -1 < x < 1, \ \frac{d}{dx}\left(\sin^{-1} x\right) = \frac{1}{\sqrt{1-x^2}}.$$

Example 6.4.1

Find (a) $\dfrac{d}{dx}\left(\cos^{-1} x\right)$, (b) $\dfrac{d}{dx}\left(\sec^{-1} x\right)$.

(a) Using the complement rule,

$$\frac{d}{dx}\left(\cos^{-1} x\right) = \frac{d}{dx}\left(\tfrac{1}{2}\pi - \sin^{-1} x\right) = 0 - \frac{1}{\sqrt{1-x^2}} = -\frac{1}{\sqrt{1-x^2}}.$$

(b) Using the reciprocal rule and the result of (a),

$$\frac{d}{dx}\left(\sec^{-1} x\right) = \frac{d}{dx}\left(\cos^{-1}\frac{1}{x}\right) = -\frac{1}{\sqrt{1-\frac{1}{x^2}}} \times \left(\frac{1}{x^2}\right) = \frac{\frac{1}{x^2}}{\sqrt{\frac{x^2-1}{x^2}}} = \frac{1}{x^2} \times \frac{\sqrt{x^2}}{\sqrt{x^2-1}}$$

$$= \frac{\sqrt{x^2}}{x^2} \times \frac{1}{\sqrt{x^2-1}} = \frac{1}{\sqrt{x^2}} \times \frac{1}{\sqrt{x^2-1}} = \frac{1}{|x|\sqrt{x^2-1}}.$$

Notice that this gives a positive derivative, whether $x > 1$ or $x < -1$. This is as you would expect from the graph of $\sec^{-1} x$ (see Fig. 6.2).

Example 6.4.2

Find $\displaystyle\int \tan^{-1} x \, dx$.

In P3 Example 8.2.3, $\displaystyle\int \ln x \, dx$ was found by writing the integrand as $\ln x \times 1$ and using integration by parts. This works because the derivative of $\ln x$ is a rational function of x, and doesn't involve a logarithm.

You can find $\displaystyle\int \tan^{-1} x \, dx$ in a similar way, and for the same reason.

Writing $u = \tan^{-1} x$ and $\dfrac{dv}{dx} = 1$, so that $v = x$,

$$\int \tan^{-1} x \, dx = \tan^{-1} x \times x - \int \frac{1}{1+x^2} \times x \, dx.$$

You should recognise this last integral, $\displaystyle\int \frac{x}{1+x^2} \, dx$, as a constant multiple of the

form $\displaystyle\int \frac{f'(x)}{f(x)} \, dx$, which is $\ln|f(x)| + k$ (see P3 Section 10.3). So

$$\int \frac{x}{1+x^2} \, dx = \tfrac{1}{2} \int \frac{2x}{1+x^2} \, dx = \tfrac{1}{2} \ln\left(1+x^2\right) + k.$$

So $\displaystyle\int \tan^{-1} x \, dx = x \tan^{-1} x - \tfrac{1}{2} \ln\left(1+x^2\right) - k.$

Exercise 6C

1 State the values of

(a) $\sec^{-1}(-2)$,   (b) $\operatorname{cosec}^{-1}\!\left(\tfrac{2}{3}\sqrt{3}\right)$,   (c) $\cot^{-1}1$,   (d) $\cot^{-1}\!\left(-\sqrt{3}\right)$.

2 (a) If $\sec^{-1} x = a$, express $\sin^{-1}\!\left(\dfrac{1}{x}\right)$ in terms of a.

(b) If $\tan^{-1} y = b$, express $\cot^{-1}\!\left(\dfrac{1}{y}\right)$ in terms of b.

3 Write an equation connecting x and y not involving trigonometric functions if

(a) $\sec^{-1} x = \operatorname{cosec}^{-1} y$,   (b) $\cot^{-1} x = \tan^{-1} y$,   (c) $\sin^{-1} x = \sec^{-1} y$.

4 Express in the form $\tan^{-1} x$

(a) $2 \tan^{-1} \tfrac{1}{5}$,   (b) $4 \tan^{-1} \tfrac{1}{5}$,   (c) $4 \tan^{-1} \tfrac{1}{5} - \tfrac{1}{4}\pi$.

5 Write an equation connecting x, y and z if

(a) $\tan^{-1} x + \tan^{-1} y + \tan^{-1} z = \tfrac{1}{2}\pi$,   (b) $\sin^{-1} x + \cos^{-1} y = \sin^{-1} z$.

6 Find the derivatives of the following with respect to x.

(a) $\operatorname{cosec}^{-1} x$ (b) $\tan^{-1} 2x$ (c) $\sin^{-1} \tfrac{1}{3}x$ (d) $\sec^{-1} 3x$

(e) $x \tan^{-1} x$ (f) $\left(\sin^{-1} x\right)^2$ (g) $\sin^{-1} \sqrt{x}$ (h) $\tan^{-1}\!\left(x\sqrt{x}\right)$

(i) $\cot^{-1}(1-x)$ (j) $\sin^{-1} \sqrt{1-x^2}$

7 Find the following integrals.

(a) $\displaystyle\int x \tan^{-1} x \, dx$ (b) $\displaystyle\int \sin^{-1} x \, dx$ (c) $\displaystyle\int x \sin^{-1} x \, dx$

8 Find the maximum value of $f(x) = \left(\sin^{-1} x\right)^2 \cos^{-1} x$ in the interval $0 < x < 1$.

9 Use a substitution to find an exact expression for the area under the graph of $y = \sec^{-1} x$ from $x = 1$ to $x = 2$.

10 The region bounded by the axes and the graph of $y = \cos^{-1} x$ is rotated about the x-axis to form a solid of revolution. Find its volume.

6.5 Trigonometric substitutions

It is important to recognise the results obtained in the last section in their integral forms:

$$\int \frac{1}{1+x^2}\,dx = \tan^{-1} x + k, \qquad \int \frac{1}{\sqrt{1-x^2}}\,dx = \sin^{-1} x + k.$$

You can also get these results by the method of substitution. For example, writing $x = \tan u$ converts $\int \dfrac{1}{1+x^2}\,dx$ into

$$\int \frac{1}{1+\tan^2 u}\times(\sec^2 u\,du = \int \frac{1}{\sec^2 u}\times \sec^2 u\,du = \int 1\,du = u + k;$$

so, converting back to a function of x,

$$\int \frac{1}{1+x^2}\,dx = \tan^{-1} x + k.$$

Similarly you can find $\int \dfrac{1}{\sqrt{1-x^2}}\,dx$ by substituting $x = \sin u$. Try this for yourself.

The effectiveness of these substitutions depends on Pythagoras' identities. You can often use them successfully with more complicated integrals.

To find an integral involving $\begin{Bmatrix} 1+x^2 \\ \sqrt{1-x^2} \\ \sqrt{x^2-1} \end{Bmatrix}$, try substituting $\begin{Bmatrix} x = \tan u \\ x = \sin u \\ x = \sec u \end{Bmatrix}$.

Notice that the second and third substitutions are only recommended when $1-x^2$ and x^2-1 appear in a square root. Otherwise it is usually easier to factorise them as the difference of two squares, and then use techniques such as partial fractions. But $1+x^2$ cannot be factorised.

Example 6.5.1

Evaluate $\displaystyle\int_0^1 \frac{1}{\left(1+x^2\right)^{\frac{3}{2}}}\,dx$.

The substitution $x = \tan u$ converts this integral into

$$\int_0^{\frac{1}{4}\pi} \frac{1}{\left(\sec^2 u\right)^{\frac{3}{2}}} \times \sec^2 u\,du = \int_0^{\frac{1}{4}\pi} \frac{\sec^2 u}{\sec^3 u}\,du = \int_0^{\frac{1}{4}\pi} \cos u\,du = [\sin u]_0^{\frac{1}{4}\pi} = \frac{1}{\sqrt{2}}.$$

Example 6.5.2

Find $\displaystyle\int \frac{1}{\sqrt{x^2-1}}\,dx$ for $x > 1$.

The substitution $x = \sec u$ converts the integral into

$$\int \frac{1}{\sqrt{\sec^2 u - 1}} \times \sec u \tan u\,du \quad \text{(see Exercise 6A Question 1(b))}$$

$$= \int \frac{1}{\tan u} \times \sec u \tan u\,du$$

$$= \int \sec u\,du = \ln(\sec u + \tan u) + k \quad \text{(see Exercise 6A Question 1(i)).}$$

Notice that all values of x greater than 1 can be obtained by taking u between 0 and $\frac{1}{2}\pi$. In that case it is correct to take $\sqrt{\sec^2 u - 1}$ to be $+\tan u$, and the integration $\int \sec u\,du$ is valid. Also $\tan u = \sqrt{x^2-1}$, so

$$\int \frac{1}{\sqrt{x^2-1}}\,dx = \ln\left(x + \sqrt{x^2-1}\right) + k.$$

You can extend this method further to cover more general quadratic expressions than $\pm 1 \pm x^2$, by using the completed square method. A preliminary algebraic substitution can then be applied to get the integral into one of the standard forms.

Example 6.5.3

Find $\displaystyle\int \frac{1}{\sqrt{a^2 - b^2 x^2}}\,dx$, where a and b are positive constants.

If bx is written as au, then $\sqrt{a^2 - b^2 x^2}$ becomes $\sqrt{a^2 - a^2 u^2}$, which simplifies to $a\sqrt{1-u^2}$. So, substituting $x = \dfrac{au}{b}$,

$$\int \frac{1}{\sqrt{a^2 - b^2 x^2}}\,dx = \int \frac{1}{a\sqrt{1-u^2}} \times \frac{a}{b}\,du = \frac{1}{b}\int \frac{1}{\sqrt{1-u^2}}\,du$$

$$= \frac{1}{b}\sin^{-1} u + k = \frac{1}{b}\sin^{-1}\frac{bx}{a} + k.$$

Example 6.5.4

Find $\displaystyle\int_{-1}^{1} \frac{1}{9x^2 + 6x + 5}\,dx$.

Since $9x^2 + 6x + 5 = (3x+1)^2 + 4$, substitute $3x+1 = 2u$. Then $\dfrac{dx}{du} = \dfrac{2}{3}$; also when $x = -1$ and 1, $u = -1$ and 2 respectively. So the integral becomes

$$\int_{-1}^{2} \frac{1}{4u^2 + 4} \times \tfrac{2}{3}\,du = \tfrac{1}{6}\int_{-1}^{2} \frac{1}{u^2 + 1}\,du = \tfrac{1}{6}\Big[\tan^{-1} u\Big]_{-1}^{2}$$

$$= \tfrac{1}{6}\left(\tan^{-1} 2 - \tan^{-1}(-1)\right) = \tfrac{1}{6}\left(\tan^{-1} 2 + \tan^{-1} 1\right).$$

If you want a numerical answer, don't forget to put your calculator into radian mode. The value is 0.315, correct to 3 decimal places.

You could also use the formula for $\tan^{-1} a + \tan^{-1} b$ in Section 6.3 to write the answer as $\tfrac{1}{6}\left(\tan^{-1}\dfrac{2+1}{1-2} + \pi\right) = \tfrac{1}{6}\left(\pi - \tan^{-1} 3\right)$.

Example 6.5.5

Find $\displaystyle\int \sqrt{\frac{x}{1-x}}\,dx$.

To take advantage of one of Pythagoras' identities for this integral you can substitute $x = \sin^2 u$. This converts the integral to

$$\int \sqrt{\frac{\sin^2 u}{\cos^2 u}} \times 2\sin u \cos u\,du = \int \frac{\sin u}{\cos u} \times 2\sin u \cos u\,du$$

$$= \int 2\sin^2 u\,du = \int (1 - \cos 2u)\,du$$

$$= u - \tfrac{1}{2}\sin 2u + k = u - \sin u \cos u + k.$$

In terms of x, this is

$$\int \sqrt{\frac{x}{1-x}}\,dx = \sin^{-1}\sqrt{x} - \sqrt{x}\sqrt{1-x} + k = \sin^{-1}\sqrt{x} - \sqrt{x(1-x)} + k.$$

Excrcise 6D

1 Use substitutions to evaluate the following definite integrals.

(a) $\displaystyle\int_{0}^{1} \frac{1}{1+x^2}\,dx$ (b) $\displaystyle\int_{1}^{2} \frac{1}{\sqrt{4-x^2}}\,dx$ (c) $\displaystyle\int_{1}^{3} \frac{1}{x^2+3}\,dx$ (d) $\displaystyle\int_{0}^{\infty} \frac{1}{9x^2+16}\,dx$

(e) $\displaystyle\int_{0}^{1} \left(1-x^2\right)^{\frac{3}{2}}\,dx$ (f) $\displaystyle\int_{2}^{\infty} \left(x^2-1\right)^{-\frac{3}{2}}\,dx$ (g) $\displaystyle\int_{2}^{4} \frac{1}{\sqrt{x^2-4}}\,dx$ (h) $\displaystyle\int_{2}^{4} \frac{1}{x\sqrt{x^2-4}}\,dx$

(i) $\displaystyle\int_{0}^{1} \frac{1}{1+\sqrt{1-x^2}}\,dx$ (j) $\displaystyle\int_{1}^{\sqrt{2}} \frac{1}{1+\sqrt{x^2-1}}\,dx$

2 Find the following indefinite integrals.

(a) $\displaystyle\int \frac{1}{\sqrt{9-4x^2}}\,dx$

(b) $\displaystyle\int \frac{1}{9+4x^2}\,dx$

(c) $\displaystyle\int \frac{1}{a^2+b^2x^2}\,dx$

(d) $\displaystyle\int \frac{1}{x\sqrt{x^2-9}}\,dx$

(e) $\displaystyle\int \frac{x}{\sqrt{x^2-9}}\,dx$

(f) $\displaystyle\int \frac{1}{x^2+4x+5}\,dx$

(g) $\displaystyle\int \frac{1}{4x^2-4x+5}\,dx$

(h) $\displaystyle\int \frac{1}{\sqrt{x(2-x)}}\,dx$

(i) $\displaystyle\int \frac{1}{\sqrt{20-24x-9x^2}}\,dx$

3 Find the relative error, to 2 significant figures, if the trapezium rule with 5 intervals is used to evaluate the following integrals.

(a) $\displaystyle\int_0^5 \frac{1}{4x^2+25}\,dx$

(b) $\displaystyle\int_{\frac{1}{2}}^{\frac{3}{4}} \frac{1}{\sqrt{x-x^2}}\,dx$

4 Use integration by parts to show that $\displaystyle\int \sec^3 u\,du = \tfrac{1}{2}\left(\sec u \tan u + \ln(\sec u + \tan u)\right) + k$ for

$0 < u < \tfrac{1}{2}\pi$, and deduce an expression for $\displaystyle\int \sec u \tan^2 u\,du$. Hence find, for positive values

of x, expressions for $\displaystyle\int \sqrt{1+x^2}\,dx$, $\displaystyle\int \sqrt{x^2-1}\,dx$, $\displaystyle\int \sqrt{\frac{x}{1+x}}\,dx$ and $\displaystyle\int \sqrt{\frac{x}{x-1}}\,dx$. Check

your answers by differentiation.

Miscellaneous exercise 6

1 By using the substitution $u = \sin x$, find $\displaystyle\int \sin^3 x \sin 2x\,dx$, giving your answer in

terms of x.   (OCR)

2 A region R in the first quadrant is bounded by the curve $y = \tan x$, the x-axis and the line $x = \tfrac{1}{4}\pi$. Show that the exact value of the volume of the solid formed when R is rotated completely about the x-axis is $\pi - \tfrac{1}{4}\pi^2$.   (OCR)

3 Find the exact value of $\displaystyle\int_0^3 \sqrt{x(4-x)}\,dx$, using the substitution $x = 4\sin^2 u$.   (OCR)

4 Find $\displaystyle\int \cos x\sqrt{1-\cos x}\,dx$, using the substitution $u = \cos\tfrac{1}{2}x$.   (OCR)

5 Find the exact value of $\displaystyle\int_0^{\frac{1}{4}\pi} \frac{\sin 2x}{3-\cos 2x}\,dx$.   (OCR)

6 If $x = 5\sin\theta - 3$, show that $16 - 6x - x^2 = 25\cos^2\theta$. Hence find $\displaystyle\int \frac{1}{\sqrt{16-6x-x^2}}\,dx$.

(OCR)

7 Using the substitution $x = 3 + \tan\theta$, find $\displaystyle\int \frac{1}{x^2-6x+10}\,dx$.   (OCR)

8 Use the expressions for $\sin x$ and $\cos x$ in terms of $\tan\frac{1}{2}x$ to find three different sets of Pythagorean triples. (A Pythagorean triple is a set of natural numbers a, b, c such that $a^2 + b^2 = c^2$.)

9 Find the cartesian equation of the curve for which parametric equations are $x = 8\operatorname{cosec} u$, $y = 6\cot u$ for $-\pi < u < \pi$, $u \neq 0$. By writing $t = \tan\frac{1}{2}u$, find an alternative pair of parametric equations for the curve. Use these to make a sketch of the curve.

Find the equation of the tangent to the curve at the point where $t = p$. Hence find the point on the curve at which the tangent passes through $(4, -3)$.

10 Find the solution of the differential equation $\dfrac{dy}{dx} = \dfrac{8x\cos^2 x}{y}$ which satisfies $y = \sqrt{3}$ when $x = 0$. (MEI)

11 The variables x and y are related by the differential equation $\dfrac{dy}{dx} = \sin x \sin 2y$ $(0 < y < \frac{1}{2}\pi)$, and $y = \frac{1}{4}\pi$ when $x = 0$. Show that, when $x = \pi$, the value of y is $\tan^{-1} e^4$. (OCR)

12 For $x > 0$ and $0 < y < \frac{1}{2}\pi$, the variables y and x are connected by the differential equation $\dfrac{dy}{dx} = \dfrac{\ln x}{\cot y}$, and $y = \frac{1}{6}\pi$ when $x = e$. Find the value of y when $x = 1$, giving your answer correct to three significant figures. Use the differential equation to show that this value of y is a stationary value, and determine its nature. (MEI)

13 A rugby goal has posts erected at A and B. A point C lies on AB produced so that $AC = a$ and $BC = b$. A player wishes to place the ball at the point P on the straight line through C perpendicular to AB, so that the angle APB is a maximum. Show that, if $CP = y$ and angle $APB = \theta$, then $\theta = \tan^{-1}\dfrac{y}{b} - \tan^{-1}\dfrac{y}{a}$, and deduce that the maximum value of θ occurs when $y^2 = ab$. (OCR, adapted)

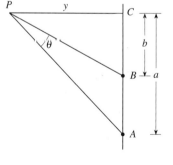

14 Given that $y = x - \sqrt{1 - x^2}\,\sin^{-1} x$, show that $\dfrac{dy}{dx} = \dfrac{x\sin^{-1} x}{\sqrt{1 - x^2}}$. Hence evaluate

$$\int_0^{\frac{1}{4}\sqrt{3}} \dfrac{2x\sin^{-1} 2x}{\sqrt{1 - 4x^2}}\,dx,$$ giving your answer in terms of π and $\sqrt{3}$. (OCR)

15 Given that x and y satisfy the equation $\tan^{-1} x + \tan^{-1} y + \tan^{-1}(xy) = \frac{11}{12}\pi$, prove that, when $x = 1$, $\dfrac{dy}{dx} = -1 - \frac{1}{2}\sqrt{3}$. (OCR)

16 Show that $\displaystyle\int_0^{\sqrt{3}} \sin^{-1}\tfrac{1}{2}x\,dx = \frac{\pi}{\sqrt{3}} - 1.$ (MEI)

17 (a) Show that $\cos x - \sin x = \sqrt{2}\cos\!\left(x + \tfrac{1}{4}\pi\right)$ and hence integrate $\displaystyle\int_0^{X} \frac{dx}{\cos x - \sin x}$, where

    $0 < X < \tfrac{1}{4}\pi$. By letting $X \to \tfrac{1}{4}\pi$ in your answer find if $\displaystyle\int_0^{\frac{1}{4}\pi} \frac{dx}{\cos x - \sin x}$ exists.

  (b) Evaluate $\displaystyle\int_0^{X} \frac{dx}{(\cos x - \sin x)^2}$, $\;0 < X < \tfrac{1}{4}\pi$.

  (c) The graph of $\cos x - \sin x$ cuts the axes at $P(0,1)$ and $Q\!\left(\tfrac{1}{4}\pi, 0\right)$. By considering the

    chord PQ and the tangent at P, show that $1 - \dfrac{4x}{\pi} < \cos x - \sin x < 1 - x$ for

    $0 < x < \tfrac{1}{4}\pi$. Hence find numbers A, B such that $A < \displaystyle\int_0^{\frac{1}{4}\pi} \frac{dx}{\sqrt{\cos x - \sin x}} < B$, and

    deduce that the integral exists.   (OCR)

7 Maclaurin expansions

You have already used series expansions in connection with geometric series and binomial expansions. In this chapter the idea is extended to other functions. When you have completed it, you should

- be able to find Maclaurin polynomials, and understand why they give good approximations to functions
- know the Maclaurin expansions for a number of functions
- understand what is meant by the interval of validity of an expansion
- be able to find expansions of composite functions
- know how to find expansions using integrals.

7.1 Agreement between functions

If $f(x)$ denotes the function $\sqrt{1+x}$, or $(1+x)^{\frac{1}{2}}$, then it can be expressed using the binomial expansion as

$$f(x) = 1 + \tfrac{1}{2}x - \tfrac{1}{8}x^2 + \tfrac{1}{16}x^3 - \dots .$$

Fig. 7.1, Fig. 7.2 and Fig. 7.3 show the graph of $f(x)$ compared with graphs of the polynomial functions

$$p_1(x) = 1 + \tfrac{1}{2}x,$$
$$p_2(x) = 1 + \tfrac{1}{2}x - \tfrac{1}{8}x^2,$$
$$p_3(x) = 1 + \tfrac{1}{2}x - \tfrac{1}{8}x^2 + \tfrac{1}{16}x^3.$$

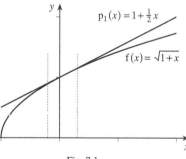

Fig. 7.1

The dotted lines indicate the intervals of values of x for which you can't distinguish the pairs of graphs by eye. You can see that the more terms of the expansion you take, the wider the interval over which the polynomial gives a good approximation to $\sqrt{1+x}$.

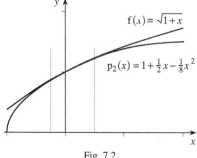

Fig. 7.2

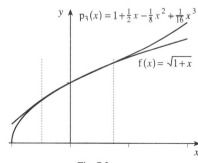

Fig. 7.3

The polynomial $p_1(x)$ has the same value as $f(x)$ when $x = 0$, and also the same gradient. Thus $f(0) = \sqrt{1+0} = 1$ and $p_1(0) = 1$. Also, since

$$f'(x) = \tfrac{1}{2}(1+x)^{-\frac{1}{2}} \quad \text{and} \quad p_1{}'(x) = \tfrac{1}{2},$$

you find that $f'(0) = p_1{}'(0) = \tfrac{1}{2}$.

The reason why $p_2(x)$ fits $f(x)$ better than $p_1(x)$ is that, by adding a term in x^2, the graph can be made to bend into a curve. The coefficient of x^2 has been chosen so that the two graphs bend at the same rate when $x = 0$; that is, their second derivatives are the same. Thus

$$f''(x) = -\tfrac{1}{4}(1+x)^{-\frac{3}{2}} \quad \text{and} \quad p_2{}''(x) = -\tfrac{1}{4},$$

so that $f''(0) = p_2{}''(0) = -\tfrac{1}{4}$.

The functions $p_3(x)$ and $f(x)$ agree even better, since they not only bend at the same rate at $x = 0$, but also their rates of bending are changing at the same rate. You can check for yourself that $f'''(0) = p_3{}'''(0) = \tfrac{3}{8}$.

The ideas above can be summarised with the help of a definition:

Definition   The functions f and g **agree to the nth degree** at $x = 0$ if

$$f(0) = g(0), \quad f'(0) = g'(0), \quad f''(0) = g''(0), \quad \dots, \quad f^{(n)}(0) = g^{(n)}(0),$$

that is if $f^{(r)}(0) = g^{(r)}(0)$ where r is an integer, and $0 \leqslant r \leqslant n$.

Thus $f(x)$ and $p_1(x)$ agree to the first degree, $f(x)$ and $p_2(x)$ agree to the second degree and $f(x)$ and $p_3(x)$ agree to the third degree.

You can extend this idea to functions other than binomial expansions.

Example 7.1.1
Find a cubic polynomial which agrees with $\tan x$ to the third degree.

Writing $\tan x$ as $f(x)$, use the chain rule and the product rule to find

$$f'(x) = \sec^2 x, \quad f''(x) = 2\sec x \times \sec x \tan x = 2\sec^2 x \tan x,$$

$$f'''(x) = 4\sec x \times \sec x \tan x \times \tan x + 2\sec^2 x \times \sec^2 x$$
$$= 2\sec^2 x \left(2\tan^2 x + \sec^2 x\right).$$

Since $\tan 0 = 0$ and $\sec 0 = 1$,

$$f(0) = 0, \quad f'(0) = 1, \quad f''(0) = 0, \quad f'''(0) = 2.$$

If the cubic polynomial is $p(x) = a + bx + cx^2 + dx^3$, then

$$p'(x) = b + 2cx + 3dx^2, \quad p''(x) = 2c + 6dx, \quad p'''(x) = 6d.$$

So $p(0) = a$, $p'(0) = b$, $p''(0) = 2c$, $p'''(0) = 6d$.

For $p(x)$ and $f(x)$ to agree at $x = 0$, you need $a = 0$, $b = 1$, $2c = 0$, $6d = 2$.

Therefore $p(x) = x + \frac{1}{3}x^3$.

It is interesting to plot the graphs of $\tan x$ *and* $p(x) = x + \frac{1}{3}x^3$ *on a graphic calculator, and to suggest an interval over which you would consider that* $p(x)$ *is a good approximation to* $\tan x$.

7.2 Maclaurin polynomials

You can generalise the argument in the last section to give polynomial approximations to any function $f(x)$ around $x = 0$, provided that all the derivatives of the function are defined.

The result is stated in the form of the following theorem.

Theorem The polynomial of degree n which agrees with $f(x)$ to the nth degree at $x = 0$ is

$$p_n(x) = f(0) + \frac{f'(0)}{1!}x + \frac{f''(0)}{2!}x^2 + \ldots + \frac{f^{(r)}(0)}{r!}x^r + \ldots + \frac{f^{(n)}(0)}{n!}x^n.$$

The polynomial $p_n(x)$ in the theorem is called the **Maclaurin polynomial for $f(x)$ of degree n**. In sigma notation it can be written as $\sum_{r=0}^{n} \frac{f^{(r)}(0)}{r!}x^r$. It is named after Colin Maclaurin, a Scottish mathematician who lived in the first half of the 18th century.

Example 7.2.1
Find the Maclaurin polynomial of degree 4 for the function $f(x) = (1 + x)^{-3}$.

The first four derivatives are $f'(x) = -3(1 + x)^{-4}$, $f''(x) = 12(1 + x)^{-5}$, $f'''(x) = -60(1 + x)^{-6}$, $f^{(4)}(x) = 360(1 + x)^{-7}$. Therefore $f(0) = 1$, $f'(0) = -3$, $f''(0) = 12$, $f'''(0) = -60$, $f^{(4)}(0) = 360$. This gives

$$p_4(x) = 1 + \frac{(-3)}{1!}x + \frac{12}{2!}x^2 + \frac{(-60)}{3!}x^3 + \frac{360}{4!}x^4$$

$$= 1 - 3x + 6x^2 - 10x^3 + 15x^4.$$

You can check that this is the same as the binomial expansion of $(1 + x)^{-3}$ up to and including the term in x^4.

Before giving the proof of the theorem, it will be useful to establish two mini-theorems (or 'lemmas'). These are set out in a general notation, but if you have difficulty following this, try writing the equations out for yourself in full using values such as $r = 3$ and $n = 5$.

Mini-theorem   If $g(x) = x^r$, where $r \in \mathbb{N}$, then $g^{(r)}(0) = r!$ and $g^{(i)}(0) = 0$ if $i < r$ or $i > r$.

     Proof   Generalising from $g'(x) = rx^{r-1}$, $g''(x) = r(r-1)x^{r-2}, \ldots$ you get

$$g^{(i)}(x) = r(r-1)(r-2)\ldots(r-(i-1))x^{r-i},$$

provided that $i \leqslant r$. If $i < r$, the power of x is positive, so that $g^{(i)}(0) = 0$. But when $i = r$, so that $r - i = 0$, $g^{(i)}(x)$ has the constant value

$$g^{(i)}(x) = r(r-1)(r-2)\ldots 1 = r!.$$

The formula for $g^{(i)}(x)$ no longer holds when $i > r$. Since $g^{(r)}(x)$ is constant, $g^{(r+1)}(x) = 0$ and all subsequent derivatives are 0 for all x.

So $g^{(i)}(0) = 0$ for $i > r$.

The next mini-theorem extends this result to a polynomial of degree n. To do this it is convenient to use a new notation for the coefficients of a polynomial, denoting the coefficient of the term in x^r by a_r so that

$$p(x) = a_0 + a_1 x + a_2 x^2 + \ldots + a_r x^r + \ldots + a_n x^n.$$

The term $a_r x^r$ is called the **general term** of $p(x)$. You can use sigma notation to abbreviate this equation to

$$p(x) = \sum_{r=0}^{n} a_r x^r.$$

Mini-theorem   If $p(x) = \sum_{r=0}^{n} a_r x^r$, then $p^{(r)}(0) = a_r r!$ for $0 \leqslant r \leqslant n$.

     Proof   When you find the rth derivative of $p(x)$, all the terms of the form $a_i x^i$ with $i < r$ and $i > r$ have rth derivatives which are 0 when $x = 0$, by the previous mini-theorem. Only the term $a_r x^r$ has an rth derivative which is not 0 when $x = 0$, and the value of this derivative is $a_r r!$.

You now have everything you need to prove the main result.

     Proof of the main theorem   Denoting $p_n(x)$ by $\sum_{r=0}^{n} a_r x^r$ you require

$p_n^{(r)}(0) = f^{(r)}(0)$ for $0 \leqslant r \leqslant n$. By the previous mini-theorem, $p_n^{(r)}(0) = a_r r!$.

Therefore $a_r r! = f^{(r)}(0)$, so that $a_r = \dfrac{f^{(r)}(0)}{r!}$ for $0 \leqslant r \leqslant n$.

1 For the following expressions $f(x)$ write down the binomial expansions as far as the term in x^3. Denoting this expansion by $p_3(x)$, verify that $f(x)$ and $p_3(x)$ agree to the third degree at $x = 0$. Display graphs of $f(x)$ and $p_3(x)$ on a graphic calculator, and estimate the interval over which you cannot distinguish between the graphs.

   (a) $(1+x)^{\frac{3}{2}}$ (b) $(1-x)^{-\frac{3}{2}}$ (c) $(1+2x)^{-3}$ (d) $\left(1+x^2\right)^{\frac{1}{2}}$

2 For the following expressions $f(x)$ find the Maclaurin polynomial $p_n(x)$ of the given degree n. Illustrate your answers by comparing the graphs of $f(x)$ and $p_n(x)$.

   (a) $\sin x$, $n = 5$ (b) $\sin 2x$, $n = 5$ (c) e^x, $n = 4$

   (d) e^{-3x}, $n = 4$ (e) $\sin^2 x$, $n = 3$ (f) $\cos^2 x$, $n = 3$

   (g) $\ln(1-x)$, $n = 4$ (h) $\dfrac{1}{\sqrt{1-2x}}$, $n = 3$ (i) $e^{-\frac{1}{2}x^2}$, $n = 4$

   (j) $\ln\left(1+x^2\right)$, $n = 4$

3 Show that it is possible to find numbers a and b such that $ax + bx^2$ and $e^x \ln(1+x)$ agree to degree 2 at $x = 0$.

4 Show that it is possible to find numbers a and b such that $a + bx^2$ and $\sec x$ agree to degree 3 at $x = 0$.

5 Show that it is possible to find numbers a and b such that $ax + bx^3$ and $\dfrac{e^x - 1}{e^x + 1}$ agree to degree 3 at $x = 0$.

6 Find the Maclaurin polynomial of degree 4 for $(1+x)^m$, where m is not a positive integer. Verify that this agrees with the first five terms of the binomial expansion of $(1+x)^m$.

7 Show that $\dfrac{d}{dx}(f(ax)) = af'(ax)$, and that $\dfrac{d}{dx}\left(f\left(x^2\right)\right) = 2xf'\left(x^2\right)$. Hence show that

   (a) if $f(x)$ and $g(x)$ agree to degree 3 at $x = 0$, then $f(ax)$ and $g(ax)$ agree to degree 3;

   (b) if $f(x)$ and $g(x)$ agree to degree 2 at $x = 0$, then $f\left(x^2\right)$ and $g\left(x^2\right)$ agree to degree 4.

7.3 Expansions and intervals of validity

The expression

$$f(0) + \frac{f'(0)}{1!}x + \frac{f''(0)}{2!}x^2 + \ldots + \frac{f^{(r)}(0)}{r!}x^r + \ldots,$$

continued indefinitely, is called the **Maclaurin expansion** of $f(x)$. By cutting off the expansion after the second, third, fourth, ... terms you get a sequence of Maclaurin polynomials $p_1(x)$, $p_2(x)$, $p_3(x)$, ...

Fig. 7.1, Fig. 7.2 and Fig. 7.3 showed how such a sequence of polynomials can give better and better approximations to $f(x)$ for certain values of x. In such cases you can say that $f(x)$ is the limit of the sequence of polynomial values as n tends to infinity.

This can be written

$$f(x) = \lim_{n \to \infty} p_n(x) = \lim_{n \to \infty} \sum_{r=0}^{n} \frac{f^{(r)}(0)}{r!} x^r, \text{ or } \sum_{r=0}^{\infty} \frac{f^{(r)}(0)}{r!} x^r.$$

It means that, by taking n large enough, you can (for a particular value of x) make $p_n(x)$ as close as you like to $f(x)$.

For many functions this is true for some but not all values of x. For example, if $f(x) = \ln(1+x)$, then $f'(x) = (1+x)^{-1}$, $f''(x) = -(1+x)^{-2}$, $f'''(x) = 2(1+x)^{-3}, \dots$, so that $f'(0) = 1$, $f''(0) = -1$, $f'''(0) = 2, \dots$. The general term is positive when r is odd and negative when r is even, and it is not difficult to check that

$$f^{(r)}(x) = (-1)^{r-1}(r-1)!(1+x)^{-r}, \text{ so that}$$

$$\frac{f^{(r)}(0)}{r!} = \frac{(-1)^{r-1}(r-1)!}{r!} = (-1)^{r-1} \frac{1}{r}.$$

The Maclaurin expansion is therefore

$$\ln(1+x) = x - \tfrac{1}{2}x^2 + \tfrac{1}{3}x^3 - \tfrac{1}{4}x^4 + \dots.$$

Fig. 7.4 shows a comparison of the graphs of $\ln(1+x)$ and the 10th Maclaurin polynomial, ending with the term $-\frac{1}{10}x^{10}$. It is striking how closely the Maclaurin polynomial follows the function from just above -1 to just below 1, but that beyond 1 the two functions separate very sharply. However many terms you take, you can never get $p_n(x)$ to come close to $\ln(1+x)$ for $x > 1$.

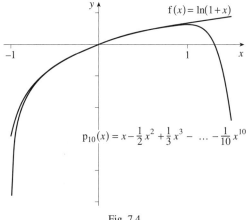

Fig. 7.4

Contrast this with the function $f(x) = \sin x$. Since the derivatives are successively $\cos x$, $-\sin x$, $-\cos x$, $\sin x$, ... and then repeat through the same cycle, the values of $f^{(r)}(0)$ are successively $1, 0, -1, 0, 1, 0, \dots$. Also $f(0) = 0$. The Maclaurin expansion is therefore

$$\sin x = \frac{x}{1!} - \frac{x^3}{3!} + \frac{x^5}{5!} - \frac{x^7}{7!} \dots.$$

Fig. 7.5 shows a comparison of the graphs of $\sin x$ and the 10th Maclaurin polynomial. (The last non-zero term of $p_{10}(x)$ is $\dfrac{x^9}{9!}$,

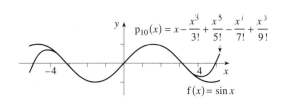

Fig. 7.5

because $f^{(10)}(0) = 0$.) You can see that already the graphs cannot be distinguished from each other by eye between about -4 and $+4$. And in fact, by taking enough terms, you can get a Maclaurin polynomial which fits the $\sin x$ graph over as wide an interval as you like.

The set of values of x for which the Maclaurin expansion can be made to fit a function, provided that enough terms are taken, is called the **interval of validity** of the expansion. For the function $\ln(1+x)$ the interval of validity is $-1 < x \leqslant 1$; the expansion of $\sin x$ is valid for all real values of x, so its interval of validity is $\mathbb{R}$.

The only condition for a function to have a Maclaurin expansion is that $f(0)$ and all the derivatives $f^{(r)}(0)$ must be defined. So $\operatorname{cosec} x$ and $\ln x$ do not have Maclaurin expansions, because they are not defined when $x = 0$; and $|x|$ does not have one, since $\dfrac{d}{dx}(|x|)$ is not defined when $x = 0$.

But many of the standard functions do have Maclaurin expansions, and the most important ones are listed below. Before reading on, you should check these for yourself; it is worth remembering the first few terms of each expansion, but not the expression for the general term. You will have to take the intervals of validity on trust, but you could try using a computer or a graphic calculator to produce graphs like Figs. 7.4 and 7.5.

$$e^x = 1 + \frac{x}{1!} + \frac{x^2}{2!} + \frac{x^3}{3!} + \ldots + \frac{x^r}{r!} + \ldots, \quad \text{for } x \in \mathbb{R}.$$

$$\sin x = \frac{x}{1!} - \frac{x^3}{3!} + \frac{x^5}{5!} - \frac{x^7}{7!} + \ldots + (-1)^r \frac{x^{2r+1}}{(2r+1)!} + \ldots, \quad \text{for } x \in \mathbb{R}.$$

$$\cos x = 1 - \frac{x^2}{2!} + \frac{x^4}{4!} - \frac{x^6}{6!} + \ldots + (-1)^r \frac{x^{2r}}{(2r)!} + \ldots, \quad \text{for } x \in \mathbb{R}.$$

$$\ln(1+x) = x - \tfrac{1}{2}x^2 + \tfrac{1}{3}x^3 - \tfrac{1}{4}x^4 + \ldots + (-1)^{r-1}\tfrac{1}{r}x^r + \ldots, \quad \text{for } -1 < x \leqslant 1.$$

$$(1+x)^n = 1 + nx + \frac{n(n-1)}{2!}x^2 + \frac{n(n-1)(n-2)}{3!}x^3 + \ldots$$

$$+ \frac{n(n-1)(n-2)\ldots(n-(r-1))}{r!}x^r + \ldots, \quad \text{for } x \in \mathbb{R} \text{ if } n \in \mathbb{N},$$

otherwise for $-1 < x < 1$ (and, in some cases, also for $x = -1$ or $x = 1$).

Example 7.3.1

Find the values of e and $\dfrac{1}{e}$, correct to 4 decimal places.

You can evaluate these by substituting $x = 1$ and $x = -1$ in the expansion for e^x:

$$e = 1 + \frac{1}{1!} + \frac{1}{2!} + \frac{1}{3!} + \frac{1}{4!} + \ldots,$$

$$\frac{1}{e} = 1 - \frac{1}{1!} + \frac{1}{2!} - \frac{1}{3!} + \frac{1}{4!} - \ldots .$$

$1 = 1$	$\dfrac{1}{1!} = 1$
$\dfrac{1}{2!} = 0.5$	$\dfrac{1}{3!} = 0.166\,667$
$\dfrac{1}{4!} = 0.041\,667$	$\dfrac{1}{5!} = 0.008\,333$
$\dfrac{1}{6!} = 0.001\,389$	$\dfrac{1}{7!} = 0.000\,198$
$\dfrac{1}{8!} = 0.000\,025$	$\dfrac{1}{9!} = 0.000\,003$
$1.543\,081$	$1.175\,201$

Table 7.6

The calculation is very simple, since $(r+1)! = (r+1)r!$, so that you can find

$\dfrac{1}{(r+1)!}$ by dividing $\dfrac{1}{r!}$ by $r+1$. Table 7.6 lists values of $\dfrac{1}{r!}$ up to $r = 9$.

So $e \approx 1.543\,081 + 1.175\,201 \approx 2.7183,$

$\dfrac{1}{e} \approx 1.543\,081 - 1.175\,201 \approx 0.3679$, correct to 4 decimal places.

Exercise 7B

1 Use Maclaurin expansions to find, correct to 4 decimal places, the values of

 (a) $\sqrt{e}$,   (b) $\sin 1$,   (c) $\sqrt[3]{0.9}$,   (d) $\cos 20°$,

 (e) $\ln 0.95$,   (f) $\ln 2.25$,   (g) $\cos 3$.

2 Find the Maclaurin expansion for $\ln\dfrac{1+x}{1-x}$, and state its interval of validity. By choosing a suitable value for x, calculate the value of $\ln 3$, correct to 3 decimal places.

 Why can't you find $\ln 3$ directly from the Maclaurin expansion for $\ln(1+x)$?

3 Use the standard expansions to find the first two non-zero terms in the expansion of $x\cos x - \sin x$. Hence find the limit, as $x \to 0$, of $\dfrac{x\cos x - \sin x}{x^3}$.

4 Use the method of Question 3 to find the limit, as $x \to 0$, of

 (a) $\dfrac{e^x - e^{-x}}{x}$, (b) $\dfrac{1 - \cos x}{x^2}$, (c) $\dfrac{\ln(1+x)}{x}$, (d) $\dfrac{\ln(1+x) - x}{x^2}$.

5 Show that, if you assume that a function can be differentiated by differentiating each term of its Maclaurin expansion, you get correct results for

 (a) $\dfrac{d}{dx}\left(e^x\right)$, (b) $\dfrac{d}{dx}(\sin x)$, (c) $\dfrac{d}{dx}(\ln(1+x))$, (d) $\dfrac{d}{dx}\left(\sqrt{(1+x)}\right)$.

6 An approximate value for π can be found by putting $x = \frac{1}{2}\pi$ in the Maclaurin expansion of $\cos x$ and neglecting all the terms of degree greater than 4, and then solving a quartic polynomial equation for π. To how many significant figures is the approximation accurate?

 An alternative method is to use the substitution $x = \frac{1}{3}\pi$. To how many significant figures is the resulting approximation accurate?

 Which method gives the better approximation? Suggest a reason why.

7* Prove that, if $x = 10$, the terms of the Maclaurin expansion for $\cos x$ decrease in absolute value from $\dfrac{x^{12}}{12!}$ onwards. Deduce that the errors in replacing $\cos 10$ by its Maclaurin polynomials $p_{30}(10)$ and $p_{40}(10)$ are less than $\dfrac{10^{32}}{32!}$ and $\dfrac{10^{42}}{42!}$ respectively in absolute value. Evaluate these expressions correct to 1 significant figure, and explain why your answers suggest that the expansion is valid for $x = 10$.

 By generalising this argument, say what this suggests about the interval of validity of the Maclaurin expansion for $\cos x$.

7.4 Maclaurin expansions for composite functions

If you want to find the Maclaurin expansion for a function such as $\sin 5x$ or $\ln(1+x^2)$, you could use the general expression at the beginning of Section 7.3 with $f(x) = \sin 5x$ or $f(x) = \ln(1+x^2)$. This is quite easy for $\sin 5x$, since the derivatives are successively $5\cos 5x$, $-5^2 \sin 5x$, $-5^3 \cos 5x$, ... , whose values for $x = 0$ are 5, 0, -5^3, ... It is easy to see how this continues. The Maclaurin expansion then begins

$$\frac{5}{1!}x - \frac{5^3}{3!}x^3 + \frac{5^5}{5!}x^5 - \dots .$$

You can write this as

$$\frac{(5x)}{1!} - \frac{(5x)^3}{3!} + \frac{(5x)^5}{5!} - \dots ,$$

which is (as you would probably expect) what you would get by simply replacing x by $5x$ in the Maclaurin expansion of $\sin x$.

Differentiating $\ln(1+x^2)$ several times is a lot more difficult, and you might not recognise the general pattern. But, just as you could with $\sin 5x$, you can find the Maclaurin expansion by substitution, in this case by simply replacing x by x^2 in the Maclaurin expansion of $\ln(1+x)$. This gives

$$\ln(1+x^2) = (x^2) - \tfrac{1}{2}(x^2)^2 + \tfrac{1}{3}(x^2)^3 - \tfrac{1}{4}(x^2)^4 + \dots$$
$$= x^2 - \tfrac{1}{2}x^4 + \tfrac{1}{3}x^6 - \tfrac{1}{4}x^8 + \dots .$$

Since the expansion of $\ln(1+x)$ is valid when $-1 < x \leqslant 1$, this expansion is valid when $-1 < x^2 < 1$, that is when $-1 \leqslant x \leqslant 1$.

Sometimes it is worth using some special property of the function before finding the Maclaurin expansion, as in the following example.

Example 7.4.1
Find Maclaurin expansions for (a) $\sin(x + \tfrac{1}{4}\pi)$,   (b) $\ln(2 - 4x)$.

(a) By the addition formula, $\sin(x + \tfrac{1}{4}\pi) = \sin x \cos \tfrac{1}{4}\pi + \cos x \sin \tfrac{1}{4}\pi$.

Since $\sin \tfrac{1}{4}\pi = \cos \tfrac{1}{4}\pi = \dfrac{1}{\sqrt{2}}$,

$$\sin(x + \tfrac{1}{4}\pi) = \frac{1}{\sqrt{2}}(\sin x + \cos x)$$

$$= \frac{1}{\sqrt{2}}\left(\left(\frac{x}{1!} - \frac{x^3}{3!} + \frac{x^5}{5!} - \dots\right) + \left(1 - \frac{x^2}{2!} + \frac{x^4}{4!} - \dots\right)\right)$$

$$= \frac{1}{\sqrt{2}}\left(1 + x - \frac{x^2}{2!} - \frac{x^3}{3!} + \frac{x^4}{4!} + \frac{x^5}{5!} - \dots\right).$$

(b) Use the multiplication rule of logarithms to write

$$\ln(2 - 4x) = \ln 2 + \ln(1 - 2x).$$

Then use the Maclaurin series for $\ln(1 + x)$, replacing x by $-2x$, to get

$$\ln(2 - 4x) = \ln 2 + (-2x) - \tfrac{1}{2}(-2x)^2 + \tfrac{1}{3}(-2x)^3 - \tfrac{1}{4}(-2x)^4 - \dots$$
$$= \ln 2 - 2x - 2x^2 - \tfrac{8}{3}x^3 - 4x^4 - \dots.$$

This expansion is valid if $-1 < -2x \leqslant 1$, that is if $\dfrac{(-1)}{(-2)} > x \geqslant \dfrac{1}{(-2)}$, or $-\tfrac{1}{2} \leqslant x < \tfrac{1}{2}$.

Example 7.4.2

Find the Maclaurin polynomials of degree 4 for (a) $\ln\cos x$,   (b) $e^{\cos x}$,   (c) $x\operatorname{cosec} x$.

The composite functions in this example each involve two expansions. The work can be eased by discarding powers of x higher than x^4 as you go along, but you need to be careful in (c) where division is involved.

(a) $\ln\cos x = \ln\left(1 - \dfrac{x^2}{2!} + \dfrac{x^4}{4!} - \dots\right)$

$$= \ln\left(1 + \left(-\tfrac{1}{2}x^2 + \tfrac{1}{24}x^4 - \dots\right)\right)$$

$$= \left(-\tfrac{1}{2}x^2 + \tfrac{1}{24}x^4 - \dots\right) - \tfrac{1}{2}\left(-\tfrac{1}{2}x^2 + \tfrac{1}{24}x^4 - \dots\right)^2 + \dots$$

$$= \left(-\tfrac{1}{2}x^2 + \tfrac{1}{24}x^4\right) - \tfrac{1}{2}\left(\tfrac{1}{4}x^4\right) \text{ to degree 4}$$

$$= -\tfrac{1}{2}x^2 + \left(\tfrac{1}{24} - \tfrac{1}{8}\right)x^4 = -\tfrac{1}{2}x^2 - \tfrac{1}{12}x^4.$$

(b) If you try to use a method similar to that in (a), writing $e^{\cos x}$ as

$$\exp\left(1 - \dfrac{x^2}{2!} + \dfrac{x^4}{4!} - \dots\right) \text{ and expanding this as}$$

$$1 + \dfrac{\left(1 - \dfrac{x^2}{2!} + \dfrac{x^4}{4!} - \dots\right)}{1!} + \dfrac{\left(1 - \dfrac{x^2}{2!} + \dfrac{x^4}{4!} - \dots\right)^2}{2!} - \dots,$$

then you run into a problem. However far you continue with the exponential

expansion, every term is of the form $\dfrac{\left(1 - \dfrac{x^2}{2!} + \dfrac{x^4}{4!} - \dots\right)^r}{r!}$, which when expanded

contributes to the constant term and the terms in x^2 and x^4 of the expansion.

The way round this is to begin by using the multiplication rule for indices to write the expansion as

$$\exp(1) \times \exp\left(-\dfrac{x^2}{2!}\right) \times \exp\left(\dfrac{x^4}{4!}\right) \times \dots.$$

The dots at the end of this product represent factors like $\exp\left(-\dfrac{x^6}{6!}\right)$ which when expanded contribute only the first term, 1, to the powers of x of degree up to 4. Then

$$e^{\cos x} = e \times \left(1 + \frac{1}{1!}\left(-\frac{x^2}{2}\right) + \frac{1}{2!}\left(-\frac{x^2}{2}\right)^2 + \dots\right) \times \left(1 + \frac{1}{1!}\left(\frac{x^4}{24}\right) + \dots\right) \times \dots$$

$$= e\left(1 - \tfrac{1}{2}x^2 + \tfrac{1}{8}x^4 - \dots\right) \times \left(1 + \tfrac{1}{24}x^4 + \dots\right) \times \dots$$

$$= e\left(1 - \tfrac{1}{2}x^2 + \left(\tfrac{1}{24} + \tfrac{1}{8}\right)x^4\right) \text{ to degree } 4$$

$$= e\left(1 - \tfrac{1}{2}x^2 + \tfrac{1}{6}x^4\right).$$

(c) The first step is to write $x \operatorname{cosec} x$ as $\dfrac{x}{\sin x}$ and to replace $\sin x$ by its Maclaurin expansion. There will then be factors of x in both numerator and denominator, which will cancel out. So you have to keep the x^5 term in the $\sin x$ expansion, which will become x^4 after cancellation.

$$x \operatorname{cosec} x = \frac{x}{\sin x} = \frac{x}{\left(x - \dfrac{x^3}{3!} + \dfrac{x^5}{5!} - \dots\right)} = \frac{1}{1 - \dfrac{x^2}{6} + \dfrac{x^4}{120} - \dots}$$

$$= \left(1 - \left(\tfrac{1}{6}x^2 - \tfrac{1}{120}x^4 + \dots\right)\right)^{-1}.$$

Now replace u in the binomial expansion $(1-u)^{-1} = 1 + u + u^2 + \dots$ by $\frac{1}{6}x^2 - \frac{1}{120}x^4 + \dots$ to obtain

$$x \operatorname{cosec} x = 1 + \left(\tfrac{1}{6}x^2 - \tfrac{1}{120}x^4 + \dots\right) + \left(\tfrac{1}{6}x^2 \dots\right)^2$$

$$= 1 + \tfrac{1}{6}x^2 + \left(-\tfrac{1}{120} + \tfrac{1}{36}\right)x^4 \text{ to degree } 4$$

$$= 1 + \tfrac{1}{6}x^2 + \tfrac{7}{360}x^4.$$

There is no easy way of knowing the interval of validity of these composite expansions because you don't have an expression for the general term. The value of the expansions lies in their use as polynomial approximations to the functions when x is small.

Exercise 7C

1 Each of the following expressions $f(x)$ can be written as $g(h(x))$, where g is one of the functions whose Maclaurin expansion is listed on page 93. Expand $f(x)$ as far as the term in x^4 by two methods: (i) by finding $f^{(r)}(x)$ for $r = 1, 2, 3, 4$ and using the general formula for a Maclaurin expansion, and (ii) by substituting $h(x)$ in place of x in the expansion of $g(x)$. Verify that both methods give the same answer.

(a) $f(x) = (1 + 2x)^{\frac{3}{2}}$ (b) $f(x) = e^{-2x}$

(c) $f(x) = \ln(1 + x^3)$ (d) $f(x) = \sin x^3$

2 Write the Maclaurin expansion of the following, giving the first three non-zero terms, an expression for the general term and the interval of validity.

(a) e^{3x} (b) $\cos\frac{1}{2}x$ (c) $\sqrt{x}\sin\sqrt{x}$ (d) $\ln(1-x)$

(e) $\ln(1+2x)$ (f) e^{1+x} (g) $\cos^2 x$ (h) $\ln(e+x)$

(i) $\cos(1+x)$

3 Find the Maclaurin polynomials of degree 4 for the following.

(a) $e^{(1+x)^2}$ (b) $e^{\sqrt{1+x}}$ (c) $\cos(\sin x)$ (d) $\sin(\cos x)$

(e) $\sec x$ (f) $\dfrac{x^2}{\ln(1+x^2)}$ (g) $\tan x$ (h) $\ln(1+e^x)$

(i) $\sqrt{\dfrac{1+x}{1-x}}$

4 Find functions whose Maclaurin expansions are

(a) $1+\dfrac{x^2}{1!}+\dfrac{x^4}{2!}+\ldots+\dfrac{x^{2r}}{r!}+\ldots,$ (b) $1+\dfrac{x^2}{2!}+\dfrac{x^4}{4!}+\ldots+\dfrac{x^{2r}}{(2r)!}+\ldots,$

(c) $1+\dfrac{x}{2!}+\dfrac{x^2}{4!}+\ldots+\dfrac{x^r}{(2r)!}+\ldots.$

7.5* Integrals as functions

You know that $\displaystyle\int_a^b f(x)\,dx$ can be calculated as $I(b)-I(a)$, where $I(x)$ is a function such that $I'(x)=f(x)$. Changing the notation, you can say that $\displaystyle\int_a^x f(t)\,dt$ can be calculated as $I(x)-I(a)$. (Notice that the variable in the integrand has been changed from x to t. When you write a definite integral it doesn't matter what letter you use in the integrand. Thus $\displaystyle\int_1^4 x^2\,dx$ has the value 21, and so does $\displaystyle\int_1^4 u^2\,du$ and $\displaystyle\int_1^4 t^2\,dt$. But it confuses the issue to use the same letter in the integrand as you have used for one of the limits of integration. The variable t here is another example of a dummy variable.)

Now $\displaystyle\int_a^x f(t)\,dt$ is itself a function of x; for each value of x the integral has a unique value. If it is denoted by $F(x)$, then

$$F(x)=\int_a^x f(t)\,dt = I(x)-I(a),\text{ so that } F'(x)=I'(x)=f(x).$$

This can be summarised in the important result:

$$\frac{d}{dx}\int_a^x f(t)\,dt = f(x).$$

From this you can derive a theorem which is useful in obtaining expansions in some cases when Maclaurin's result is difficult to apply directly.

Theorem If two functions $f(x)$ and $g(x)$ agree to the nth degree at $x = 0$, then

$$F(x) = \int_a^x f(t)\,dt \quad \text{and} \quad G(x) = \int_a^x g(t)\,dt \quad \text{agree to the } (n+1)\text{th degree.}$$

Proof Notice first that $F(0) = G(0) = 0$. Also $F'(x) = f(x)$ and $G'(x) = g(x)$, so that $F^{(r+1)}(x) = f^{(r)}(x)$ and $G^{(r+1)}(x) = g^{(r)}(x)$. Therefore, since $f(0) = g(0)$ and $f^{(r)}(0) = g^{(r)}(0)$ for $1 \leqslant r \leqslant n$, it follows that $F^{(r+1)}(0) = G^{(r+1)}(0)$ for $0 \leqslant r \leqslant n$. That is, $F^{(r)}(0) = G^{(r)}(0)$ for $1 \leqslant r \leqslant n+1$.

Suppose now that $g(x)$ is the Maclaurin polynomial of $f(x)$ of degree n. This theorem then shows that the Maclaurin polynomial of $\int_a^x f(t)\,dt$ of degree $n+1$ can be found by integrating the Maclaurin polynomial g from 0 to x.

Also, since this holds for any n, you can find the expansion of $\int_a^x f(t)\,dt$ (continued indefinitely) by integrating the terms of the Maclaurin expansion of $f(x)$.

Example 7.5.1
Find the expansion of $\tan^{-1} x$.

Since $\int_0^x \dfrac{1}{1+t^2}\,dt = \left[\tan^{-1} t\right]_0^x = \tan^{-1} x - \tan^{-1} 0 = \tan^{-1} x$, you can find the expansion of $\tan^{-1} x$ by integrating the terms of the binomial expansion for $\left(1+t^2\right)^{-1} = 1 - t^2 + t^4 - t^6 + \ldots$ from 0 to x.

That is,

$$\tan^{-1} x = x - \tfrac{1}{3}x^3 + \tfrac{1}{5}x^5 - \tfrac{1}{7}x^7 + \ldots$$

$$= \sum_{r=0}^{\infty} (-1)^r \frac{1}{2r+1} x^{2r+1}.$$

It can be proved that when you integrate an expansion in this way, the interval of validity of the result is at least as wide as that of the original expansion. In Example 7.5.1, the binomial expansion is valid for $-1 < x < 1$, but the $\tan^{-1} x$ expansion is also valid when $x = \pm 1$. The value $x = 1$ produces the delightful (but not very useful) result

$$\tfrac{1}{4}\pi = 1 - \tfrac{1}{3} + \tfrac{1}{5} - \tfrac{1}{7} + \ldots.$$

Example 7.5.2

Find the value of $\dfrac{1}{\sqrt{2\pi}}\displaystyle\int_{-1}^{1} e^{-\frac{1}{2}t^2}\, dt$.

This integral is important in probability. It gives the probability that a normal random variable takes a value within one standard deviation of the mean.

Integrating the expansion $e^{-\frac{1}{2}t^2} = 1 - \dfrac{1}{1!}\dfrac{t^2}{2} + \dfrac{1}{2!}\left(\dfrac{t^2}{2}\right)^2 - \ldots$ gives

$$\int_0^x e^{-\frac{1}{2}t^2}\, dt \approx \left[t - \dfrac{1}{2}\dfrac{t^3}{3} + \dfrac{1}{8}\dfrac{t^5}{5} - \dfrac{1}{48}\dfrac{t^7}{7} + \dfrac{1}{384}\dfrac{t^9}{9} - \dfrac{1}{3840}\dfrac{t^{11}}{11} + \ldots \right]_0^x ,$$

which, evaluating at $x = 1$,

$$= 1 - \tfrac{1}{6} + \tfrac{1}{40} - \tfrac{1}{336} + \tfrac{1}{3456} - \tfrac{1}{42240} + \ldots = 0.85562\ldots .$$

Since $e^{-\frac{1}{2}t^2}$ is an even function, the integral from -1 to 1 is double the integral from 0 to 1. The probability required is therefore

$$\dfrac{1}{\sqrt{2\pi}} \times 2 \times 0.85562\ldots \approx 0.683, \text{ correct to 3 decimal places.}$$

Exercise 7D*

1 Use the property $\sin^{-1} x = \displaystyle\int_0^x \dfrac{1}{\sqrt{1-t^2}}\, dt$ to find the Maclaurin expansion of $\sin^{-1} x$. Hence

   find the expansion of $\cos^{-1} x$. By taking $x = \tfrac{1}{2}$, use your Maclaurin expansion to find the value of π, correct to 4 decimal places.

2 In Exercise 6C Question 4 you showed that $4\tan^{-1}\tfrac{1}{5} - \tfrac{1}{4}\pi = \tan^{-1}\tfrac{1}{239}$. Use this, with the Maclaurin expansion of $\tan^{-1} x$, to find a 5 decimal place approximation to π.

3 A function called the *sine integral* is defined by $\mathrm{Si}\,(x) = \displaystyle\int_0^x \dfrac{\sin u}{u}\, du$. Find the Maclaurin expansion of $\mathrm{Si}\,(x)$, and use this to obtain the graph of $y = \mathrm{Si}\,(x)$ for $x > 0$.

4 Find the Maclaurin expansion of $\displaystyle\int_0^x \dfrac{e^t - 1}{t}\, dt$. Hence evaluate $\displaystyle\int_0^{\frac{1}{2}} \dfrac{e^t - 1}{t}\, dt$, correct to 3 decimal places.

5 The following construction is suggested to trisect a given angle θ. Make a triangle ABC with angle BAC equal to θ and angle ABC a right angle. Divide the side BC into three equal parts at X and Y, so that $BX = XY = YC$. Then angle XAY is approximately $\tfrac{1}{3}\theta$. Prove that angle XAY is exactly $\tan^{-1}\left(\tfrac{2}{3}\tan\theta\right) - \tan^{-1}\left(\tfrac{1}{3}\tan\theta\right)$. Find the Maclaurin polynomial of degree 3 for this function, and use this to estimate the greatest value of θ for which the construction is accurate to within 5%.

6 Use the sum of the geometric series $1 - u + u^2 - \ldots + (-1)^{n-1}u^{n-1}$ to find an expression for the error in using the Maclaurin polynomial of degree n as an approximation to $\ln(1+x)$.

7 Prove that the difference between $\tan^{-1} x$ and the first n non-zero terms of its Maclaurin expansion has absolute value $\displaystyle\int_0^{|x|} \frac{t^{2n}}{1+t^2}\, dt$, and show that this is less than $\dfrac{|x|^{2n+1}}{2n+1}$.

Use this to estimate the largest number of terms of the $\tan^{-1} x$ expansion that you might need to use to compute $\tan^{-1} 0.2$ with an error of less than 10^{-10}.

Miscellaneous exercise 7

1 Obtain the first three terms in the Maclaurin series for $\ln(3+x)$. (OCR)

2 Show that, if x is small, $e^{-\frac{1}{2}x} - \dfrac{1}{\sqrt{1+x}} \approx ax^2$ where the value of the constant a should be stated. (OCR)

3 It is given that the series expansions of $(1+x)^p$ and $1 + \ln(1+qx)$ are identical, up to and including the terms in x^2. Find the values of the non-zero constants p and q. (OCR)

4 The function $f(x)$, defined by $f(x) = x(1+4x)^p + q\ln(1+x)$, where p and q are constants, is expanded in ascending powers of x. It is given that the coefficient of x^2 in the expansion of $f(x)$ is zero. Show that $q = 8p$.

It is also given that the coefficient of x in the expansion of $f(x)$ is 13. Find the numerical value of the coefficient of x^3 in the expansion of $f(x)$. (OCR)

5 Find the values of the constants A, B and C such that the series expansion of $A\cos x + Be^x + C$ is the same as the series expansion of $4\sqrt{1+x}$, given that x is so small that terms in x^3 and higher powers of x may be neglected. (OCR)

6 Use the Maclaurin series for $\ln(1+x)$ and $\ln(1-x)$ to show that, for small values of x,

$$\ln\left(\frac{1+x}{1-x}\right) \approx 2\left(x + \tfrac{1}{3}x^3\right).$$ (OCR)

It is desired to use the approximation to find an estimate for $\ln 1.25$. Find the appropriate value for x, and hence find the estimate for $\ln 1.25$ giving your answer to six decimal places. (OCR)

7 Find the Maclaurin series of $e^{\sin x}$ up to and including the term in x^2. Show that, when $x = 0.5$, the relative error in the approximation obtained is 0.6%, correct to one significant figure. (OCR)

8 *PMQ* is a minor arc of a circle with centre O and radius r. N is the mid-point of the arc
PQ and the angle MOQ is θ radians. The lengths of the chords MQ and PQ are denoted
by a and b respectively. In the series for $\sin x$, put x equal to θ and $\frac{1}{2}\theta$ in turn, to find
approximations for a and b in terms of r and θ, up to the terms in θ^5. Deduce the series
expansion of $\frac{1}{3}(8a-b)$ up to the term in θ^5. Hence show that $\frac{1}{3}(8a-b)$ is approximately
equal to the length of the arc PMQ, and give an estimate of the error in terms of r and θ.

Calculate the percentage error when $\theta = \frac{1}{6}\pi$, giving your answer to two significant figures.

Write down a formula, in terms of a, b and r, which gives an approximation to the area
of the sector POQ.   (OCR)

9 By expanding $\left(1-4x^2\right)^{-\frac{1}{2}}$ and integrating term by term, find the series expansion for
$\sin^{-1} 2x$ when $|x| < \frac{1}{2}$ as far as the term in x^7.   (MEI)

10 Show that, if q and r are natural numbers, then $(q+r)! \geqslant q! \times (q+1)^r$. Show further that
the symbol $\geqslant$ can be replaced by $>$ if $r > 1$. Hence show that

$$\frac{q!}{(q+1)!} + \frac{q!}{(q+2)!} + \frac{q!}{(q+3)!} + \ldots < \frac{1}{q}.$$

Suppose that e is a rational number $\dfrac{p}{q}$, where p and q are natural numbers. Deduce that

$q!$e is a natural number. Also, by using the Maclaurin expansion of e^x, deduce that $q!$e is
not a natural number. What conclusion can you draw from this contradiction?

8 Polar coordinates

This chapter introduces a new kind of coordinate system, which is particularly suitable for curves which are drawn around one special point. When you have completed it, you should

- know how to plot points from their polar coordinates
- understand conventions which ensure that points have unique coordinates
- be able to draw graphs from their polar equations
- be able to convert coordinates and equations from cartesian to polar form and vice versa
- be able to calculate areas of sectors and areas inside closed curves using integration
- understand that conventions may be breached if necessary to produce more complete graphs.

8.1 Definitions and conventions

There are two ways of pin-pointing a position on a walking map. You can give a map reference, or you can choose a well-known landmark and give the distance and bearing of the position from it.

In mathematics the equivalent of a map reference is the pair of cartesian coordinates (x, y). But it is sometimes better to give the position of a point in **polar coordinates** (r, θ), which correspond in mathematics to distance and bearing.

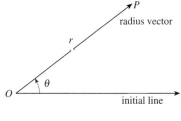

Fig. 8.1

You have to begin by choosing an origin O (sometimes called the **pole**) and a line in a fixed direction, called the **initial line** (see Fig. 8.1). The convention is to take this as the positive x-axis. The position of a point P is then defined by the distance $r = OP$, and the angle θ which the vector $\overrightarrow{OP}$ (sometimes called the **radius vector**) makes with the initial line. The convention is for this angle to be positive if the rotation from the initial line to the radius vector is anticlockwise, negative if the rotation is clockwise.

For example, to locate the point with polar coordinates $\left(4, \frac{3}{4}\pi\right)$, you begin at O, facing along the initial line, and rotate through an angle of $\frac{3}{4}\pi$ anticlockwise. You then move 4 units in the direction in which you are now facing. Clearly any pair of coordinates (r, θ) fixes the position of the corresponding point.

Unfortunately, the converse of this last statement is not true. That is, a particular point can have many polar coordinates. For example, the coordinates $\left(2, \frac{1}{2}\pi\right)$, $\left(2, \frac{5}{2}\pi\right)$, $\left(2, -\frac{3}{2}\pi\right)$, ... all define the same point. This is the point whose cartesian coordinates are $(0, 2)$.

This is sometimes inconvenient, and it can be avoided by restricting the angle θ so that it lies within an interval of width 2π. There are two obvious ways of doing this. You can require either that $0 \leqslant \theta < 2\pi$ or that $-\pi < \theta \leqslant \pi$. Which you choose is simply a convention; it will be useful to refer to these possibilities as the '2π-convention' and the 'π-convention' respectively.

With these conventions, any point other than O has a unique description (r,θ) in polar coordinates, with $r > 0$ and θ within an interval defined by the chosen convention.

For example, the point with cartesian coordinates $(0,-3)$ would have polar coordinates $\left(3,\frac{3}{2}\pi\right)$ using the 2π-convention, or $\left(3,-\frac{1}{2}\pi\right)$ using the π-convention.

The point O remains an exception. It has polar coordinates $(0,\theta)$ where θ can have any value. In practice this is not a problem, since polar coordinates are normally used for curves for which the origin is a special point.

8.2 Polar and cartesian coordinates

It is useful to be able to calculate the cartesian coordinates of a point from its polar coordinates, and vice versa. Suppose that a point P has cartesian coordinates (x, y) and polar coordinates (r,θ) (see Fig. 8.2). The problem is to find expressions for x and y in terms of r and θ, and for r and θ in terms of x and y.

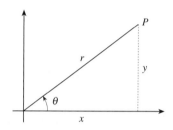

Fig. 8.2

The definitions of cosine and sine given in P1 Sections 11.1 and 11.2 can be interpreted as showing that a point with polar coordinates $(1,\theta)$ has cartesian coordinates $(\cos\theta,\sin\theta)$. (At that stage in the course angles were in degrees, but the definitions apply equally with θ in radians.) If the associated Fig. 11.1 were enlarged by a scale factor of r, then it would follow that a point with polar coordinates (r,θ) has cartesian coordinates $(r\cos\theta, r\sin\theta)$.

The reverse process needs a little more care. Since the distance from $(0,0)$ to (x, y) is $\sqrt{x^2 + y^2}$, and since by convention $r > 0$, it follows that $r = \sqrt{x^2 + y^2}$. Therefore, since $x = r\cos\theta$ and $y = r\sin\theta$,

$$\cos\theta = \frac{x}{\sqrt{x^2 + y^2}} \quad \text{and} \quad \sin\theta = \frac{y}{\sqrt{x^2 + y^2}}.$$

Also, since $\tan\theta = \dfrac{\sin\theta}{\cos\theta}$,

$$\tan\theta = \frac{y}{x} \quad \text{(provided that } x \neq 0\text{)}.$$

However, no one of these equations is sufficient by itself to find θ, since each of them has (in general) two solutions for θ in any interval of width 2π. It would be wrong to use the notation $\cos^{-1}$, $\sin^{-1}$ or $\tan^{-1}$ to give an explicit expression for θ in terms of x and y. The best you can do is to state that θ is the angle defined (within the chosen convention) by

$$\cos\theta : \sin\theta : 1 = x : y : \sqrt{x^2 + y^2}.$$

If the cartesian and polar coordinates of a point are (x, y) and (r, θ) respectively, then

$$x = r\cos\theta, \quad y = r\sin\theta, \quad r = \sqrt{x^2 + y^2},$$

and (except at the origin)

$$\cos\theta : \sin\theta : 1 = x : y : \sqrt{x^2 + y^2}.$$

Example 8.2.1

Find the polar coordinates of the point with cartesian coordinates $(3, -4)$.

The formula for r gives $r = \sqrt{3^2 + (-4)^2} = \sqrt{25} = 5$, so that

$$\cos\theta = \tfrac{3}{5} = 0.6 \quad \text{and} \quad \sin\theta = -\tfrac{4}{5} = -0.8.$$

Now $\cos^{-1} 0.6 = 0.9273$ (to 4 decimal places), but $\sin 0.9273 = 0.8$, not -0.8 as required. The correct value of θ using the π-convention is -0.9273. The equivalent angle using the 2π-convention is $2\pi - 0.9273 = 5.3559$.

Some calculators have special keys for making these conversions, and it is worthwhile learning to use these. (They can also be used in mechanics for other vector quantities such as force and velocity, to find components and resultants.)

Exercise 8A

1 Using centimetre units, plot the points with the following polar coordinates.

(a) $(5, 0)$ (b) $(3, \pi)$ (c) $(4, 1)$

(d) $\left(6, \tfrac{3}{2}\pi\right)$ (e) $\left(4.5, -\tfrac{1}{3}\pi\right)$ (f) $\left(2, \tfrac{3}{4}\pi\right)$

2 Find the cartesian coordinates of the points whose polar coordinates are

(a) $\left(10, \tfrac{1}{2}\pi\right)$,   (b) $\left(2, \tfrac{5}{6}\pi\right)$,   (c) $\left(4, \tfrac{5}{4}\pi\right)$,

(d) $\left(6, -\tfrac{2}{3}\pi\right)$,   (e) $(5, \pi)$,   (f) $(3, 2)$.

3 Find the polar coordinates of the points with the following cartesian coordinates. Give your answers using (i) the 2π-convention, (ii) the π-convention.

(a) $(-3, 0)$ (b) $(12, 5)$ (c) $(2, -2)$

(d) $(0, -4)$ (e) $(-3, -4)$ (f) $\left(-1, \sqrt{3}\right)$

4 Find the distance between the points whose polar coordinates are $\left(2, -\tfrac{4}{9}\pi\right)$ and $\left(3, \tfrac{8}{9}\pi\right)$.

5 Find in polar coordinates the mid-point of the line segment joining the points (r, α) and (r, β),

(a) if $0 < \beta - \alpha < \pi$,   (b) if $\pi < \beta - \alpha < 2\pi$.

6 Prove that a necessary and sufficient condition for a point to be represented by the same number-pair (a, b) in both cartesian and polar coordinates is that it lies on the initial line.

8.3 Graphs with polar equations

A graph can be defined in polar coordinates just as for cartesian coordinates, as the set of points whose coordinates satisfy an equation of the form $r = f(\theta)$.

You can use a graphic calculator or computer software to produce polar graphs, but first it is worthwhile drawing a few by hand. To do this it helps to use polar graph paper. Just as cartesian graph paper has printed lines with equations $x = \text{constant}$ (up the page) and $y = \text{constant}$ (across the page), so polar paper has lines radiating from O with equations $\theta = \text{constant}$ and circles centre O with equations $r = \text{constant}$.

Example 8.3.1
Draw the graph with equation $r = 2 + \cos\theta$.

Since $\cos\theta = \cos(-\theta)$, it is convenient to use the π-convention. The first step is to make a table of values of r for typical values of θ, as shown in Table 8.3.

θ	0	$\pm\frac{1}{6}\pi$	$\pm\frac{1}{3}\pi$	$\pm\frac{1}{2}\pi$	$\pm\frac{2}{3}\pi$	$\pm\frac{5}{6}\pi$	$\pm\pi$
r	3	2.866	2.5	2	1.5	1.134	1

Table 8.3

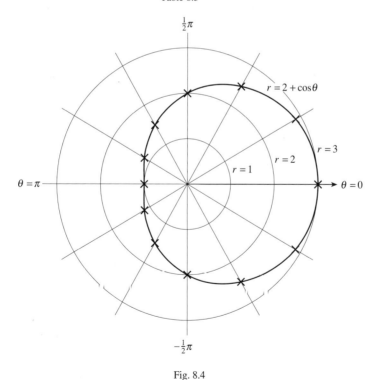

Fig. 8.4

Fig. 8.4 shows these points plotted on polar graph paper, and joined with a curve.

Notice that the largest value of r is 3, when $\theta = 0$. This is the point of the graph furthest away from O. The closest point to O is when $\theta = \pi$, which gives $r = 1$.

Another point to notice is that the graph is symmetrical about the initial line. If you consider the point Q on the graph in the direction $-\theta$, the value of r is $2 + \cos(-\theta)$; since $\cos(-\theta) \equiv \cos\theta$, this value of r is $2 + \cos\theta$, the same as for the point P in the direction θ (see Fig. 8.5a). So $OP = OQ$, which means that P and Q are symmetrical about the initial line. Since this holds for all values of θ, the whole graph is symmetrical about the initial line.

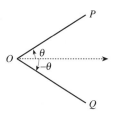

Fig. 8.5a

This argument can be generalised to provide a test for symmetry of any graph $r = f(\theta)$ about a line $\theta = \alpha$ (see Fig. 8.5b). Consider points P and Q on the graph which are at equal angles from the line $\theta = \alpha$. If P is in the direction θ, the radius vector $\overrightarrow{OP}$ makes an angle $\theta - \alpha$ with the line $\theta = \alpha$. So the direction of Q is $\alpha - (\theta - \alpha)$, which is $2\alpha - \theta$. So if $f(2\alpha - \theta) = f(\theta)$, then $OQ = OP$. It follows that, if this is true for all values of θ (that is, as an identity in θ), then the whole graph is symmetrical about the line $\theta = \alpha$.

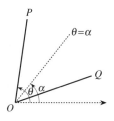

Fig. 8.5b

> If $f(2\alpha - \theta) \equiv f(\theta)$ for all values of θ, the graph with polar equation $r = f(\theta)$ is symmetrical about the line $\theta = \alpha$.

Example 8.3.2
Draw the graph with equation $r = 2\sin 2\theta$ for $0 \le \theta \le \frac{1}{2}\pi$. Prove that it is symmetrical about the line $\theta = \frac{1}{4}\pi$.

In this example θ has been restricted to an interval over which $r \ge 0$. In this interval r increases from 0 to 2 and then decreases to 0.

Table 8.6 gives a table of typical values, and the plotted points are joined by the curve in Fig. 8.7.

θ	0	$\frac{1}{12}\pi$	$\frac{1}{6}\pi$	$\frac{1}{4}\pi$	$\frac{1}{3}\pi$	$\frac{5}{12}\pi$	$\frac{1}{2}\pi$
r	0	1	1.732	2	1.732	1	0

Table 8.6

To establish the symmetry property, you need to show that $f\left(2 \times \frac{1}{4}\pi - \theta\right) \equiv f(\theta)$ with $f(\theta) = 2\sin 2\theta$, for all values of θ. Starting from the left side,

$$f\left(\tfrac{1}{2}\pi - \theta\right) \equiv 2\sin 2\left(\tfrac{1}{2}\pi - \theta\right)$$
$$\equiv 2\sin(\pi - 2\theta)$$
$$\equiv 2\sin 2\theta \equiv f(\theta),$$

as required.

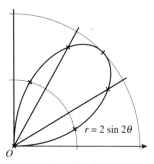

$r = 2\sin 2\theta$

Fig. 8.7

Notice that in this example $r = 0$ when $\theta = 0$, but r is positive right down to $\theta = 0$; similarly, $r = 0$ when $\theta = \frac{1}{2}\pi$ but r is positive right up to $\theta = \frac{1}{2}\pi$. This can only happen (for a continuous function) if the lines $\theta = 0$ and $\theta = \frac{1}{2}\pi$ are tangents to the curve. This is an example of a general feature of polar graphs, illustrated in Fig. 8.8.

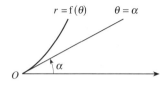

Fig. 8.8

> If $f(\alpha) = 0$ but $f(\theta) > 0$ in an interval $\alpha < \theta < \dots$ or $\dots < \theta < \alpha$, then the line $\theta = \alpha$ is a tangent to the graph of $r = f(\theta)$ at the origin.

Example 8.3.3

For the graph with polar equation $r = 1 + \cos 3\theta$

(a) find the greatest and least values of r,

(b) find the equations of the tangents at the pole,

(c) show that all lines with equations $r = \frac{1}{3}k\pi$, where k is an integer, are lines of symmetry.

(a) Since $\cos 3\theta$ lies between -1 and 1, r lies between 0 and 2. The greatest value of r is 2, when $\theta = 0$ or $\theta = \pm\frac{2}{3}\pi$ (using the π-convention). The least value is 0, when $\theta = \pi$ or $\theta = \pm\frac{1}{3}\pi$.

(b) Denoting $r = 1 + \cos 3\theta$ by $f(\theta)$, it is shown in part (a) that $f(\theta) = 0$ when $\theta = \pi$ or $\theta = \pm\frac{1}{3}\pi$, and that $f(\theta) > 0$ when $-\pi < \theta < -\frac{1}{3}\pi$, $-\frac{1}{3}\pi < \theta < \frac{1}{3}\pi$ or $\frac{1}{3}\pi < \theta < \pi$. It follows that the tangents at the pole are $\theta = -\frac{1}{3}\pi$, $\theta = \frac{1}{3}\pi$ and $\theta = \pi$.

(c) You have to prove that $f\left(\frac{2}{3}k\pi - \theta\right) \equiv f(\theta)$ for all values of θ. Starting from the left side,

$$f\left(\tfrac{2}{3}k\pi - \theta\right) \equiv 1 + \cos(2k\pi - 3\theta) \equiv 1 + \cos 3\theta \equiv f(\theta).$$

So all lines with equations $r = \frac{1}{3}k\pi$ are lines of symmetry.

Using the information in Example 8.3.3, try to sketch the graph for yourself.

8.4 Equations in polar and cartesian coordinates

The connections found in Section 8.2 between the cartesian and polar coordinates of points can also be used to convert equations of curves from cartesian to polar forms, and vice versa.

Example 8.4.1

Find the polar equations of

(a) the line $x \cos \alpha + y \sin \alpha = p$, where $p > 0$,   (b) the parabola $y = x^2$.

(a) Writing $x = r \cos \theta$ and $y = r \sin \theta$, the equation becomes

$$r \cos \theta \cos \alpha + r \sin \theta \sin \alpha = p, \text{ that is } r \cos(\theta - \alpha) = p.$$

This polar equation is illustrated in Fig. 8.9.
Notice that the line has gradient $-\cot\alpha$, so that
the perpendicular from O to the line has gradient
$\tan\alpha$. This perpendicular therefore makes an
angle α with the x-axis. Since $r = OP$, the
length of the perpendicular is $r\cos(\theta - \alpha)$. This
shows that the constant p in the equation is the
length of the perpendicular from the origin to the
line.

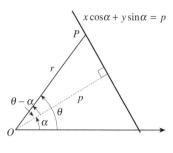

Fig. 8.9

(b) The equation becomes $r\sin\theta = (r\cos\theta)^2$. If $r \neq 0$ and $\cos\theta \neq 0$,

$$r = \frac{\sin\theta}{\cos^2\theta} = \sec\theta\tan\theta.$$

Although the value $r = 0$ was excluded in obtaining this equation, the origin does
in fact appear if you substitute $\theta = 0$ or $\theta = \pi$ in the equation. Notice that these
values of θ give the tangent at the origin to the parabola. There is, however, no
point on the parabola corresponding to $\theta = \frac{1}{2}\pi$, where $\cos\theta = 0$.

Example 8.4.2

Find the cartesian equations of the curves with polar equations
(a) $r = 2a\cos\theta$, for $-\frac{1}{2}\pi \leqslant \theta \leqslant \frac{1}{2}\pi$,   (b) $r^2 = a^2\sin 2\theta$.

Both these equations contain a constant a which defines a scale to which the
curve is drawn. In (a) the maximum value of r is $2a$, when $\theta = 0$; in (b) it is a,
when $\theta = \frac{1}{4}\pi$ or $\theta = \frac{5}{4}\pi$.

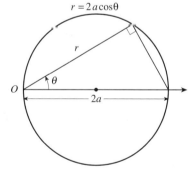

$r = 2a\cos\theta$

(a) Since $\cos\theta = \dfrac{x}{r}$, the equation is $r^2 = 2ax$.

Writing r^2 as $x^2 + y^2$ leads to the cartesian
equation

$$x^2 + y^2 = 2ax.$$

You should recognise this as the equation of a
circle, $(x-a)^2 + y^2 = a^2$, with centre $(a, 0)$ and
radius a. Fig. 8.10 shows why the circle has the
equation $r = 2a\cos\theta$, based on the property that
the angle in a semicircle is a right angle.

Fig. 8.10

(b) Since $2\sin\theta\cos\theta = 2\left(\dfrac{y}{r}\right)\left(\dfrac{x}{r}\right) = \dfrac{2xy}{r^2}$, you can write the equation as
$r^4 = 2a^2xy$ or

$$\left(x^2 + y^2\right)^2 = 2a^2xy.$$

You can see from this equation that $xy \geqslant 0$, so that the graph lies entirely in the
first and third quadrants. This fits with the polar equation, since (using the 2π-
convention) $\sin 2\theta$ is positive only for $0 < \theta < \frac{1}{2}\pi$ or $\pi < \theta < \frac{3}{2}\pi$.

8.5*   Parabolas, polars and parameters

This section revises a number of topics in coordinate geometry, by applying a variety of methods to find some properties of parabolas.

Fig. 8.11 shows the graph of

$$r = \frac{2a}{1 + \cos\theta} \text{ for } -\pi < \theta < \pi.$$

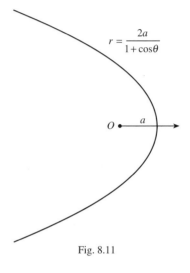

$$r = \frac{2a}{1 + \cos\theta}$$

Notice that θ cannot take the value π, since $1 + \cos\pi = 0$. Also, since $1 + \cos\theta$ decreases from 2 to 0 as θ increases from 0 to π, r increases from a without limit. The equation has the form $r = g(\cos\theta)$, and $\cos(-\theta) = \cos\theta$, so the graph is symmetrical about the initial line.

If you guessed that this graph is a parabola you would be right. Writing the equation as $r = 2a - r\cos\theta$, the cartesian equation is

$$\sqrt{x^2 + y^2} = 2a - x, \text{ or}$$

$$x^2 + y^2 = 4a^2 - 4ax + x^2, \text{ which is}$$

$$y^2 = 4a(a - x).$$

Fig. 8.11

P3 Example 4.4.1 dealt with a parabola with parametric equations $x = at^2$, $y = 2at$ (Fig. 8.12). You can eliminate t by writing it as $\dfrac{y}{2a}$ and substituting:

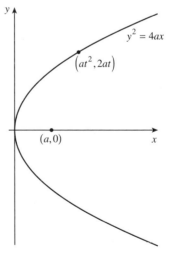

$$x = a\left(\frac{y}{2a}\right)^2, \text{ that is } y^2 = 4ax.$$

How are the graphs of $y^2 = 4ax$ and $y^2 = 4a(a - x)$ related? If in the second equation you replace x by $-x$, it becomes $y^2 = 4a(x + a)$. If you then replace x by $(x - a)$, the equation becomes $y^2 = 4ax$. So these equations represent essentially the same curve; you get the first from the second by reflecting in the y-axis and then translating a distance a in the x-direction.

Fig. 8.12

The point which was the origin in the polar form has, as usual, a place of special importance for the curve. It is called the **focus** of the parabola. On the graph of $y^2 = 4ax$ this corresponds to the point $(a, 0)$.

Now that you know the equation of the parabola in cartesian, parametric and polar forms, you can use whichever is most convenient to find geometrical properties of the curve. Here are two properties which involve the focus.

Theorem　If F is the focus of a parabola, and PQ is any chord through F, then
$$\frac{1}{FP} + \frac{1}{FQ} \text{ is constant.}$$

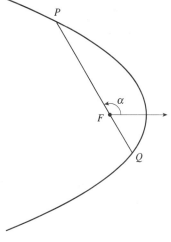

Fig. 8.13

Proof　Since this involves distances from the focus, it is best to use the polar equation. In Fig. 8.13, P corresponds to $\theta = \alpha$, where $0 < \alpha < \pi$, and Q to $\theta = \alpha - \pi$. Then since $r = \dfrac{2a}{1 + \cos\theta}$,

$$FP = \frac{2a}{1 + \cos\alpha} \text{ and}$$

$$FQ = \frac{2a}{1 + \cos(\alpha - \pi)} = \frac{2a}{1 - \cos\alpha}.$$

Therefore

$$\frac{1}{FP} + \frac{1}{FQ} = \frac{1}{2a}\big((1 + \cos\alpha) + (1 - \cos\alpha)\big)$$

$$= \frac{1}{2a} \times 2 = \frac{1}{a}.$$

Theorem　If a source of light is placed at the focus of a mirror in the shape of a parabola rotated about its axis of symmetry, all the light from the source will be reflected parallel to the axis.

Proof　The rule of reflection is that a ray and its reflection make the same angle with the tangent to the mirror (Fig. 8.14). You do not know how to find tangents in polar coordinates, so it is better to use parameters.

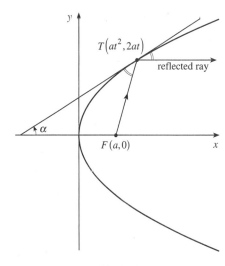

Fig. 8.14

The gradient of the tangent at the point T, with coordinates $(at^2, 2at)$, is

$$\frac{dy}{dx} = \frac{dy}{dt} \Big/ \frac{dx}{dt} = \frac{2a}{2at} = \frac{1}{t}.$$

If this tangent makes an angle α with the x-axis, then $\tan\alpha = \dfrac{1}{t}$.

If F is the focus $(a, 0)$, the line FT has gradient

$$\frac{2at - 0}{at^2 - a} = \frac{2t}{t^2 - 1}.$$

Dividing numerator and denominator by t^2, this can be written as

$$\frac{2/t}{1-1/t^2} = \frac{2\tan\alpha}{1-\tan^2\alpha} = \tan 2\alpha.$$

This shows that FT makes an angle 2α with the x-axis.

The ray FT therefore makes an angle $2\alpha - \alpha = \alpha$ with the tangent, so the ray is also reflected at an angle α. This means that the reflected ray is parallel to the x-axis.

Exercise 8B

1   Draw the curves with the following polar equations. Check your answers with a graphic calculator.

(a) $r = 3 + \sin\theta$

(b) $r = \cos^2\theta$

(c) $r = \dfrac{1}{2 + \cos\theta}$

(d) $r = \tan\theta$ for $0 \leqslant \theta < \frac{1}{2}\pi$

(e) $r = \sin\theta$ for $0 \leqslant \theta \leqslant \pi$

(f) $r = \sec\theta$ for $\frac{1}{2}\pi < \theta < \frac{1}{2}\pi$

(g) $r = 1 + \dfrac{\theta}{\pi}$ for $0 \leqslant \theta < 2\pi$

(h) $r = \cos\frac{1}{2}\theta$ for $-\pi < \theta \leqslant \pi$

2   For each of the following curves (i) draw a sketch, (ii) find the least and greatest values of r, (iii) state any tangents at the pole, (iv) identify (with proof) any lines of symmetry.

(a) $r = \theta^2$ for $-\pi < \theta \leqslant \pi$

(b) $r = 1 + \sin 2\theta$

(c) $r = \dfrac{1}{1 + 2\cos\theta}$ for $-\frac{2}{3}\pi < \theta < \frac{2}{3}\pi$

(d) $r = 1 - \sin^3\theta$

3   Find the cartesian equations of the curves with the following polar equations.

(a) $r = 2\sin\theta$ for $0 \leqslant \theta < \pi$

(b) $r = a\cos 2\theta$ for $-\frac{1}{4}\pi \leqslant \theta \leqslant \frac{1}{4}\pi$

(c) $r = a\operatorname{cosec}\theta$ for $0 < \theta < \pi$

(d) $r = \dfrac{4}{3 + \cos\theta}$

4   Find the polar equations of the curves with the following cartesian equations.

(a) $y = \dfrac{1}{x}$ for $x > 0$

(b) $x^2 + y^2 = 4$

(c) $(x-1)^2 + (y-1)^2 = 2$

(d) $\dfrac{1}{x} + \dfrac{1}{y} = \dfrac{1}{a}$, where $a > 0$, for $x > 0$, $y > 0$

5* For the parabola in Section 8.5, show that $r + x = 2a$. Use this to show that, for any point P on the parabola in Fig. 8.11, the distance OP is equal to the perpendicular distance from P to a certain line. Describe the position of this line (the *directrix*) precisely.

8.6 Finding areas using polar coordinates

With cartesian graphs you know how to use integration to calculate areas and volumes of revolution contained between given values of x. A similar method can be used with polar graphs to find areas contained between given values of θ. That is, in Fig. 8.15, to find the area of the sector bounded by the graph $r = f(\theta)$ and the radii $\theta = \alpha$ and $\theta = \beta$.

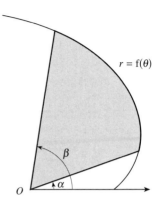

Fig. 8.15

The method is very similar to that for cartesian graphs. If A denotes the area of the sector from $\theta = \alpha$ as far as any general value of θ, then A is a function of θ (see Fig. 8.16). If θ increases by $\delta\theta$, then r increases by δr and A increases by δA; and Fig. 8.17 shows that δA lies between the areas of two circular sectors with angle $\delta\theta$ and radii r and $r + \delta r$. So δA lies between $\frac{1}{2}r^2\delta\theta$ and $\frac{1}{2}(r + \delta r)^2\delta\theta$.

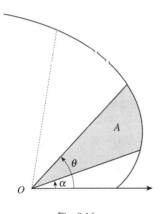

Fig. 8.16

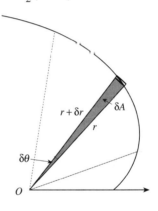

Fig. 8.17

That is, $\dfrac{\delta A}{\delta\theta}$ lies between $\frac{1}{2}r^2$ and $\frac{1}{2}(r + \delta r)^2$.

The next step is to consider the limit as $\delta\theta \to 0$. Then $\dfrac{\delta A}{\delta\theta}$ tends to $\dfrac{dA}{d\theta}$, and $\delta r \to 0$, so

$$\frac{dA}{d\theta} = \tfrac{1}{2}r^2.$$

You will recognise that this is the same kind of argument as was used for areas in P1 Section 10.2 and for volumes in P2 Section 7.1. It follows that the area of the sector in Fig. 8.15 can be found as a definite integral:

> The area of the region bounded by the graph $r = f(\theta)$ and the radii $\theta = \alpha$ and $\theta = \beta$ is
>
> $$\int_\alpha^\beta \tfrac{1}{2}r^2\,d\theta = \int_\alpha^\beta \tfrac{1}{2}(f(\theta))^2\,d\theta.$$

Example 8.6.1

Fig. 8.18 shows the graph of $r = a\theta$ for $0 < \theta < 2\pi$. Find the area of the shaded region.

If you imagine the radius OP rotating from $\theta = 0$ to $\theta = 2\pi$, it will sweep out the shaded region. So the area is

$$\int_0^{2\pi} \tfrac{1}{2}(a\theta)^2 \, d\theta = \int_0^{2\pi} \tfrac{1}{2}a^2\theta^2 \, d\theta$$

$$= \left[\tfrac{1}{6}a^2\theta^3\right]_0^{2\pi}$$

$$= \tfrac{1}{6}a^2(2\pi)^3$$

$$= \tfrac{4}{3}\pi^3 a^2.$$

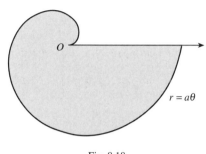

$r = a\theta$

Fig. 8.18

Example 8.6.2

Find the area enclosed by the curve $r = 2 + \cos\theta$ (see Example 8.3.1).

This graph was drawn in Fig. 8.4 using the π-convention. The 'sector' beginning at $\theta = -\pi$ and ending at $\theta = \pi$ makes up the whole region inside the curve. So the area enclosed is

$$\int_{-\pi}^{\pi} \tfrac{1}{2}(2 + \cos\theta)^2 \, d\theta = \int_{-\pi}^{\pi}\left(2 + 2\cos\theta + \tfrac{1}{2}\cos^2\theta\right)d\theta$$

$$= \int_{-\pi}^{\pi}\left(2 + 2\cos\theta + \tfrac{1}{4}(1 + \cos 2\theta)\right)d\theta$$

$$= \left[\tfrac{9}{4}\theta + 2\sin\theta + \tfrac{1}{8}\sin 2\theta\right]_{-\pi}^{\pi}$$

$$= \tfrac{9}{4}(\pi - (-\pi))$$

$$= \tfrac{9}{2}\pi.$$

The equation $\dfrac{dA}{d\theta} = \tfrac{1}{2}r^2$ has important applications to the motion of planets and satellites. In about the year 1600 Kepler discovered from observations that the rate at which the radius from the sun to a planet sweeps out area is constant. That is, if O is the sun and r is the distance from the sun to the planet, then $\dfrac{dA}{dt} = \text{constant}$. Since $\dfrac{dA}{dt}$ can be written as $\dfrac{dA}{d\theta} \times \dfrac{d\theta}{dt}$, Kepler's law corresponds to the equation

$$\tfrac{1}{2}r^2 \dfrac{d\theta}{dt} = \text{constant}.$$

For example, when a comet comes close to the sun, the radius rotates very much more rapidly than it does when the comet is at a great distance.

Exercise 8C

1 Calculate the areas enclosed by the following curves and radii. Illustrate each calculation with a sketch.

(a) $r = e^{\theta}$, $\theta = 0, \theta = \pi$

(b) $r = \theta^2$, $\theta = -\pi, \theta = \pi$

(c) $r = a + b\theta$, $\theta = 0, \theta = 2\pi$

(d) $r = a\cos\theta$, $\theta = -\frac{1}{4}\pi, \theta = \frac{1}{4}\pi$

(e) $r = a + b\sin\theta$, $\theta = 0, \theta = \pi$

2 Find the area enclosed by the curve with equation $r^2 = a^2 \sin 2\theta$ for $0 \le \theta \le \frac{1}{2}\pi$. (See Example 8.4.2(b).)

3 Find the area of the loop of $r = 2\sin 2\theta$ for $0 \le \theta \le \frac{1}{2}\pi$. (See Fig. 8.7.)

4 Sketch the curve (a *cardioid*) with polar equation $r = a(1 + \cos\theta)$. Show that it encloses an area of $\frac{3}{2}\pi a^2$.

5 Find the area enclosed within the curve $r = a\cos\frac{1}{2}\theta$ for $-\pi < \theta \le \pi$.

6 Prove that, in Fig. 8.13, the area enclosed between the chord PQ and the parabola is $\frac{8}{3}a^2\mathrm{cosec}^3\alpha$.

8.7* Breaching the conventions

You may omit this section if you wish.

The reason for introducing conventions restricting the values of r and θ is to ensure that each point (other than O) has unique polar coordinates. But when you draw polar graphs these conventions sometimes put up unnecessary barriers.

For example, if the function $f(\theta)$ has a period of 2π (such as $r = 2 + \cos\theta$, see Example 8.3.1) or a divisor of 2π (such as $r = \tan^2\theta$ with period π), then allowing θ to continue outside the interval defined by the convention will not produce any more points; the point (r, θ) will simply trace out the same graph again. But if $f(\theta)$ is not periodic, new points will continue to be added to the graph.

Example 8.7.1

Draw the graph of $r = \dfrac{\theta}{2\pi}$ for $\theta \ge 0$.

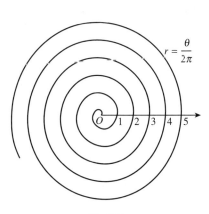

$r = \dfrac{\theta}{2\pi}$

The graph starts at $(0,0)$, and after one rotation of the radius it reaches $(1, 2\pi)$. As θ continues to increase, the value of r is greater by 1 than it was the previous time that the radius vector pointed in the same direction.

The graph is shown in Fig. 8.19. It is called the spiral of Archimedes, because he wrote a book about its properties.

Fig. 8.19

There are also some graphs which look incomplete unless r is allowed to take negative values. The interpretation is that, in plotting the point (r,θ), you face in the direction of the radius vector at an angle θ, but move backwards in that direction if r is negative. In Figs. 8.20 to 8.23 the graphs are shown with the portions for which $r < 0$ drawn dotted.

Example 8.7.2

Draw the graph of $r = 1 + 2\cos\theta$, using the π-convention.

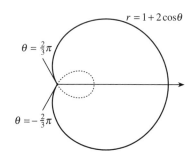

Notice that $r = 0$ when $\cos\theta = -\frac{1}{2}$, that is when $\theta = -\frac{2}{3}\pi$ or $\frac{2}{3}\pi$. Between these values of θ, r is positive; but for $-\pi < \theta < -\frac{2}{3}\pi$ and $\frac{2}{3}\pi < \theta \leqslant \pi$, r is negative. When $\theta = \pi$, $r = -1$. The graph is shown in Fig. 8.20.

Fig. 8.20

Example 8.7.3

Draw the graphs, using the 2π-convention, of   (a) $r = \sin 4\theta$,   (b) $r = \sin 3\theta$.

The period of the function $\sin n\theta$ is $\dfrac{2\pi}{n}$, which is a divisor of 2π if n is an integer, so the graphs are certainly completed once $\theta = 2\pi$ is reached. Values of r are positive from 0 to $\dfrac{\pi}{n}$, negative from $\dfrac{\pi}{n}$ to $\dfrac{2\pi}{n}$, and so on alternately.

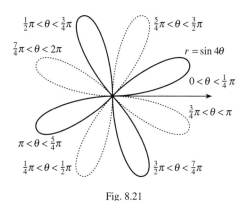

Fig. 8.21

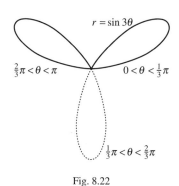

Fig. 8.22

The graphs are shown in Figs. 8.21 and 8.22; an interesting difference is that (a) continues to produce new points up to $\theta = 2\pi$, but (b) is complete once you reach $\theta = \pi$ and then repeats the same points between π and 2π.

The next example is a graph which for completeness requires the conventions restricting both r and θ to be breached.

Example 8.7.4

Draw the graph of $r = \sin\frac{1}{2}\theta$.

This function has period 4π; r is positive for $0 < \theta < 2\pi$ and negative for $2\pi < \theta < 4\pi$. The graph is shown in Fig. 8.23.

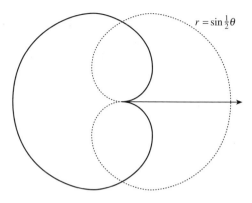

Fig. 8.23

Exercise 8D*

1 Sketch the graph of $r = e^{\theta}$ for $\theta \in \mathbb{R}$. Show that any portion of the curve defined by $\alpha \leqslant \theta \leqslant \alpha + \beta$ is an enlargement or contraction of the portion defined by $0 \leqslant \theta \leqslant \beta$.

2 Show that, as $\theta \to 0$, the graph of $r = \dfrac{2\pi}{\theta}$ approaches the line $y = 2\pi$. Draw a sketch to indicate the shape of the complete graph for $\theta > 0$.

3 Use a graphic calculator to show the complete graphs (with no restrictions on r or θ) of

   (a) $r = \sin\frac{1}{3}\theta$,   (b) $r = \sin\frac{1}{4}\theta$,   (c) $r = \sin\frac{2}{3}\theta$,   (d) $r = \sin\frac{3}{4}\theta$.

4 Draw sketches to show the different possible shapes of graphs (*limaçons*) with equation $r = k + \cos\theta$ for $k \geqslant 0$. What area is represented by $\displaystyle\int_{-\pi}^{\pi} \frac{1}{2}(k + \cos\theta)^2 \, d\theta$ for various values of k?

5 Find the total area enclosed inside the graph of $r = \sin n\theta$, where $n \in \mathbb{N}$ and $n \geqslant 1$.

6 Sketch the curves (*conchoids*) with polar equations $r = \sec\theta + k$, where r may take both positive and negative values, in the cases

   (a) $k = 0$,   (b) $k = 1$,   (c) $k = -1$,   (d) $k = -2$.

Where appropriate, state the tangents at the pole.

Show that one of the curves includes a loop, and find the area enclosed by it.

7 A $45°$ set square ABC has a right angle at B and $AB = BC = a$. Initially A is at the origin, B is at the point with cartesian coordinates $(a, 0)$ and C is at $(a, -a)$. The corner C moves up the line $x = a$ until it reaches $(a, 0)$, and the set square moves so that the edge AB always passes through the origin. Show that B describes a curve whose polar equation is $r = a(\sec\theta - \tan\theta)$ for $0 \leqslant \theta < \frac{1}{2}\pi$.

Draw the whole of this curve (a *strophoid*) with the given equation for values of θ between 0 and 2π, allowing r to take both positive and negative values. Show that the curve includes a loop, and find the area enclosed by it.

Miscellaneous exercise 8

1   O is the pole, and A and B have polar coordinates $\left(8, -\frac{1}{12}\pi\right)$ and $\left(5, \frac{1}{4}\pi\right)$. Find

   (a) the distance AB,   (b) the area of the triangle OAB.

2   Sketch, on the same diagrams, the graphs of

   (a) $r = \cos 2\theta$ and $r = \sec 2\theta$,   (b) $r = 1 - 2\cos\theta$ and $r = \dfrac{1}{1 - 2\cos\theta}$.

   In each case, consider the values of θ between $-\pi$ and π for which $r > 0$.

3   Find the cartesian equations of the curves with polar equations

   (a) $r = \cos^3\theta$,   (b) $r = \sec^3\theta$.

4   Find the polar equation of the curve with cartesian equation $\dfrac{1}{x^2} + \dfrac{1}{y^2} = 1$. Use your answer to draw a sketch of the curve.

5   Sketch the curve with polar equation $r = \cos\theta(1 - \sin\theta)$ for $-\frac{1}{2}\pi \le \theta \le \frac{1}{2}\pi$. Find

   (a) the area enclosed by the curve,

   (b) the polar coordinates of the point of the curve furthest from the origin.

6   Draw on one diagram the curves G and H with polar equations $r = 2\cos\theta$ (Fig. 8.10) and $r = 1 + 2\cos\theta$ (Fig. 8.20).

   Let C be the point with polar coordinates $r = 1$, $\theta = 0$. Draw a line through C making an angle α with the initial line. Let this line meet the curve H at P, and let OP meet the curve G at Q. Denote the angle QCP by β. Identify two isosceles triangles in your figure, and deduce that $\alpha = 3\beta$.

   Show how this can be used to give a construction to trisect an angle. (For this reason the curve H is called a *trisectrix*.)

7   A curve C has cartesian equation $x^2 + y^2 = a(x - y)$. It is rotated about the origin through $45°$ anticlockwise to give a curve C'. Find the polar equation of C, and hence find the polar and cartesian equations of C'.

8   Find the polar equation of the curve H with cartesian equation $x^2 - y^2 = a^2$. Hence find the cartesian equation of the curve obtained by rotating H about the origin through an angle of $45°$ anticlockwise.

9   Sketch the curve E with cartesian equation $\dfrac{x^2}{25} + \dfrac{y^2}{9} = 1$. Write the equation of the curve E' obtained by translating E by -4 in the x-direction. Show that the polar equation of E' can be written as $r = \dfrac{9}{5 + 4\cos\theta}$.

   For the curve E, F is the point $(4, 0)$ and PQ is a chord which passes through F. Prove that $\dfrac{1}{FP} + \dfrac{1}{FQ}$ is constant.

   Deduce from the polar equation of E' that $r = \frac{4}{5}\left(\frac{9}{4} - x\right)$. Hence show that, if P is any point on the curve E, the distance of P from F is $\frac{4}{5}$ of its perpendicular distance from the line $x = 6\frac{1}{4}$.

10 Find the cartesian equation of the curve with polar equation $r = \cos^2 \theta$. Hence show that the equation of the tangent to the curve at the point $\left(\frac{1}{2}, \frac{1}{4}\pi\right)$ is $r = \dfrac{1}{\sqrt{2}(3\sin\theta - \cos\theta)}$.

11* In suitable units the vertical cross-section through the axis of symmetry of an airship has polar equation $r = 2\cos\theta + 3\cos 3\theta$, where r may take both positive and negative values. Find the values of θ in the interval $0 \leqslant \theta \leqslant \pi$ for which r is zero, and show that the curve consists of three loops.

If the area of the top half of the large loop is given by $\displaystyle\int_0^\alpha f(\theta)\,d\theta$, write down the expression $f(\theta)$ and the value of α. Find the area of the large loop. $\hspace{1cm}$ (OCR, adapted)

12* Sketch the curve (a *strophoid*) with equation $r = \dfrac{a\cos 2\theta}{\cos\theta}$, where r can take both positive and negative values. Show that the whole curve lies within the interval $-a \leqslant x \leqslant a$, and that for $-\frac{1}{4}\pi \leqslant \theta \leqslant \frac{1}{4}\pi$ the curve describes a loop. Calculate the area of the loop. (Compare with Exercise 8D Question 7.)

13* Plot the points on the curve with equation $r = \cos 2\theta + 2\cos\theta$ from $\theta = -\pi$ to $\theta = \pi$ at intervals of $\frac{1}{4}\pi$ allowing r to take both positive and negative values. Use these to draw a sketch of the complete curve.

There are four regions which are completely bounded by parts of the curve. Show that one of these has the points with cartesian coordinates $(1,0)$, $(3,0)$, $(1,1)$ and $(1,-1)$ on its boundary. Find the area of this region.

14* Show that parametric equations for the curve in Fig. 8.20 are
$$x = 1 + \cos\theta + \cos 2\theta, \quad y = \sin\theta + \sin 2\theta.$$
Find the minimum value of x, and the angle $\theta = \alpha$ between $\frac{1}{2}\pi$ and π for which x takes this value.

An apple-shaped surface is formed by rotating the outer loop of this curve about the initial line. Explain why the volume it encloses can be calculated as
$$\int_\alpha^0 \pi y^2 \frac{dx}{d\theta}\,d\theta - \int_0^{\frac{2}{3}\pi} \pi y^2 \frac{dx}{d\theta}\,d\theta,$$
and evaluate this.

9 First order differential equations

This chapter describes methods of solving more complicated differential equations than those met earlier in the course. When you have completed it, you should

- be able to solve linear first order equations by using an integrating factor
- be able to use a substitution to solve other first order equations.

9.1 Solution using the product rule

In P3 Chapter 9 you solved differential equations like $\dfrac{dy}{dx} = \cos x$ and $\dfrac{dy}{dx} = y^2$ (so $\dfrac{dx}{dy} = \dfrac{1}{y^2}$). P3 Chapter 11 introduced more general equations like $\dfrac{dy}{dx} = y^2 \cos x$, where the variables are said to be 'separable'. An equation like this can be written as $\dfrac{1}{y^2} \dfrac{dy}{dx} = \cos x$, where the left side is the derivative with respect to x of a function of y alone, and the right side is the derivative of a function of x. Thus $\dfrac{1}{y^2} \dfrac{dy}{dx} = \dfrac{d}{dx}\left(-\dfrac{1}{y}\right)$ and $\cos x = \dfrac{d}{dx}(\sin x)$, so the solution is $-\dfrac{1}{y} = \sin x + k$. Using this method you can solve any equation of the form $\dfrac{dy}{dx} = \dfrac{f(x)}{g(y)}$ as long as you can do the actual integration.

All these equations are examples of **first order equations**, because they involve only the first derivative $\dfrac{dy}{dx}$. But not all first order equations can be separated in this way.

For example, if you have the equation

$$3x^2 y + x^3 \frac{dy}{dx} = x^4$$

to solve, no amount of algebraic manoeuvre will enable you to get $\dfrac{dy}{dx}$ into the form $\dfrac{f(x)}{g(y)}$.

In fact, this equation is easy to solve, because you should recognise the left side as the derivative of the product of two functions. Thus

$$3x^2 y + x^3 \frac{dy}{dx} \quad \text{is} \quad \frac{d}{dx}\left(x^3\right) \times y + x^3 \frac{dy}{dx}, \quad \text{which is} \quad \frac{d}{dx}\left(x^3 y\right),$$

so the equation can be written as $\dfrac{d}{dx}\left(x^3 y\right) = x^4$. The solution is

$$x^3 y = \tfrac{1}{5} x^5 + k, \quad \text{or more conveniently} \quad y = \tfrac{1}{5} x^2 + \frac{k}{x^3}.$$

The trouble is that it is most unlikely that you will be asked to solve

$$3x^2y + x^3\frac{dy}{dx} = x^4,$$

because all the terms of this equation have a common factor x^2. It is more likely that the equation will be presented as

$$3y + x\frac{dy}{dx} = x^2,$$

and then the left side is not the derivative of a product. How could you tell that the key to solving this equation is to multiply each term by x^2? Read on!

9.2 Integrating factors

The first part of this chapter is concerned with the general problem of solving differential equations of the form

$$\frac{dy}{dx}f(x) + yg(x) = h(x),$$

where f, g and h are given functions. A differential equation like this is said to be **linear**, because $\frac{dy}{dx}$ and y appear only to the first degree; the equation has no terms involving $\left(\frac{dy}{dx}\right)^m$ or y^m with $m \neq 1$, nor are there any products like $y\frac{dy}{dx}$.

It isn't necessary to write this equation with three given functions, because you can divide through by $f(x)$ to get

$$\frac{dy}{dx} + y\frac{g(x)}{f(x)} = \frac{h(x)}{f(x)}$$

and then express $\frac{g(x)}{f(x)}$ as a single function $p(x)$, and $\frac{h(x)}{f(x)}$ as $q(x)$.

> The **standard form** of a first order linear differential equation is
>
> $$\frac{dy}{dx} + yp(x) = q(x)$$
>
> where $p(x)$ and $q(x)$ are given functions of x.

For example, the standard form of the equation discussed in Section 9.1 would be

$$\frac{dy}{dx} + y \times \frac{3}{x} = x.$$

You already know that this can be integrated by multiplying by x^3, which makes the left side $\dfrac{dy}{dx} \times x^3 + y \times 3x^2 = \dfrac{d}{dx}(yx^3)$. The question is, how can you find this multiplying factor x^3 from the knowledge that $p(x) = \dfrac{3}{x}$?

The answer comes in two steps. First, notice that

$$\int \frac{3}{x}\,dx = 3\ln x + k = \ln x^3 + k.$$

So you could say that the 'simplest' integral of $\dfrac{3}{x}$ is $\ln x^3$.

The second step is to get from $\ln x^3$ to the multiplying factor x^3, and to do this you simply have to take the exponential, since $e^{\ln x^3} = x^3$.

This works as a general rule. The multiplier x^3 is an example of an **integrating factor**. It is a function that you can use to convert a first order differential equation in standard form into a form which can be integrated.

To find an integrating factor for the differential equation

$$\frac{dy}{dx} + y p(x) = q(x),$$

first find the simplest integral of $p(x)$, and call it $I(x)$; then $e^{I(x)}$ is an integrating factor.

Example 9.2.1

Find the general solution of the differential equation $\dfrac{dy}{dx} - \dfrac{y}{x} = x$.

This is already in standard form, with $p(x) = -\dfrac{1}{x}$. So find the simplest integral of $-\dfrac{1}{x}$, which is $-\ln x$, or $\ln\dfrac{1}{x}$. An integrating factor is therefore $e^{\ln\frac{1}{x}}$, which is simply $\dfrac{1}{x}$.

Multiplying the differential equation by $\dfrac{1}{x}$ gives

$$\frac{dy}{dx} \times \frac{1}{x} + y \times \left(-\frac{1}{x^2}\right) = 1.$$

The left side of this is $\dfrac{d}{dx}\left(y \times \dfrac{1}{x}\right)$, so the equation can be written as $\dfrac{d}{dx}\left(y \times \dfrac{1}{x}\right) = 1$.

This can be integrated as

$$y \times \frac{1}{x} = x + k, \quad \text{or more conveniently} \quad y = x^2 + kx.$$

In an example like this, since the process is quite complicated, it is a good idea to check the answer by direct substitution. If $y = x^2 + kx$, then $\dfrac{dy}{dx} = 2x + k$ and $\dfrac{y}{x} = x + k$, so

$\dfrac{dy}{dx} - \dfrac{y}{x} = (2x + k) - (x + k) = x$, as required.

Example 9.2.2

Find the curve through $(0,1)$ whose equation satisfies the differential equation $\dfrac{dy}{dx} + y = e^x$.

For this differential equation $p(x)$ is simply 1, and the simplest integral of this is x. So an integrating factor is e^x.

Multiplying the equation by e^x gives $\dfrac{dy}{dx} \times e^x + y \times e^x = e^{2x}$.

The left side is $\dfrac{d}{dx}\left(ye^x\right)$, so the equation can be written as $\dfrac{d}{dx}\left(ye^x\right) = e^{2x}$, and then integrated to give

$$ye^x = \tfrac{1}{2}e^{2x} + k.$$

The question asks for the solution for which $y = 1$ when $x = 0$, so substitute these values to obtain $1 = \tfrac{1}{2} + k$, giving $k = \tfrac{1}{2}$. The solution is therefore

$$ye^x = \tfrac{1}{2}e^{2x} + \tfrac{1}{2}, \quad \text{which is best written as} \quad y = \tfrac{1}{2}e^x + \tfrac{1}{2}e^{-x}.$$

It is important to remember that, to use this method, you have to begin with the differential equation in standard form. But it is always worth checking first that the equation isn't already in a form which can be integrated directly, as was the case with the example in Section 9.1. This is the point of the first step in the following algorithm.

To solve the differential equation $\dfrac{dy}{dx}f(x) + y\,g(x) = h(x)$ using an integrating factor:

Step 1 If $g(x) = f'(x)$, write the equation as $\dfrac{d}{dx}(y\,f(x)) = h(x)$ and go to Step 6.

Step 2 Divide the equation by $f(x)$ to obtain $\dfrac{dy}{dx} + y\,p(x) = q(x)$.

Step 3 Find the simplest integral of $p(x)$; denote it by $I(x)$.

Step 4 Write $u(x) = e^{I(x)}$, and simplify this if possible.

Step 5 Multiply the equation (in its form after Step 2) by $u(x)$, and write the

equation as $\dfrac{d}{dx}(y\,u(x)) = q(x)\,u(x)$.

Step 6 Integrate the equation with respect to x, including an arbitrary constant.

Step 7 Put the solution into the form $y = \ldots$ by dividing by the function which multiplies y (that is $u(x)$ or $f(x)$).

Example 9.2.3

Find the general solution of $\dfrac{dy}{dx}\cos x + y\sin x = \tan x$.

Step 1 $f'(x)$ is $\dfrac{d}{dx}(\cos x) = -\sin x$, which does not equal $g(x) = \sin x$.

Step 2 Divide by $\cos x$ to obtain $\dfrac{dy}{dx} + y\tan x = \tan x \sec x$.

Step 3 $p(x) = \tan x$; $\displaystyle\int \tan x\, dx = \ln\sec x + k$, so take $I(x) = \ln\sec x$.

Step 4 The integrating factor is $u(x) = e^{\ln\sec x} = \sec x$.

Step 5 Multiply by $\sec x$: $\dfrac{dy}{dx}\sec x + y\sec x\tan x = \tan x\sec^2 x$, which is

$$\frac{d}{dx}(y\sec x) = \tan x\sec^2 x.$$

Step 6 Integrating, $y\sec x = \tfrac{1}{2}\tan^2 x + k$.

Step 7 Dividing by $\sec x$, $y = \dfrac{\sin^2 x}{2\cos x} + k\cos x$.

This can be simplified as $y = \dfrac{1 - \cos^2 x}{2\cos x} + k\cos x$, which is

$$y = \tfrac{1}{2}(\sec x - \cos x) + k\cos x = \tfrac{1}{2}\sec x + \left(k - \tfrac{1}{2}\right)\cos x.$$

Since k is an arbitrary constant, $k - \tfrac{1}{2}$ can be replaced by a single arbitrary constant c, giving the simplest form of the solution as

$$y = \tfrac{1}{2}\sec x + c\cos x.$$

After such a complicated calculation it is worth checking the answer to make sure you have not made a mistake. If $y = \tfrac{1}{2}\sec x + c\cos x$, then $\dfrac{dy}{dx} = \tfrac{1}{2}\sec x\tan x - c\sin x$, so that the left side of the original equation is

$$\left(\tfrac{1}{2}\sec x\tan x - c\sin x\right)\cos x + \left(\tfrac{1}{2}\sec x + c\cos x\right)\sin x$$
$$= \tfrac{1}{2}\tan x - c\sin x\cos x + \tfrac{1}{2}\tan x + c\cos x\sin x$$
$$= \tan x, \quad \text{as required.}$$

One small point to notice at Step 3 is that strictly the integral of $\tan x$ is $\ln|\sec x|$; that is, it is $\ln\sec x$ or $\ln(-\sec x)$ depending on whether $\sec x$ is positive or negative. If you use the minus sign, then at Step 4 you get $u(x) = -\sec x$ rather than $\sec x$. But this is not important, since it clearly makes no difference at Step 5 whether you multiply the equation by $\sec x$ or $-\sec x$.

9.3* Why the method works

You may omit this section if you wish.

It is quite easy to see why the rule for finding the integrating factor works. Since $I(x)$ is an integral of $p(x)$, it follows that $p(x) = I'(x)$. The left side of the differential equation, in standard form, is therefore

$$\frac{dy}{dx} + yI'(x).$$

After multiplying by $e^{I(x)}$, this becomes

$$\frac{dy}{dx}e^{I(x)} + ye^{I(x)}I'(x).$$

Now if $u(x) = e^{I(x)}$, then differentiation by the chain rule gives $u'(x) = e^{I(x)} \times I'(x)$.

So

$$\frac{dy}{dx}e^{I(x)} + ye^{I(x)}I'(x) = \frac{dy}{dx}u(x) + yu'(x), \text{ which is } \frac{d}{dx}(yu(x)).$$

You may also question why the algorithm in Section 9.2 specifies that you should choose $I(x)$ to be the *simplest* integral of $p(x)$. The answer is that you needn't. But if you chose some other integral of $p(x)$, this would have the form $I(x) + c$, for some constant c. The integrating factor would then be $e^{I(x)+c}$, which is $e^{I(x)} \times e^c$. So the only effect of taking one of the other integrals of $p(x)$ for $I(x)$ is to multiply the equation through by an additional numerical constant e^c, which is pointless.

Exercise 9A

1 Find general solutions of the following differential equations.

(a) $y + x\dfrac{dy}{dx} = x^2$

(b) $x\cos t + \dfrac{dx}{dt}\sin t = 1$

(c) $\dfrac{1}{x}\dfrac{dy}{dx} - \dfrac{1}{x^2}y = \dfrac{1}{x^3}$

(d) $e^{x^2}\dfrac{du}{dx} + 2xe^{x^2}u = 2$

2 Find the equation of the solution curve through the given point for each of the following differential equations.

(a) $2xy + x^2\dfrac{dy}{dx} = 1$ through $(1,0)$

(b) $2y\sin x \cos x + \dfrac{dy}{dx}\sin^2 x = \cos x$ through $\left(\tfrac{1}{2}\pi, 1\right)$

(c) $\dfrac{y}{\sqrt{x}} + 2\sqrt{x}\dfrac{dy}{dx} = x$ through $(1,1)$

3 Use integrating factors to find the general solutions of the following differential equations. Check your answers by substituting back into the original equations.

(a) $\dfrac{du}{dx} + \dfrac{2u}{x} = 1$

(b) $\dfrac{dy}{dx} - y\tan x = 2\sin x$

(c) $\dfrac{dx}{dt} - 4x = e^{2t}$

(d) $\dfrac{dy}{dx} - \dfrac{3y}{x} = x$

(e) $\dfrac{dy}{dt} + y\tan t = \cos t$

(f) $\dfrac{dy}{dx}\sin x + y\sec x = \cos^2 x$

4 For the following differential equations, find the equations of the solution curves which pass through the given points. Illustrate your answers with sketch graphs.

(a) $\dfrac{dy}{dx} + 3y = 9x$ through $(0,-2), (0,-1), (0,0), (0,1), (0,2)$

(b) $x\dfrac{dy}{dx} + 2y = x^2$, for $x > 0$, through $(1,0), (1,1), (1,2), (2,0), (2,1), (2,2)$

(c) $y\sin x + \dfrac{dy}{dx}\cos x = 2\tan x$, for $-\tfrac{1}{2}\pi < x < \tfrac{1}{2}\pi$, through $(0,-2),(0,-1),(0,0),(0,1),(0,2)$

(d) $x\dfrac{dy}{dx} = 3y + 2x$, for $x \neq 0$, through $(-1,-1), (-1,0), (-1,1), (1,-1), (1,0), (1,1)$

5 A curve passing through the point $(1,1)$ has the property that, at each point P of the curve, the gradient of the curve is 1 less than the gradient of OP. Find the equation of the curve, and illustrate your answer with a graph.

6 A sack containing a liquid chemical is placed in a tank. The chemical seeps out of the sack at a rate of $0.1x$ litres per hour, where x is the number of litres of the chemical remaining in the sack after t hours. The chemical in the tank evaporates at a rate $0.2y$ litres per hour, where y is the number of litres of the chemical in the tank after t hours. If the sack originally contained 50 litres of the chemical, find differential equations for x and for y, and solve them. Find the greatest amount of chemical in the tank, and when this occurs.

7 A will-o'-the-wisp is oscillating in a straight line so that its displacement from the origin at time t is $a + b\sin ct$, where a, b and c are positive constants. It is chased by a kitten which moves so that its velocity at any time is equal to cy, where y is the displacement of the will-o'-the-wisp from the kitten. If x denotes the displacement of the kitten from the origin at time t, find a differential equation connecting x and t. Show that, after some time, x is approximately equal to $a + \dfrac{1}{\sqrt{2}}b\sin\left(ct - \tfrac{1}{4}\pi\right)$. Draw graphs to illustrate the positions of the kitten and the will-o'-the-wisp during the chase.

8 A rope hangs over a rough circular peg of radius r. It is just about to slip with a vertical length p on one side and a vertical length q on the other, where $q > p$. It can be shown that, if the coefficient of friction is 1, the quantity $u = \dfrac{T}{\gamma g}$ satisfies the differential equation $\dfrac{du}{d\theta} - u = r(\cos\theta - \sin\theta)$. ($\gamma$ is the mass of the rope per unit length, g is the acceleration due to gravity, θ is the angle that the radius to a point on the peg makes with the vertical and T is the tension in the rope at that point.) Given that $u = p$ when $\theta = -\tfrac{1}{2}\pi$, and $u = q$ when $\theta = \tfrac{1}{2}\pi$, prove that $q = pe^\pi + r\left(1 + e^\pi\right)$.

9 Find the general solution of the differential equation $x\dfrac{dy}{dx} = 2(y - x)$ for $x \neq 0$. Investigate the regions in which the gradient of the solution curve is positive, and those in which it is negative,

(a) from the equation of the solution,

(b) from the differential equation.

Illustrate your answers with sketches of some solution curves.

10 Find the general solution of the differential equation $x\dfrac{dy}{dx} + y = \dfrac{1}{x^2}$ for $x > 0$. Use the differential equation to show that the stationary points on the solution curves all lie on $y = \dfrac{1}{x^2}$, and verify this from your equation for the general solution. Draw graphs to illustrate this property.

By differentiating the differential equation, show that $\dfrac{d^2 y}{dx^2} = \dfrac{2}{x^2}\left(y - \dfrac{2}{x^2}\right)$. Hence identify the regions in which the solution curves bend upwards, and those in which they bend downwards. Check your answer from your graphs.

9.4 Transforming equations by substitution

You have now met most of the common types of first order differential equation, but occasionally more complicated equations turn up. You can sometimes solve these by substituting a new variable for y, so as to reduce the equation to one of the types which you can already solve. Here are four examples which illustrate some of the possibilities; but the skill of finding the right substitution is something which comes only with experience, and calls for some ingenuity.

Example 9.4.1

Use the substitution $y = \dfrac{1}{z}$ to solve the equation $\dfrac{dy}{dx} - \dfrac{y}{x} = 2y^2$.

Notice that the given differential equation is not linear, because it includes a term containing y^2. The effect of the substitution is to convert it into a linear equation for z in terms of x.

If $y = \dfrac{1}{z}$, $\dfrac{dy}{dx} = -\dfrac{1}{z^2}\dfrac{dz}{dx}$. If you substitute these expressions for y and $\dfrac{dy}{dx}$ in the differential equation, you get

$$-\frac{1}{z^2}\frac{dz}{dx} - \frac{1}{xz} = \frac{2}{z^2},$$

which you can rearrange as

$$\frac{dz}{dx} + \frac{z}{x} = -2.$$

This is a linear first order equation for z as a function of x. You can easily check that the integrating factor is x, and that

$$x\frac{dz}{dx} + z = -2 \quad \text{can be written as} \quad \frac{d}{dx}(xz) = -2.$$

Integration gives $xz = k - x^2$,   so $z = \dfrac{k - x^2}{x}$ and $y = \dfrac{1}{z} = \dfrac{x}{k - x^2}$.

The solution of the given differential equation is $y = \dfrac{x}{k - x^2}$, where k is an arbitrary constant.

Example 9.4.2

A curve passes through $(1,0)$ and, at each point P, the direction of the tangent makes an angle of $\frac{1}{4}\pi$ with the direction OP, as shown in Fig. 9.1. Find the equation of the curve.

If OP makes an angle θ with the x-axis, and the tangent makes an angle α with the x-axis, then $\alpha = \frac{1}{4}\pi + \theta$, so that

$$\frac{dy}{dx} = \tan\alpha = \tan\left(\tfrac{1}{4}\pi + \theta\right)$$

$$= \frac{\tan\frac{1}{4}\pi + \tan\theta}{1 - \tan\frac{1}{4}\pi \tan\theta} = \frac{1 + \dfrac{y}{x}}{1 - \dfrac{y}{x}} = \frac{x + y}{x - y}.$$

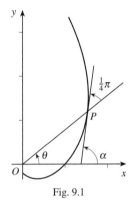

Fig. 9.1

Equations for which $\dfrac{dy}{dx}$ can be expressed in terms of $\dfrac{y}{x}$

can be solved by introducing a new variable $u = \dfrac{y}{x}$, so that $y = xu$. Then, by the

product rule, $\dfrac{dy}{dx} = u + x\dfrac{du}{dx}$. You can then substitute for y and $\dfrac{dy}{dx}$ in the differential

equation to get

$$u + x\frac{du}{dx} = \frac{1 + u}{1 - u}, \quad \text{so} \quad x\frac{du}{dx} = \frac{1 + u}{1 - u} - u = \frac{1 + u - u(1 - u)}{1 - u} = \frac{1 + u^2}{1 - u}.$$

You can rearrange this as $\dfrac{1 - u}{1 + u^2}\dfrac{du}{dx} = \dfrac{1}{x}$, which is an equation with separable variables.

Now $\displaystyle\int \frac{1 - u}{1 + u^2}\, du = \int\left(\frac{1}{1 + u^2} - \frac{u}{1 + u^2}\right) du$

$$= \tan^{-1} u - \tfrac{1}{2}\ln\left(1 + u^2\right) + k.$$

The equation can therefore be integrated with respect to x as

$$\tan^{-1} u - \tfrac{1}{2}\ln\left(1 + u^2\right) + k = \ln|x|.$$

To find k note that the curve passes through $(1,0)$, so that $u = \frac{0}{1} = 0$ when $x = 1$. So

$$\tan^{-1} 0 - \tfrac{1}{2}\ln(1+0^2) + k = \ln|1|, \text{ giving } k = 0.$$

Finally, substitute back u as $u = \dfrac{y}{x}$, which gives the solution

$$\tan^{-1}\frac{y}{x} = \tfrac{1}{2}\ln\left(1 + \frac{y^2}{x^2}\right) + \ln|x|.$$

Writing $|x|$ as $\sqrt{x^2}$ and combining the logarithms,

$$\tan^{-1}\frac{y}{x} = \ln\left(\sqrt{\left(1 + \frac{y^2}{x^2}\right)} \times \sqrt{x^2}\right)$$

$$= \ln\sqrt{\left(1 + \frac{y^2}{x^2}\right) \times x^2} = \ln\sqrt{x^2 + y^2}.$$

This equation would look far less formidable if it were written in polar coordinates. If you replace $\tan^{-1}\dfrac{y}{x}$ by θ, and $\sqrt{x^2 + y^2}$ by r, it becomes

$$\theta = \ln r, \quad \text{or} \quad r = e^\theta.$$

The curve is called an equiangular spiral, because the tangent always makes the same angle with the radius.

Example 9.4.3

An object slides down a track whose shape is part of a circle of radius r, as shown in Fig. 9.2. Its velocity at the top of the track is u. The velocity v when the radius makes an angle θ with the vertical satisfies the differential equation

$$2v\frac{dv}{d\theta} - v^2 = gr(2\sin\theta - \cos\theta).$$

(This is the equation with a coefficient of friction of $\frac{1}{2}$; g is the constant acceleration of gravity.) Investigate the subsequent motion.

This is not a linear equation, since it contains terms in v^2 and a product $2v\dfrac{dv}{d\theta}$. But you should recognise that $2v\dfrac{dv}{d\theta}$ is $\dfrac{d}{d\theta}(v^2)$. So if w is written in place of v^2, the equation becomes

$$\frac{dw}{d\theta} - w = gr(2\sin\theta - \cos\theta),$$

which is linear.

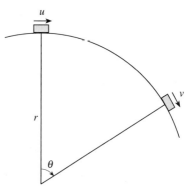

Fig. 9.2

The integrating factor is $e^{I(\theta)}$, where $I(\theta)$ is the simplest integral of -1 with respect to θ, so that $I(\theta) = -\theta$. After multiplication by the integrating factor $e^{-\theta}$, the equation becomes

$$\frac{d}{d\theta}\left(we^{-\theta}\right) = gre^{-\theta}(2\sin\theta - \cos\theta).$$

You could integrate $e^{-\theta}\sin\theta$ and $e^{-\theta}\cos\theta$ by two applications of integration by parts, as was shown in Example 6.1.4(c). It turned out in that example that the result is a combination of functions of the same kind, so that

$$\int e^{-\theta}(2\sin\theta - \cos\theta) = e^{-\theta}(a\sin\theta + b\cos\theta).$$

The quickest way to find the numbers a and b is to differentiate:

$$e^{-\theta}(2\sin\theta - \cos\theta) = -e^{-\theta}(a\sin\theta + b\cos\theta) + e^{-\theta}(a\cos\theta - b\sin\theta).$$

The coefficients of $e^{-\theta}\sin\theta$ and $e^{-\theta}\cos\theta$ must agree, so that

$$2 = -a - b \text{ and } -1 = -b + a, \text{ giving } a = -\tfrac{3}{2},\ b = -\tfrac{1}{2}.$$

The solution of the differential equation is therefore

$$we^{-\theta} = gre^{-\theta}\left(-\tfrac{3}{2}\sin\theta - \tfrac{1}{2}\cos\theta\right) + k,$$

where k is chosen so that w (or v^2) is equal to u^2 when $\theta = 0$:

$$u^2 = -\tfrac{1}{2}gr + k, \quad \text{or} \quad k = u^2 + \tfrac{1}{2}gr.$$

Substituting back w as v^2, and rearranging,

$$v^2 = \tfrac{1}{2}gre^{\theta}\left(\frac{2u^2}{gr} - \left(e^{-\theta}(3\sin\theta + \cos\theta) - 1\right)\right).$$

You might well ask what is the use of this solution. There is no great merit in knowing the speed of the object at any point along the track. What is of interest is the general form of the solution, which can be written as

$$v = Ce^{\frac{1}{2}\theta}\sqrt{A - f(\theta)},$$

where $C = \sqrt{\tfrac{1}{2}gr}$, $A = \dfrac{2u^2}{gr}$ and $f(\theta) = e^{-\theta}(3\sin\theta + \cos\theta) - 1$.

Fig. 9.3 shows the graph of $f(\theta)$. You will see that $f(0) = 0$, and you can easily check for yourself that the maximum value occurs when $\tan\theta = \tfrac{1}{2}$, and that the maximum value is about 0.4. Thus there are two possibilities.

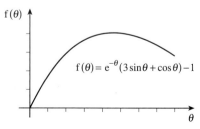

$f(\theta) = e^{-\theta}(3\sin\theta + \cos\theta) - 1$

Fig. 9.3

If $A < 0.4$, v will become zero for some value of θ less than $\tan^{-1} \frac{1}{2}$, after which the differential equation no longer applies. If $A > 0.4$, the expression $A - f(\theta)$ first decreases but, after $\theta = \tan^{-1} \frac{1}{2}$, it starts to increase. Since the other factor $e^{\frac{1}{2}\theta}$ is also increasing, v itself increases.

So, if $\dfrac{2u^2}{gr} < 0.4$, that is $u < \sqrt{0.2gr}$, the object will be brought to rest by the friction from the track at some point before $\theta < \tan^{-1} \frac{1}{2}$. If $u > \sqrt{0.2gr}$, it will slow down at first but will then pick up speed as gravity overcomes the force of friction.

Example 9.4.4

Find the general solution of the differential equation $x^4 \dfrac{dy}{dx} = x^2 y^2 + 2xy + x^2 + 1$.

If you compare the form of this equation with the general linear equation at the beginning of Section 9.2, you will see that, in addition to terms of the form $\dfrac{dy}{dx} f(x)$, $yg(x)$ and $h(x)$, there is also a term of the form $y^2 k(x)$. Equations of this kind are called Riccati equations, after the Venetian mathematician who published a paper about them in 1724.

There is no general method for finding solutions of Riccati equations. But they have the surprising property that, if you can find one solution $y = F(x)$, then the general solution can be got by making a substitution $y = F(x) + \dfrac{1}{z}$, where z is a function of x.

So begin by trying to guess a solution. Since all the functions of x which appear in the equation are powers of x, it is possible that it might be satisfied by a function such as $y = ax^m$ for some numbers a and m. If this is so, then the identity

$$x^4 \left(amx^{m-1} \right) \equiv x^2 \left(ax^m \right)^2 + 2x \left(ax^m \right) + x^2 + 1$$

would have to hold for all values of x. This can be written as

$$amx^{m+3} \equiv a^2 x^{2m+2} + 2ax^{m+1} + x^2 + x^0.$$

It is not hard to see that, since there must be other terms to balance the terms x^2 and x^0, this can happen only if $m + 3 = 2$ and $m + 1 = 0$, so that $m = -1$. The identity then becomes

$$-ax^2 = a^2 + 2a + x^2 + 1, \quad \text{or} \quad (a+1)x^2 + (a+1)^2 = 0.$$

Both coefficients are 0 if $a = -1$, so the equation is satisfied by $y = -\dfrac{1}{x}$.

To find the general solution, make the substitution $y = -\dfrac{1}{x} + \dfrac{1}{z}$. Then

$\dfrac{dy}{dx} = \dfrac{1}{x^2} - \dfrac{1}{z^2}\dfrac{dz}{dx}$. The right side of the differential equation can be written as

$(xy+1)^2 + x^2$, and $xy + 1 = \dfrac{x}{z}$. So the equation becomes

$$x^4\left(\dfrac{1}{x^2} - \dfrac{1}{z^2}\dfrac{dz}{dx}\right) = \left(\dfrac{x}{z}\right)^2 + x^2, \quad \text{which simplifies to} \quad \dfrac{dz}{dx} = -\dfrac{1}{x^2}.$$

This is easy to integrate, as

$$z = \dfrac{1}{x} + k, \quad \text{or} \quad z = \dfrac{1 + kx}{x}.$$

Therefore, substituting back $y = -\dfrac{1}{x} + \dfrac{1}{z}$, the general solution of the original

equation is

$$y = -\dfrac{1}{x} + \dfrac{x}{1 + kx}.$$

Exercise 9B

1 Use the substitution $y = xu$ to find the general solution of the differential equation

$$(x + y)\dfrac{dy}{dx} = y.$$

2 Find the general solution of the differential equation $\dfrac{dy}{dx} = \dfrac{x^2 + y^2}{2xy}$ by using the substitutions

(a) $y = xu$, (b) $y = \sqrt{v}$.

3 Find the general solution of the differential equation $x\dfrac{dy}{dx} + 2xy^2 = y$ by using the substitution $y = \dfrac{1}{u}$. Check your answer in the original equation.

4 Find the solution of the differential equation $\dfrac{dy}{dx} + \dfrac{y}{x} = \sqrt{\dfrac{y}{x}}$ for $x > 1$, given that $y = 0$ when $x = 1$, by using the substitution $y = u^2$.

5 Find the value of q such that the substitution $y = u^q$ converts the differential equation $x\dfrac{dy}{dx} + 2y = x^2 y^3$ into a linear differential equation connecting u and x. Hence find the general solution of the original equation.

6 Use the method of Question 5 to find the solution curve of the differential equation $x\dfrac{dy}{dx} - y = \dfrac{x}{y^2}$ which passes through the point $(2, 5)$.

7 Show that the differential equation $\dfrac{dy}{dx} + y = x^m y^n$, where m is a positive integer, can be solved by using the substitution $y = u^q$ where $q = -\dfrac{1}{n-1}$. Hence find the general solutions of the differential equations

(a) $\dfrac{dy}{dx} + y = x^2 y^3$, (b) $\dfrac{dy}{dx} + y = x\sqrt{y}$.

8 A curve C has the property that, at any point P on the curve, the angle which the tangent makes with the x-axis is twice the angle which OP makes with the x-axis. Show that C satisfies the differential equation $\dfrac{dy}{dx} = \dfrac{2xy}{x^2 - y^2}$. Use the method of Example 9.4.2 to solve this equation. Identify the solution geometrically, and use a geometrical argument to show that the curve you have identified has the property described.

9 Show that one solution of $\dfrac{dy}{dx} = 1 - 2x(x-y)^2$ is $y = x$. Use the substitution $y = x + \dfrac{1}{u}$ to find the general solution.

10 The differential equation $\dfrac{dy}{dx} = 4x^2 y - y^2 + 4x(1 - x^3)$ has a solution of the form $y = ax^m$. Find the values of m and a, and then use the method of Example 9.4.4 to find the general solution. Draw graphs to illustrate the family of solution curves.

Miscellaneous exercise 9

1 Find the general solution of the differential equation $\dfrac{ds}{dt} - 3s = te^{3t}$, giving s in terms of t.

(OCR)

2 Find the general solution of the differential equation $x\dfrac{dy}{dx} + 4y = x$, giving y explicitly in terms of x. Find also the particular solution for which $y = 1$ when $x = 1$. (OCR)

3 Find the general solution of the differential equation $\dfrac{dy}{dx} - 3x^2 y = xe^{x^3}$, giving y explicitly in terms of x. Find also the particular solution for which $y = 1$ when $x = 0$. (OCR)

4 Find y in terms of x, given that $\dfrac{dy}{dx} + 2xy = 10e^{-x^2}$ and that $y = 20$ when $x = 0$. (OCR)

5 Find the general solution of the differential equation $\dfrac{dy}{dx} + y\cot x = x$. Find also the particular solution for which $y = 0$ when $x = \frac{1}{2}\pi$. (OCR)

6 The general solution of the differential equation $x\dfrac{dy}{dx} + (x+1)y = 1$ is represented by a family of curves. Find the general solution of the differential equation, and find the equation of the particular curve which passes through the point $(1, 2)$. (OCR)

7 Given that $-1 < x < 1$, find the general solution of the differential equation

$(1 - x^2)\dfrac{dy}{dx} - xy + 1 = 0$. Find the particular solution for which $y = \frac{1}{2}\pi$ when $x = 0$. (OCR)

8 The differential equation $\dfrac{dy}{dx} + \dfrac{y}{x \ln x} = \dfrac{1}{x}$, with $y = 1$ when $x = e$, is to be solved using an

integrating factor. Find the integrating factor, and solve the differential equation. Sketch the solution curve for $x > 1$. (MEI)

9 The gradient at any point $P(x, y)$ of a curve is proportional to the sum of the coordinates of P. The curve passes through the point $(1, -2)$ and its gradient at $(1, -2)$ is -4. Find the equation of the curve. Show that the line $y = -x - \frac{1}{4}$ is an asymptote to the curve. (OCR)

10 Water starts pouring into an empty open tank whose capacity is 1000 litres, and t seconds

later the volume, V litres, of water in the tank is such that $\dfrac{dV}{dt} + \frac{1}{20}V = \frac{1}{4}t + 1$. Find V in

terms of t, and hence show that, for large values of t, $V \approx 5t - 80$. Hence determine, to the nearest second, the value of t when the tank begins to overflow. (OCR)

11 A car moves from rest along a straight road. After t seconds the velocity is v metres per

second. The motion is modelled by $\dfrac{dv}{dt} + \alpha v = e^{\beta t}$, where α and β are positive constants.

Find v in terms of α, β and t and show that, as long as the above model applies, the car does not come to rest. (OCR)

12 (a) Find a particular solution of the differential equation $\dfrac{dy}{dx} + y = x^2$.

(b) Find the equation of the solution curve which passes through $(0, A)$.

(c) Explain why, if a solution curve has a stationary point, that point lies on $y = x^2$.

(d) Show that, if a solution curve has a point of inflexion, that point lies on $y = x^2 - 2x$.

(e) Plot the graphs of $y = x^2$ and $y = x^2 - 2x$ for $-3 \leqslant x \leqslant 4$. On the same diagram, sketch the solution curve which passes through $(0, 2)$. Sketch also the solution curve which passes through $(0, 1)$, indicating clearly how it satisfies the properties established in parts (c) and (d). (OCR)

13 Consider solutions to the differential equation $\dfrac{dy}{dx} + y = x$.

(a) If a solution curve has a stationary point show that the point lies on the line $y = x$.

(b) Explain why any solution curve that meets the line $y = x + 1$ cuts the line at right angles.

(c) The general solution of the differential equation has the form $y = Ae^{-x} + P(x)$, where $P(x)$ is a polynomial. Find $P(x)$.

(d) On a single diagram sketch the graphs $y = P(x)$, $y = x$, $y = x + 1$, and the solution curves through $(0, 1)$ and $(0, 0)$.

(e) Show that the solution curve through $(0, -2)$ has no stationary point, and sketch this curve. (OCR)

14 Find the general solution of the differential equation $x\dfrac{dy}{dx} + 2y = \sqrt{1+x^2}$. Find the

particular solution which satisfies the condition that $y = 1$ when $x = 1$. How does y behave when x becomes very small?

Use the first three non-zero terms in the expansion of $\left(1+x^2\right)^{\frac{3}{2}}$ to write down the power series expansion of the general solution y for small values of x up to and including the term in x^2. Hence find the particular solution of the differential equation which crosses the x-axis from the region $x > 0$ into the region $x < 0$. Is it possible to obtain other solutions of the differential equation in the region $x < 0$? Explain your answer. (MEI)

15 Use the substitutions $Y = y^3$, $X = x^2$ to reduce the equation $3y^2x^3\dfrac{dy}{dx} + 2nx^2y^3 = 2\sin x^2$

to the linear equation $\dfrac{dY}{dX} + \dfrac{n}{X}Y = \dfrac{1}{X^2}\sin X$. Integrate this equation in the case $n = 4$. In

this case, given that Y is a solution which tends to a limit as X tends to 0, find this limit.

(OCR)

16 The differential equation $\dfrac{dy}{dx}\sin x - y\cos x = e^{-kx}\sin^2 x$ ($k \geqslant 0$) is to be solved, where k

is a constant.

(a) In the case $k > 0$, show that the general solution is $y = \left(A - \dfrac{1}{k}e^{-kx}\right)\sin x$, where A is

an arbitrary constant.

(b) Find the particular solution in the cases

(i) $\dfrac{dy}{dx} = \dfrac{1}{k}$ when $x = 0$,   (ii) $\dfrac{dy}{dx} = -\dfrac{1}{k}$ when $x = 0$.

Describe the differences in the behaviour of the two solutions for large positive values of x.

(c) In the case $k = 0$, find the general solution of the equation. Describe its behaviour for large positive values of x. (MEI)

17 (a) A long pendulum swinging for a considerable length of time can be used to demonstrate the rotation of the earth. In these circumstances the appropriate equation

is assumed to be $\dfrac{d^2\theta}{dt^2} + k\left(\dfrac{d\theta}{dt}\right)^2 = -G\sin\theta$, where k and G are constants and θ is the

pendulum's displacement from the downward vertical. Use the transformations

$\omega = \dfrac{d\theta}{dt}$, $\dfrac{d^2\theta}{dt^2} = \omega\dfrac{d\omega}{d\theta}$, $\omega^2 = E$ to reduce the equation to the linear form

$\dfrac{dE}{d\theta} + 2kE = -2G\sin\theta$. Solve this equation to find E in terms of θ.

(b) Successive positions of rest are $\theta = -\alpha$ and $\theta = \beta$, where $\alpha > \beta > 0$. Find an equation relating α and β. (OCR)

18 This question is about the solutions of the differential equation $y\dfrac{dy}{dx} = 3y - 2x$.

   (a) Show that there are two (straight line) solutions of the form $y = kx$. Give the two corresponding values of k.

   (b) If $u = \dfrac{y}{x}$, find $\dfrac{dy}{dx}$ in terms of x, u and $\dfrac{du}{dx}$. Use your answer to show that u satisfies the differential equation $-xu\dfrac{du}{dx} = u^2 - 3u + 2$.

   (c) Use partial fractions to show that the general solution of the original differential equation is given by $(y - 2x)^2 = a(y - x)$ where a is a constant.

   (d) Find the equation of the solution curve through the point $(0, y_0)$ where $y_0 \neq 0$. Show that all the solution curves with $y_0 > 0$ lie in a certain half-plane.

   (e) Show that when a solution curve crosses the line $y = mx$ it does so with gradient $3 - \dfrac{2}{m}$ and use this to sketch, for $x \geq 0$, the solution curve through the point $(0, -1)$.

(OCR)

19 (a) Verify that $y = \dfrac{1}{x^3}$ is a solution of the differential equation $\dfrac{dy}{dx} = \dfrac{y}{x} - x^2 y^2 - \dfrac{3}{x^4}$. Find another solution of the form $y = \dfrac{\lambda}{x^3}$ where λ is a constant.

   (b) Show that the substitution $y = \dfrac{1}{x^3} + \dfrac{1}{z}$ reduces the original equation to the linear differential equation $\dfrac{dz}{dx} - \dfrac{z}{x} = x^2$. Solve this equation, and hence find the general solution of the original equation.

   (c) Show how the two particular solutions of part (a) arise from your general solution in part (b).

   (d) For which solutions of the original equation is it possible for y to be defined for all $x > 0$?

(OCR)

20 A function $y = f(x)$ satisfies the differential equation $\dfrac{dy}{dx} + 2xy = 1$, and $y = 1$ when $x = 0$.

Explain why it is not possible to find an algebraic expression for $f(x)$.

Use the differential equation to show that $f''(x) = -2f(x) - 2x f'(x)$, and differentiate this to find a similar equation for $f'''(x)$.

Use these results to find a Maclaurin polynomial of degree 3 which approximates to $f(x)$ when x is small.

Check your answer by taking the solution process as far as you can, and then using Maclaurin approximations for e^{x^2} and e^{-x^2}.

10 Complex numbers

In this chapter the concept of number is extended so that all numbers have square roots. When you have completed it, you should

- understand that new number systems can be created, provided that the definitions are algebraically consistent
- appreciate that complex number algebra excludes inequalities
- be able to do calculations with complex numbers
- know the meaning of conjugate complex numbers, and that non-real roots of equations with real coefficients occur in conjugate pairs
- know how to represent complex numbers as translations or as points
- know the meaning of modulus, and be able to use it algebraically
- be able to use complex numbers to prove geometrical results
- be able to solve simple equations with complex coefficients.

10.1 Extending the number system

Before negative numbers were developed, it was impossible to subtract a from b if $a > b$. If only positive numbers exist, then there is no number x such that $a + x = b$.

This was a serious drawback for mathematics and science, so a new kind of number was invented which could be either positive or negative. It was found that this results in a consistent system of numbers in which the ordinary rules of algebra apply, provided that you also make up the right rules for combining numbers, such as $b - a = -(a - b)$ and $(-a) \times (-b) = +(ab)$.

There is a similar problem with real numbers, that square roots only exist for positive numbers and zero. That is, if $a < 0$, there is no real number x such that $x^2 = a$.

The mathematical response to this is to invent a new kind of number, called a **complex number**. It turns out that this can be done very simply, by introducing just one new number, usually denoted by i, whose square is -1. If you also require that this number combines with the real numbers by the usual rules of algebra, this creates a whole new system of numbers.

Notice first that you don't need a separate symbol for the square root of -2, since the rules of algebra require that $\sqrt{-2} = \sqrt{2} \times \sqrt{-1}$, so that $\sqrt{-2}$ is just $\sqrt{2}\,i$.

Since you must be able to combine i with all the real numbers, the complex numbers must include all the products bi where b is any real number. They must also include all the sums $a + bi$, where a is any real number.

The **complex numbers** consist of numbers of the form $a+b\mathrm{i}$, where
a and b are real numbers and $\mathrm{i}^2 = -1$.

Complex numbers of the form $a+0\mathrm{i}$ are called **real numbers**;
complex numbers of the form $0+b\mathrm{i}$ are called **imaginary numbers**.

In a general complex number $a+b\mathrm{i}$, a is called the **real part** and
b the **imaginary part**. This is written $\mathrm{Re}(a+b\mathrm{i})=a$, $\mathrm{Im}(a+b\mathrm{i})=b$.

*Some people prefer to use j rather than i for the square root of -1. Also, some books
define the imaginary part of $a+b\mathrm{i}$ as $b\mathrm{i}$ rather than b.*

Two questions need to be asked before going further: is algebra with complex numbers
consistent, and are complex numbers useful? The answers are 'yes, but … ' and 'yes,
very'. Complex numbers have an important place in modern physics and electronics.

The reason for the 'but' is that with complex numbers you cannot use the inequality
symbols $>$ and $<$. One of the rules for inequalities is that, if $a>b$ and $c>0$, then
$ac>bc$. So if $a>0$ and $a>0$, then $aa>0a$, that is $a^2>0$. What about the number
i? Is $\mathrm{i}>0$ or $\mathrm{i}<0$?

Try following through the consequences of each assumption in turn:

$$\mathrm{i}>0 \ \Rightarrow \ \mathrm{i}^2>0 \ \Leftrightarrow \ -1>0;$$

$$\mathrm{i}<0 \ \Leftrightarrow \ \mathrm{i}+(-\mathrm{i})<0+(-\mathrm{i}) \ \Leftrightarrow \ 0<-\mathrm{i}$$
$$\Leftrightarrow \ -\mathrm{i}>0 \ \Rightarrow \ (-\mathrm{i})^2>0 \ \Leftrightarrow \ -1>0.$$

Either assumption leads to the conclusion that $-1>0$, which you know to be false. The
way out of the dilemma is to make the rule:

The relations $>$ and $<$ cannot be used
to compare pairs of complex numbers.

10.2 Operations with complex numbers

It is remarkable, and not at all obvious, that when you add, subtract, multiply or divide
two complex numbers $a+b\mathrm{i}$, $c+d\mathrm{i}$, the result is another complex number.

Addition and subtraction   By the usual rules of algebra,

$$(a+b\mathrm{i})\pm(c+d\mathrm{i})=a+b\mathrm{i}\pm c\pm d\mathrm{i}=a\pm c+b\mathrm{i}\pm d\mathrm{i}=(a\pm c)+(b\pm d)\mathrm{i}.$$

Since a, b, c, d are real numbers, so are $a\pm c$ and $b\pm d$. The expression at the end of
the line therefore has the form $p+q\mathrm{i}$ where p and q are real.

Uniqueness If $a + b\mathrm{i} = 0$, then $a = -b\mathrm{i}$, so that $a^2 = (-b\mathrm{i})^2 = -b^2$. Now a and b are real, so that $a^2 \geq 0$ and $-b^2 \leq 0$. They can only be equal if $a^2 = 0$ and $b^2 = 0$. That is, $a = 0$ and $b = 0$. So if a complex number is zero, both its real and imaginary parts are zero.

Combining this with the rule for subtraction shows that

$$(a + b\mathrm{i}) = (c + d\mathrm{i}) \quad \Leftrightarrow \quad (a + b\mathrm{i}) - (c + d\mathrm{i}) = 0 \quad \Leftrightarrow \quad (a - c) + (b - d)\mathrm{i} = 0$$
$$\Leftrightarrow \quad a - c = 0 \quad \text{and} \quad b - d = 0$$
$$\Leftrightarrow \quad a = c \quad \text{and} \quad b = d.$$

That is:

> If two complex numbers are equal, their real parts are equal and their imaginary parts are equal.

Multiplication By the usual rules for multiplying out brackets,

$$(a + b\mathrm{i}) \times (c + d\mathrm{i}) = ac + a(d\mathrm{i}) + (b\mathrm{i})c + (b\mathrm{i})(d\mathrm{i}) = ac + ad\,\mathrm{i} + bc\,\mathrm{i} + bd\,\mathrm{i}^2$$
$$= (ac - bd) + (ad + bc)\mathrm{i}.$$

Since a, b, c, d are real numbers, so are $ac - bd$ and $ad + bc$. The product is therefore of the form the form $p + q\mathrm{i}$ where p and q are real.

An important special case is

$$(a + b\mathrm{i}) \times (a - b\mathrm{i}) = (aa - b(-b)) + (a(-b) + ba)\mathrm{i} = (a^2 + b^2) + 0\mathrm{i},$$

a real number. So with complex numbers the sum of two squares, $a^2 + b^2$, can be factorised as $(a + b\mathrm{i})(a - b\mathrm{i})$.

Division First, there are two special cases to consider.

If $d = 0$, then

$$\frac{a + b\mathrm{i}}{c + 0\mathrm{i}} = \frac{a + b\mathrm{i}}{c} = \frac{a}{c} + \frac{b}{c}\mathrm{i}.$$

And if $c = 0$, you can simplify the expression by multiplying numerator and denominator by i:

$$\frac{a + b\mathrm{i}}{0 + d\mathrm{i}} = \frac{a + b\mathrm{i}}{d\mathrm{i}} = \frac{(a + b\mathrm{i})\mathrm{i}}{(d\mathrm{i})\mathrm{i}} = \frac{a\mathrm{i} + b\mathrm{i}^2}{d\mathrm{i}^2}$$
$$= \frac{a\mathrm{i} - b}{-d} = \frac{-b}{-d} + \left(\frac{a\mathrm{i}}{-d}\right) = \frac{b}{d} - \frac{a}{d}\mathrm{i}.$$

In the general case $\dfrac{a + b\mathrm{i}}{c + d\mathrm{i}}$ the trick is to multiply numerator and denominator by $c - d\mathrm{i}$, and to use the result just proved, that $(c + d\mathrm{i})(c - d\mathrm{i}) = c^2 + d^2$.

$$\frac{a+b\mathrm{i}}{c+d\mathrm{i}} = \frac{(a+b\mathrm{i})(c-d\mathrm{i})}{(c+d\mathrm{i})(c-d\mathrm{i})} = \frac{(ac+bd)+(-ad+bc)\mathrm{i}}{c^2+d^2}$$

$$= \frac{ac+bd}{c^2+d^2} + \left(\frac{bc-ad}{c^2+d^2}\right)\mathrm{i}.$$

In every case the result has the form $p+q\mathrm{i}$ where p and q are real numbers. The only exception is when $c^2+d^2=0$, and since c and d are both real this can only occur if c and d are both 0, so that $c+d\mathrm{i}=0+0\mathrm{i}=0$. With complex numbers, as with real numbers, you cannot divide by zero.

Do not try to remember the formulae for $(a+b\mathrm{i})(c+d\mathrm{i})$ and $\dfrac{a+b\mathrm{i}}{c+d\mathrm{i}}$ in this section.

As long as you understand the method, it is simple to apply it when you need it.

Exercise 10A

1 If $p=2+3\mathrm{i}$ and $q=2-3\mathrm{i}$, express the following in the form $a+b\mathrm{i}$, where a and b are real numbers.

(a) $p+q$ (b) $p-q$ (c) pq (d) $(p+q)(p-q)$

(e) p^2-q^2 (f) p^2+q^2 (g) $(p+q)^2$ (h) $(p-q)^2$

2 If $r=3+\mathrm{i}$ and $s=1-2\mathrm{i}$, express the following in the form $a+b\mathrm{i}$, where a and b are real numbers.

(a) $r+s$ (b) $r-s$ (c) $2r+s$ (d) $r+s\mathrm{i}$

(e) rs (f) r^2 (g) $\dfrac{r}{s}$ (h) $\dfrac{s}{r}$

(i) $\dfrac{r}{\mathrm{i}}$ (j) $(1+\mathrm{i})r$ (k) $\dfrac{s}{1+\mathrm{i}}$ (l) $\dfrac{1-\mathrm{i}}{s}$

3 If $(2+\mathrm{i})(x+y\mathrm{i})=1+3\mathrm{i}$, where x and y are real numbers, write two equations connecting x and y, and solve them.

Compare your answer with that given by dividing $1+3\mathrm{i}$ by $2+\mathrm{i}$ using the method described in the text.

4 Evaluate the following.

(a) $\mathrm{Re}(3+4\mathrm{i})$ (b) $\mathrm{Im}(1-3\mathrm{i})$ (c) $\mathrm{Re}(2+\mathrm{i})^2$

(d) $\mathrm{Im}(3-\mathrm{i})^2$ (e) $\mathrm{Re}\dfrac{1}{1+\mathrm{i}}$ (f) $\mathrm{Im}\dfrac{1}{\mathrm{i}}$

5 If $s=a+b\mathrm{i}$ and $t=c+d\mathrm{i}$ are complex numbers, which of the following are always true?

(a) $\mathrm{Re}\,s+\mathrm{Re}\,t=\mathrm{Re}(s+t)$ (b) $\mathrm{Re}\,3s=3\,\mathrm{Re}\,s$ (c) $\mathrm{Re}(\mathrm{i}\,s)=\mathrm{Im}\,s$

(d) $\mathrm{Im}(\mathrm{i}\,s)=\mathrm{Re}\,s$ (e) $\mathrm{Re}\,s\times\mathrm{Re}\,t=\mathrm{Re}(st)$ (f) $\dfrac{\mathrm{Im}\,s}{\mathrm{Im}\,t}=\mathrm{Im}\dfrac{s}{t}$

10.3 Solving equations

Now that $a + b\,\mathrm{i}$ is recognised as a number in its own right, there is no need to go on writing it out in full. You can use a single letter, such as s (or any other letter you like, except i), to represent it. If you write $s = a + b\,\mathrm{i}$, it is understood that s is a complex number and that a and b are real numbers.

Just as x is often used to stand for a general real number, it is conventional to use z for a general complex number, and to write $z = x + y\,\mathrm{i}$, where x and y are real numbers. When you see z as the unknown in an equation, you know that there is a possibility that at least some of the roots may be complex numbers. (But if you see some other letter, don't assume that the solution is not complex.)

Example 10.3.1

Solve the quadratic equation $z^2 + 4z + 13 = 0$.

> **Method 1** In the usual notation $a = 1$, $b = 4$ and $c = 13$, so that
> $b^2 - 4ac = 16 - 52 = -36$. Previously you would have said that there are no roots, but you can now write $\sqrt{-36} = 6\,\mathrm{i}$. Using the formula,
>
> $$z = \frac{-b \pm \sqrt{b^2 - 4ac}}{2a} = \frac{-4 \pm 6\,\mathrm{i}}{2} = -2 \pm 3\,\mathrm{i}.$$
>
> **Method 2** In completed square form, $z^2 + 4z + 13 = (z + 2)^2 + 9$. This is the sum of two squares, which you can now factorise, as
>
> $$((z + 2) - 3\,\mathrm{i})((z + 2) + 3\,\mathrm{i}).$$
>
> So you can write the equation as
>
> $$(z + 2 - 3\,\mathrm{i})(z + 2 + 3\,\mathrm{i}) = 0,\ \text{with roots}\ z = -2 + 3\,\mathrm{i}\ \text{and}\ -2 - 3\,\mathrm{i}.$$

You can use a similar method with any quadratic equation, $az^2 + bz + c = 0$, where the coefficients a, b and c are real. If $b^2 - 4ac > 0$ there are two roots, both real numbers. But if $b^2 - 4ac < 0$, you can write $b^2 - 4ac$ as $-\left(4ac - b^2\right)$, whose square root is $\sqrt{4ac - b^2}\,\mathrm{i}$ so that the roots are $\dfrac{-b \pm \sqrt{4ac - b^2}\,\mathrm{i}}{2a}$, both complex numbers.

Notice that, if the roots are complex numbers, then they have the form $x \pm y\,\mathrm{i}$ with the same real parts but opposite imaginary parts. Pairs of numbers like this are called **conjugate complex numbers**. If $x + y\,\mathrm{i}$ is written as z, then $x - y\,\mathrm{i}$ is denoted by $z*$ (which is read as 'z-star').

> Complex numbers $z = x + y\,\mathrm{i}$, $z* = x - y\,\mathrm{i}$ are conjugate complex numbers.
>
> Their sum $z + z* = 2x$ and product $zz* = x^2 + y^2$ are real numbers, and their difference $z - z* = 2y\,\mathrm{i}$ is an imaginary number.
>
> If a quadratic equation with real coefficients has two complex roots, these roots are conjugate.

Conjugate complex numbers have some important properties. Suppose, for example, that $s = a + b\,\mathrm{i}$ and $t = c + d\,\mathrm{i}$ are two complex numbers, so that $s^* = a - b\,\mathrm{i}$ and $t^* = c - d\,\mathrm{i}$. Using the results in the last section and replacing b by $-b$ and d by $-d$, you get

$$s \pm t = (a \pm c) + (b \pm d)\,\mathrm{i} \quad \text{and} \quad s^* \pm t^* = (a \pm c) - (b \pm d)\,\mathrm{i};$$

$$st = (ac - bd) + (ad + bc)\,\mathrm{i} \quad \text{and} \quad s^* t^* = (ac - bd) - (ad + bc)\,\mathrm{i};$$

$$\frac{s}{t} = \frac{ac + bd + (bc - ad)\,\mathrm{i}}{c^2 + d^2} \quad \text{and} \quad \frac{s^*}{t^*} = \frac{ac + bd - (bc - ad)\,\mathrm{i}}{c^2 + d^2}.$$

You can see that the outcomes in each case are conjugate pairs. That is:

> If s and t are complex numbers, then
>
> $$(s \pm t)^* = s^* \pm t^*,$$
>
> $$(st)^* = s^* t^*,$$
>
> $$\left(\frac{s}{t}\right)^* = \frac{s^*}{t^*}.$$

If in the second of these rules you set both s and t equal to z, you get $(zz)^* = z^* z^*$, that is $\left(z^2\right)^* = (z^*)^2$. Then, setting $s = z^2$ and $t = z$, it follows that $\left(z^2 z\right)^* = \left(z^2\right)^* z^* = (z^*)^2 z^*$, that is $\left(z^3\right)^* = (z^*)^3$; and so on. The general result can be proved by induction.

Theorem   If a is a real number and z a complex number, then $\left(az^n\right)^* = a(z^*)^n$ for all integers $n \geqslant 0$.

> **Proof**   The basis case, when $n = 0$, is that $\left(az^0\right)^* = a(z^*)^0$. The left side is
>
> $$\left(az^0\right)^* = (a(1))^* = a^* = (a + 0\,\mathrm{i})^* = a - 0\,\mathrm{i} = a,$$
>
> since a is real; and the right side is $a(z^*)^0 = a(1) = a$.
>
> For the inductive step, suppose $\left(az^k\right)^* = a(z^*)^k$. Then
>
> $$\left(az^{k+1}\right)^* = \left(az^k z\right)^* = \left(az^k\right)^* z^* \qquad \text{(using the rule } (st)^* = s^* t^*)$$
>
> $$= a(z^*)^k z^* = a(z^*)^{k+1} \left(az^k\right)^* = a(z^*)^k.$$
>
> So if the proposition is true for $n = k$, it is true for $n = k + 1$.
>
> So by the principle of mathematical induction the proposition is true for all $n \geqslant 0$.

Now suppose that you have a polynomial of degree n,

$$p(z) = a_n z^n + a_{n-1} z^{n-1} + \ldots + a_2 z^2 + a_1 z + a_0,$$

whose coefficients a_n, a_{n-1}, ... , a_2, a_1 and a_0 are all real numbers. Then $p(z^*)$ is the sum of $n + 1$ terms of the form $a_r (z^*)^r$, which by the theorem just proved you can write as $\left(a_r z^*\right)^r$. So each term is the conjugate of the corresponding term in $p(z)$. Since the sum of conjugate numbers is the conjugate of the sum, it follows that $p(z^*)$ is the conjugate of $p(z)$. This can also be stated as a theorem.

Theorem   If $p(z)$ is a polynomial with real coefficients, then $p(z*)$ is the conjugate of $p(z)$.

To turn the informal argument in the last paragraph into a formal proof you again have to use mathematical induction. The proposition $P(n)$ would be

For any polynomial $p(z)$ of degree n, $p(z*) = (p(z))*$.

Try writing out this proof for yourself. The inductive step should begin by observing that, if $p(z)$ is any polynomial of degree $k+1$ it can be written as $a_{k+1}z^{k+1} + q(z)$, where $q(z)$ is a polynomial of degree k.

It is only a short step from this last theorem to an important result about equations of the form $p(z) = 0$. Suppose that $z = s$ is a non-real root of this equation. Then $p(s) = 0$, so $p(s*) = (p(s))* = 0* = 0$, which means that $z = s*$ is also a root of the equation.

You saw an example of this result in Example 10.3.1 for a quadratic equation. You can now see that this was a special case of a far more general result, for polynomial equations of any degree.

If $p(z)$ is a polynomial with real coefficients, then $p(z*) = p(z)$.

If s is a non-real root of the equation $p(z) = 0$, then $s*$ is also a root;

that is, the non-real roots of the equation $p(z) = 0$ occur as conjugate pairs.

Example 10.3.2
Show that $(1+i)^4 = -4$. Hence find all the roots of the equation $z^4 + 4 = 0$.

$(1+i)^2 = 1 + 2i + i^2 = 1 + 2i - 1 = 2i$, so $(1+i)^4 = (2i)^2 = 4i^2 = -4$.

This shows that $1+i$ is a root of the equation $z^4 + 4 = 0$, so another root must be $1-i$. You can deduce that $z - 1 - i$ and $z - (1-i) = z - 1 + i$ are both factors of $z^4 + 4$.

Now $(z - 1 - i)(z - 1 + i) \equiv (z-1)^2 - i^2 \equiv z^2 - 2z + 2$. This means that $z^4 + 4$ must be the product of $z^2 - 2z + 2$ and another quadratic factor. By the usual method (see P2 Section 1.4), you can find that

$$z^4 + 4 \equiv (z^2 - 2z + 2)(z^2 + 2z + 2).$$

The other two roots are therefore the roots of the quadratic equation $z^2 + 2z + 2 = 0$, that is $z = \dfrac{-2 \pm \sqrt{4 - 4 \times 1 \times 2}}{2} = \dfrac{-2 \pm 2i}{2} = -1 \pm i$.

There are two conjugate pairs of roots: $1+i$, $1-i$, and $-1+i$, $-1-i$.

With hindsight, and a great deal of ingenuity, you might spot that if $z^4 + 4$ is written as $(z^4 + 4z^2 + 4) - 4z^2 = (z^2 + 2)^2 - (2z)^2$, then this is the difference of two squares, with factors $(z^2 + 2 - 2z)(z^2 + 2 + 2z)$.

Example 10.3.3

Solve the equation $z^5 - 6z^3 - 2z^2 + 17z - 10 = 0$.

Denote the left side by $p(z)$ and begin by trying to find some real factors, using the factor theorem.

Try $z = 1$: $p(1) = 0$, so $p(z) = (z-1)q(z)$, where $q(z) = z^4 + z^3 - 5z^2 - 7z + 10$.

Try $z = 1$ again: $q(1) = 0$, so $q(z) = (z-1)r(z)$, where $r(z) = z^3 + 2z^2 - 3z - 10$.

Try $z = 1$ again: $r(1) \neq 0$, so try $z = 2$; $r(2) = 0$, so $r(z) = (z-2)(z^2 + 4z + 5)$.

Completing the square, $z^2 + 4z + 5 = (z+2)^2 + 1 = (z+2-i)(z+2+i)$.

Thus $p(z) = (z-1)^2(z-2)(z+2-i)(z+2+i)$, and the roots are 1 (a repeated root, counted twice), 2 and the conjugate complex pair $-2 \pm i$.

Exercise 10B

1. If $p = 3 + 4i$, $q = 1 - i$ and $r = -2 + 3i$, solve the following equations for the complex number z.

   (a) $p + z = q$ (b) $2r + 3z = p$ (c) $qz = r$ (d) $pz + q = r$

2. Solve these pairs of simultaneous equations for the complex numbers z and w.

   (a) $(1+i)z + (2-i)w = 3 + 4i$
   $iz + (3+i)w = -1 + 5i$

   (b) $5z - (3+i)w = 7 - i$
   $(2-i)z + 2iw = -1 + i$

3. Solve the following quadratic equations, giving answers in the form $a + bi$, where a and b are real numbers.

   (a) $z^2 + 9 = 0$ (b) $z^2 + 4z + 5 = 0$ (c) $z^2 - 6z + 25 = 0$ (d) $2z^2 + 2z + 13 = 0$

4. Write down the conjugates of

   (a) $1 + 7i$,   (b) $-2 + i$,   (c) 5,   (d) $3i$.

   For each of these complex numbers z find the values of

   (i) $z + z^*$,   (ii) $z - z^*$,   (iii) zz^*,   (iv) $\dfrac{z}{z^*}$.

5. Write the following polynomials as products of linear factors.

   (a) $z^2 + 25$ (b) $9z^2 - 6z + 5$ (c) $4z^2 + 12z + 13$ (d) $z^4 - 16$

   (e) $z^4 - 8z^2 - 9$ (f) $z^3 + z - 10$ (g) $z^3 - 3z^2 + z + 5$ (h) $z^4 - z^2 - 2z + 2$

6. Prove that $1 + i$ is a root of the equation $z^4 + 3z^2 - 6z + 10 = 0$. Find all the roots.

7. Prove that $-2 + i$ is a root of the equation $z^4 + 24z + 55 = 0$. Find all the roots.

8. Let $z = a + bi$, where a and b are real numbers. If $\dfrac{z}{z^*} = c + di$, where c and d are real, prove that $c^2 + d^2 = 1$.

9. Prove that, for any complex number z, $zz^* = (\operatorname{Re} z)^2 + (\operatorname{Im} z)^2$.

10. If $z = a + bi$, where a and b are real, use the binomial theorem to find the real and imaginary parts of z^5 and $(z*)^5$.

10.4 Geometrical representations

There are two ways of thinking geometrically about positive and negative numbers, as translations of a line or as points on a line.

A business which loses £500 in April and then gains £1,200 in May has over the two months a net gain of £700. You could write this as $(-500) + (+1200) = (+700)$, and represent it by a diagram like Fig. 10.1. It makes no difference whether it started with its bank account in credit or with an overdraft; the diagram merely shows by how much the bank balance changes.

Fig. 10.1

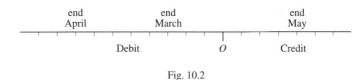

Fig. 10.2

If in fact the business had an overdraft of £300 at the beginning of April, there would be an overdraft of £800 at the end of April, and a credit balance of £400 at the end of May. You could represent the bank balance by a diagram like Fig. 10.2, in which each number is associated with a point on the line and overdrafts are treated as negative.

Similarly there are two ways of representing complex numbers, but now you need a plane rather than a line. The number $s = a + b\,\mathrm{i}$ can be shown either as a translation of the plane, a units in the x-direction and b in the y-direction (see Fig. 10.3), or as the point S with coordinates (a, b) (Fig. 10.4).

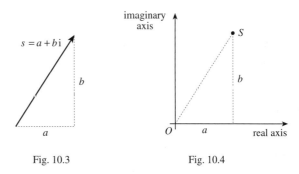

Fig. 10.3   Fig. 10.4

The second of these representations is called an **Argand diagram**, named after John-Robert Argand (1768–1822), a Parisian bookkeeper and mathematician. The axes are often called the **real axis** and the **imaginary axis**; these contain all the points representing real numbers and imaginary numbers respectively. Points representing conjugate pairs $a \pm b\,\mathrm{i}$ are reflections of each other in the real axis.

Example 10.4.1

Show in an Argand diagram the roots of
(a) $z^4 + 4 = 0$,   (b) $z^5 - 6z^3 - 2z^2 + 17z - 10 = 0$.

These are the equations in Examples 10.3.2 and 10.3.3, and the corresponding diagrams are Figs. 10.5 and 10.6. The symmetry of both diagrams about the real axis shows geometrically the property that the non-real roots occur in conjugate pairs.

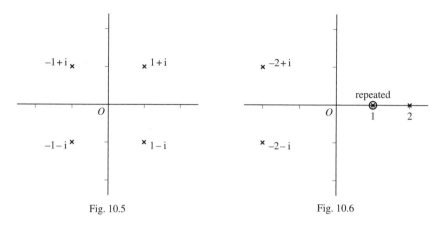

Fig. 10.5   Fig. 10.6

You have seen diagrams like Fig. 10.3 and Fig. 10.4 before. Complex numbers are represented just like vectors in two dimensions.

You can refresh your memory of adding vectors from P3 Sections 5.2 to 5.5. The equivalent operation with complex numbers is illustrated in Figs. 10.7 and 10.8.

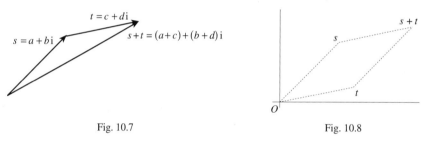

Fig. 10.7   Fig. 10.8

Complex numbers, as translations, are added by a triangle rule; in an Argand diagram you use a parallelogram rule.

For subtraction, it is enough to note that $z = t - s \iff s + z = t$. This is shown geometrically in Figs. 10.9 and 10.10.

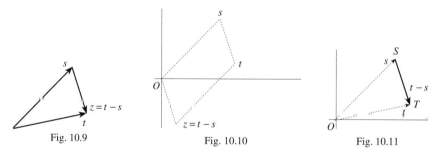

Fig. 10.9   Fig. 10.10   Fig. 10.11

You need to be able to switch between these two pictures of complex numbers. The link between them is the idea of a position vector. In an Argand diagram it doesn't matter whether you think of the complex number s as represented by the point S or by the translation $\overrightarrow{OS}$; and, as translations, $\overrightarrow{OS} + \overrightarrow{ST} = \overrightarrow{OT}$ (see Fig. 10.11). So the translation $\overrightarrow{ST}$ represents the complex number $t - s$, where S and T are the points representing the complex numbers s and t in an Argand diagram.

10.5 The modulus

In Fig. 10.3 the distance covered by the translation $s = a + b\,\text{i}$ is $\sqrt{a^2 + b^2}$. In an Argand diagram (Fig. 10.4) this is the distance of the point S from O. This is called the **modulus** of s, and is denoted by $|s|$.

You have, of course, met this notation before for the modulus of a real number. But there is no danger of confusion; if s is the real number $a + 0\,\text{i}$, then $|s|$ is $\sqrt{a^2 + 0^2} = \sqrt{a^2}$, which is $|a|$ as defined for the real number a (see P2 Section 9.7). So the modulus of a complex number is just a generalisation of the modulus you used previously.

But beware! If s is complex, then $|s|$ does not equal $\sqrt{s^2}$.

In fact, you have met the expression $a^2 + b^2$ already, as $(a + b\,\text{i})(a - b\,\text{i})$, or ss^*. So the correct generalisation of $|a| = \sqrt{a^2}$ is $|s| = \sqrt{ss^*}$. (Notice that, if a is real, then $a^* = a$, so that $a^2 = aa^*$. Thus the rule $|s| = \sqrt{ss^*}$ holds whether s is real or complex.)

You can use the modulus and an Argand diagram to link complex numbers with coordinate geometry. For example, in Fig. 10.11, if $s = a + b\,\text{i}$ and $t = c + d\,\text{i}$, then

$$\text{distance } ST = |t - s| = \sqrt{(t - s)(t - s)^*}$$
$$= \sqrt{((c - a) + (d - b)\,\text{i})((c - a) - (d - b)\,\text{i})}$$
$$= \sqrt{(c - a)^2 + (d - b)^2},$$

which is the familiar expression for the distance between the points (a, b) and (c, d).

Example 10.5.1

In an Argand diagram, points S and T represent 4 and $2\,\text{i}$ respectively (see Fig. 10.12). Identify the points P such that $PS < PT$.

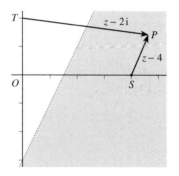

Fig. 10.12

Let P represent a complex number $z = x + y\,\text{i}$. The lengths PS and PT are given by $PS = |z - 4|$ and $PT = |z - 2\,\text{i}|$.

Then
$$PS < PT \iff |z - 4| < |z - 2\,\text{i}|$$
$$\iff |z - 4|^2 < |z - 2\,\text{i}|^2$$
$$\iff (z - 4)(z^* - 4^*) < (z - 2\,\text{i})(z^* - (2\,\text{i})^*)$$
$$\iff (z - 4)(z^* - 4) < (z - 2\,\text{i})(z^* + 2\,\text{i})$$
$$\iff zz^* - 4z - 4z^* + 16 < zz^* + 2\,\text{i}z - 2\,\text{i}z^* + 4$$
$$\iff 4(z + z^*) + 2\,\text{i}(z - z^*) > 12.$$

You can put this into cartesian form by using the relations $z + z^* = 2x$ and $z - z^* = 2y\,\text{i}$. Then

$$PS < PT \quad \Leftrightarrow \quad 8x + 2\,\mathrm{i}(2y\,\mathrm{i}) > 12$$
$$\Leftrightarrow \quad 8x - 4y > 12 \quad \Leftrightarrow \quad 2x - y > 3.$$

The line $2x - y = 3$ is the perpendicular bisector of ST, which cuts the axes at $\left(\frac{3}{2}, 0\right)$ and $(0, -3)$; as complex numbers, these are the points $\frac{3}{2}$ and $-3\,\mathrm{i}$. You can check that these points are equidistant from the points 4 and $2\,\mathrm{i}$; that is,
$$\left|\tfrac{3}{2} - 4\right| = \left|\tfrac{3}{2} - 2\,\mathrm{i}\right| \text{ and } |-3\,\mathrm{i} - 4| = |-3\,\mathrm{i} - 2\,\mathrm{i}|.$$

In examples like this, try to keep the algebra in complex number form as long as you can, before introducing x and y.

Example 10.5.2

In an Argand diagram the point S represents 3 (see Fig. 10.13). Show that the points such that $OP = 2SP$ lie on a circle.

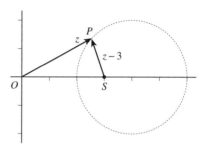

Fig. 10.13

If P represents z,

$$OP = 2SP \quad \Leftrightarrow \quad |z| = 2|z - 3|$$
$$\Leftrightarrow \quad |z|^2 = 4|z - 3|^2$$
$$\Leftrightarrow \quad zz^* = 4(z - 3)(z^* - 3^*)$$
$$\Leftrightarrow \quad zz^* = 4(z - 3)(z^* - 3)$$
$$\Leftrightarrow \quad zz^* = 4(zz^* - 3z - 3z^* + 9)$$
$$\Leftrightarrow \quad 3zz^* - 12z - 12z^* + 36 = 0$$
$$\Leftrightarrow \quad zz^* - 4z - 4z^* + 12 = 0.$$

You can now untangle this by a method similar to the completed square method for quadratics. Notice that

$$|z - 4|^2 = (z - 4)(z^* - 4) = zz^* - 4z - 4z^* + 16,$$

so that

$$OP = 2SP \quad \Leftrightarrow \quad zz^* - 4z - 4z^* + 16 = 4$$
$$\Leftrightarrow \quad |z - 4|^2 = 4 \quad \Leftrightarrow \quad |z - 4| = 2.$$

The interpretation of this last equation is that the distance of P from 4 is equal to 2. That is, P lies on a circle with centre 4 and radius 2.

Other important properties of the modulus are:

$$|st| = |s||t|, \quad \left|\frac{s}{t}\right| = \frac{|s|}{|t|}, \quad |s + t| \leqslant |s| + |t|, \quad |s - t| \geqslant |s| - |t|.$$

The first two of these are easy to prove algebraically:

$$|st|^2 = (st)(st)^* = (st)(s^* t^*) = (ss^*)(tt^*) = |s|^2 |t|^2,$$

$$\left|\frac{s}{t}\right|^2 = \left(\frac{s}{t}\right)\left(\frac{s}{t}\right)^* = \left(\frac{s}{t}\right)\left(\frac{s^*}{t^*}\right) = \frac{ss^*}{tt^*} = \frac{|s|^2}{|t|^2},$$

and the results follow by taking the square roots.

Figs. 10.7 and 10.9 show that the inequalities for the sum and difference are equivalent to the geometrical theorem that the sum of two sides of a triangle is greater than the third side. They are not so easy to prove algebraically. (See Exercise 10C Questions 10 and 12.)

Example 10.5.3

S and T are the points representing -4 and 4 in an Argand diagram. A point P moves so that $SP + TP = 10$ (see Fig. 10.14). Prove that $3 \leqslant OP \leqslant 5$.

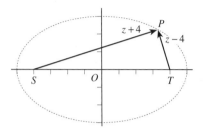

Fig. 10.14

If P represents z, then
$SP + TP = |z+4| + |z-4|$, so that z satisfies
$|z+4| + |z-4| = 10$.

Then

$$OP = |z| = \left|\tfrac{1}{2}\big((z+4)+(z-4)\big)\right|$$
$$\leqslant \tfrac{1}{2}\big(|z+4|+|z-4|\big) \qquad \text{(using } |s+t| \leqslant |s|+|t|\text{)}$$
$$= \tfrac{1}{2} \times 10 = 5.$$

Also, $\big(|z+4|+|z-4|\big)^2 = 100$, and $\big(|z+4|-|z-4|\big)^2 \geqslant 0$; adding,

$$\big(|z+4|+|z-4|\big)^2 + \big(|z+4|-|z-4|\big)^2 \geqslant 100,$$
$$2|z+4|^2 + 2|z-4|^2 \geqslant 100,$$
$$(z+4)(z^*+4^*) + (z-4)(z^*-4^*) \geqslant 50,$$
$$2zz^* + 32 \geqslant 50, \quad \text{which is} \quad |z|^2 \geqslant 9; \quad \text{that is,} \quad OP \geqslant 3.$$

You probably know that the property $SP + TP = 10$ defines an ellipse. OP takes its greatest value of 5 when S, T and P are in a straight line, at the ends of the major axis; and it takes its smallest value of 3 when $|z+4| = |z-4|$, that is when $SP = TP$, at the ends of the minor axis.

Exercise 10C

1 Draw (i) vector diagrams, (ii) Argand diagrams to represent the following relationships.

    (a) $(3+i)+(-1+2i)=(2+3i)$ (b) $(1+4i)-(3i)=(1+i)$

2 Draw Argand diagrams to illustrate the following properties of complex numbers.

    (a) $z+z^* = 2\,\mathrm{Re}\,z$ (b) $z-z^* = 2i\,\mathrm{Im}\,z$ (c) $(s+t)^* = s^*+t^*$

    (d) $\mathrm{Re}\,z \leqslant |z| \leqslant \mathrm{Re}\,z + \mathrm{Im}\,z$ (e) $(kz)^* = kz^*$, where k is a real number

3 Draw Argand diagrams showing the roots of the following equations.

    (a) $z^4 - 1 = 0$ (b) $z^3 + 1 = 0$ (c) $z^3 + 6z + 20 = 0$

    (d) $z^4 + 4z^3 + 4z^2 - 9 = 0$ (e) $z^4 + z^3 + 5z^2 + 4z + 4 = 0$

4 Represent the roots of the equation $z^4 - z^3 + z - 1 = 0$ in an Argand diagram, and show that they all have the same modulus.

5 Identify in an Argand diagram the points corresponding to the following equations.

    (a) $|z| = 5$ (b) $\operatorname{Re} z = 3$ (c) $z + z^* = 6$

    (d) $z - z^* = 2i$ (e) $|z - 2| = 2$ (f) $|z - 4| = |z|$

    (g) $|z + 2i| = |z + 4|$ (h) $|z + 4| = 3|z|$ (i) $1 + \operatorname{Re} z = |z - 1|$

6 Identify in an Argand diagram the points corresponding to the following inequalities.

    (a) $|z| > 2$ (b) $|z - 3i| \leqslant 1$ (c) $|z + 1| \leqslant |z - i|$ (d) $|z - 3| > 2|z|$

7 P is a point in an Argand diagram corresponding to a complex number z, and $|z - 5| + |z + 5| = 26$. Prove that $12 \leqslant OP \leqslant 13$, and draw a diagram to illustrate this result.

8 P is a point in an Argand diagram corresponding to a complex number z which satisfies the equation $|4 + z| - |4 - z| = 6$. Prove that $|4 + z|^2 - |4 - z|^2 \geqslant 48$, and deduce that $\operatorname{Re} z \geqslant 3$. Draw a diagram to illustrate this result.

9 Use mathematical induction to prove that, if z is a complex number and n is a positive integer, $|z^n| = |z|^n$.

    Show that all the roots of the equation $z^n + a^n = 0$, where a is a positive real number, have modulus a.

10 Assuming that the inequality $|s + t| \leqslant |s| + |t|$ holds for any two complex numbers s and t, prove that $|z - w| \geqslant |z| - |w|$ holds for any two complex numbers z and w.

11 If s and t are two complex numbers, prove the following.

    (a) $|s + t|^2 = |s|^2 + |t|^2 + (st^* + s^*t)$

    (b) $|s - t|^2 = |s|^2 + |t|^2 - (st^* + s^*t)$

    (c) $|s + t|^2 + |s - t|^2 = 2|s|^2 + 2|t|^2$

    Interpret the result of part (c) as a geometrical theorem.

12 If s and t are two complex numbers, prove the following.

    (a) $(s^*t)^* = st^*$.

    (b) $st^* + s^*t$ is a real number, and $st^* - s^*t$ is an imaginary number.

    (c) $(st^* + s^*t)^2 - (st^* - s^*t)^2 = (2|st|)^2$.

    (d) $(|s| + |t|)^2 - |s + t|^2 = 2|st| - (st^* + s^*t)$.

    Use these results to deduce that $|s + t| \leqslant |s| + |t|$.

10.6 Equations with complex coefficients

Complex numbers were introduced so that all real numbers should have square roots. But do complex numbers themselves have square roots?

Example 10.6.1

Find the square roots of   (a) $8i$,   (b) $3 - 4i$.

The problem is to find real numbers a and b such that $(a + bi)^2$ is equal to (a) $8i$ and (b) $3 - 4i$. To do this, note that $(a + bi)^2 = (a^2 - b^2) + 2abi$ and remember that, for two complex numbers to be equal, their real and imaginary parts must be equal.

(a) If $(a + bi)^2 = 8i$, then $a^2 - b^2 = 0$ and $2ab = 8$. Therefore $b = \dfrac{4}{a}$, and so

$$a^2 - \left(\frac{4}{a}\right)^2 = 0, \text{ or } a^4 = 16.$$ Since a is real, this implies that $a^2 = 4$, $a = \pm 2$.

If $a = 2$, $b = \dfrac{4}{a} = 2$; if $a = -2$, $b = -2$. So $8i$ has two square roots, $2 + 2i$ and $-2 - 2i$.

(b) If $(a + bi)^2 = 3 - 4i$, then $a^2 - b^2 = 3$ and $2ab = -4$. Therefore $b = -\dfrac{2}{a}$, and

so $a^2 - \left(-\dfrac{2}{a}\right)^2 = 3$, or $a^4 - 3a^2 - 4 = 0$.

This is a quadratic equation in a^2, which can be solved by factorising the left side, $(a^2 - 4)(a^2 + 1) = 0$. Since a is real, a^2 cannot equal -1, but for $a^2 = 4$, $a = \pm 2$.

If $a = 2$, $b = -\dfrac{2}{a} = -1$; if $a = -2$, $b = 1$. So $3 - 4i$ has two square roots, $2 - i$ and $-2 + i$.

You can use this method to find the square root of any complex number. The equation for a^2 will always have two roots, one of which is positive, leading to two values of a, and hence two square roots.

You will see also that, if one root is $a + bi$ the other is $-a$ bi, so that the roots can be written as $\pm(a + bi)$. But of course you cannot say that one of the roots is 'positive' and the other 'negative', because these words have no meaning for complex numbers.

In Section 10.3 you saw that complex numbers make it possible to solve any quadratic equation with real coefficients. Now that you can find square roots of complex numbers, you can solve any quadratic equation even if the coefficients are complex numbers.

Example 10.6.2

Solve the quadratic equation $(2-\mathrm{i})z^2+(4+3\mathrm{i})z+(-1+3\mathrm{i})=0$.

Method 1   Using the standard formula with $a=2-\mathrm{i}$, $b=4+3\mathrm{i}$ and $c=-1+3\mathrm{i}$ gives

$$z=\frac{-(4+3\mathrm{i})\pm\sqrt{(4+3\mathrm{i})^2-4\times(2-\mathrm{i})\times(-1+3\mathrm{i})}}{2(2-\mathrm{i})}$$

$$=\frac{-(4+3\mathrm{i})\pm\sqrt{7+24\mathrm{i}-4\times(1+7\mathrm{i})}}{2(2-\mathrm{i})}$$

$$=\frac{-(4+3\mathrm{i})\pm\sqrt{3-4\mathrm{i}}}{2(2-\mathrm{i})}$$

$$=\frac{-(4+3\mathrm{i})\pm(2-\mathrm{i})}{2(2-\mathrm{i})}\qquad\text{(using Example 10.6.1(b))}$$

$$=\frac{-2-4\mathrm{i}}{2(2-\mathrm{i})}\quad\text{or}\quad\frac{-6-2\mathrm{i}}{2(2-\mathrm{i})}$$

$$=\frac{-1-2\mathrm{i}}{2-\mathrm{i}}\quad\text{or}\quad\frac{-3-\mathrm{i}}{2-\mathrm{i}}$$

$$=\frac{(-1-2\mathrm{i})(2+\mathrm{i})}{(2-\mathrm{i})(2+\mathrm{i})}\quad\text{or}\quad\frac{(-3-\mathrm{i})(2+\mathrm{i})}{(2-\mathrm{i})(2+\mathrm{i})}$$

$$=\frac{-5\mathrm{i}}{5}\quad\text{or}\quad\frac{-5-5\mathrm{i}}{5}$$

$$=-\mathrm{i}\quad\text{or}\quad-1-\mathrm{i}.$$

Method 2   You can often reduce the work by first making the coefficient of z^2 real. Multiplying through by $(2-\mathrm{i})*=2+\mathrm{i}$, the equation becomes

$$(2+\mathrm{i})(2-\mathrm{i})z^2+(2+\mathrm{i})(4+3\mathrm{i})z+(2+\mathrm{i})(-1+3\mathrm{i})=0,$$

$$5z^2+(5+10\mathrm{i})z+(-5+5\mathrm{i})=0,$$

$$z^2+(1+2\mathrm{i})z+(-1+\mathrm{i})=0.$$

The standard formula with $a=1$, $b=1+2\mathrm{i}$ and $c=-1+\mathrm{i}$ then gives

$$z=\frac{-(1+2\mathrm{i})\pm\sqrt{(1+2\mathrm{i})^2-4\times1\times(-1+\mathrm{i})}}{2}$$

$$=\frac{-(1+2\mathrm{i})\pm\sqrt{-3+4\mathrm{i}-4(-1+\mathrm{i})}}{2}$$

$$=\frac{-(1+2\mathrm{i})\pm\sqrt{1}}{2}=\frac{-(1+2\mathrm{i})\pm1}{2}$$

$$=\frac{-2\mathrm{i}}{2}\quad\text{or}\quad\frac{-2-2\mathrm{i}}{2}$$

$$=-\mathrm{i}\quad\text{or}\quad-1-\mathrm{i}.$$

It is important to notice that although the quadratic equation has two roots, these are not now conjugate complex numbers. The property in Section 10.3 that the roots occur in conjugate pairs holds only for equations whose coefficients are real.

The fact that, with complex numbers, every quadratic equation has two roots is a particular case of a more general result:

Every polynomial equation of degree n has n roots.

You need to understand that for this to be true, repeated roots have to count more than once. If the polynomial $p(z)$ has a factor $(z-s)^k$ with $k > 1$, then in the equation $p(z) = 0$ the root $z = s$ has to count as k roots. For example, the equation of degree 5 in Example 10.3.3 has only 4 different roots (1, 2, $-2+i$ and $-2-i$) but the repeated root 1 counts twice because $(z-1)^2$ is a factor of $p(z)$.

This remarkable result is one of the main reasons that complex numbers are important. Unfortunately the proof is too difficult to give here.

Exercise 10D

1 Find the square roots of

    (a) $-2i$,   (b) $-3+4i$,   (c) $5+12i$,   (d) $8-6i$.

2 Solve the following quadratic equations.

    (a) $z^2 + z + (1-i) = 0$ (b) $z^2 + (1-i)z + (-6+2i) = 0$

    (c) $z^2 + 4z + (4+2i) = 0$ (d) $(1+i)z^2 + 2iz + 4i = 0$

    (e) $(2-i)z^2 + (3+i)z - 5 = 0$

3 Find the fourth roots of

    (a) -64,   (b) $7+24i$.

    Show your answers on an Argand diagram.

4 If $(x+yi)^3 = 8i$, where x and y are real numbers, prove that either $x = 0$ or $x = \pm\sqrt{3}\,y$. Hence find all the cube roots of $8i$. Show your answers on an Argand diagram.

5 If $(x+yi)^3 = 2-2i$, where x and y are real numbers, prove that
$$x(x^2 - 3y^2) = y(y^2 - 3x^2) = 2.$$

    Show that these equations have one solution in which $x = y$, and hence find one cube root of $2-2i$.

    Find the quadratic equation satisfied by the other cube roots of $2-2i$, and solve it.

    Show all the roots on an Argand diagram.

Miscellaneous exercise 10

1 Given that z is a complex number such that $z + 3z^* = 12 + 8i$, find z.　　(OCR)

2 Given that $3i$ is a root of the equation $3z^3 - 5z^2 + 27z - 45 = 0$, find the other two roots.　　(OCR)

3 Two of the roots of a cubic equation, in which all the coefficients are real, are 2 and $1 + 3i$. State the third root and find the cubic equation.　　(OCR)

4 It is given that $3 - i$ is a root of the quadratic equation $z^2 - (a + bi)z + 4(1 + 3i) = 0$, where a and b are real. In either order,

(a) find the values of a and b,

(b) find the other root of the quadratic equation, given that it is of the form ki, where k is real.　　(OCR)

5 Find the roots of the equation $z^2 = 21 - 20i$.　　(OCR)

6 Verify that $(3 - 2i)^2 = 5 - 12i$. Find the two roots of the equation $(z - i)^2 = 5 - 12i$.　　(OCR)

7 You are given the complex number $w = 1 - i$. Express w^2, w^3 and w^4 in the form $a + bi$.

(a) Given that $w^4 + 3w^3 + pw^2 + qw + 8 = 0$, where p and q are real numbers, find the values of p and q.

(b) Write down two roots of the equation $z^4 + 3z^3 + pz^2 + qz + 8 = 0$, where p and q are the real numbers found in part (a), and hence solve the equation completely.　　(MEI, adapted)

8 Two complex numbers, z and w, satisfy the inequalities $|z - 3 - 2i| \leqslant 2$ and $|w - 7 - 5i| \leqslant 1$. By drawing an Argand diagram, find the least possible value of $|z - w|$.　　(OCR)

9 A sequence of complex numbers z_1, z_2, z_3, ... is defined by $z_1 = 1 - 2i$ and
$$z_{n+1} = \frac{z_n^2 + 2z_n + 5n^2}{2n}$$
for $n \geqslant 1$. Show that $z_2 = 2z_1$ and prove by induction that $z_n = n - 2ni$.　　(MEI)

10 (a) The complex number z satisfies the equation $\left(z + \dfrac{2i}{k} \right)\left(\dfrac{1}{z} - \dfrac{2i}{k} \right) = 1$, where k is a positive real number. Obtain a quadratic equation for z, and show that its solution can be expressed in the form $ikz = a \pm \sqrt{bk^2 + ck + d}$ for suitable real numbers a, b, c, d. Show that z is purely imaginary when $k \leqslant 1$.

(b) A second complex number α is defined in terms of z by $\alpha = 1 + \dfrac{2i}{kz}$. What can be said about α when $k \leqslant 1$? Show that $|\alpha| = 1$ when $k \geqslant 1$.

(c) A third complex number β is defined by $\dfrac{1}{\beta} = 1 - \dfrac{i}{k}$. By finding the real and imaginary parts of $\beta - \frac{1}{2}ki$, show that β lies on a circle with centre $\frac{1}{2}ki$ and radius $\frac{1}{2}k$.　　(OCR)

11 Complex numbers in polar form

New insights about complex numbers come by expressing them in polar coordinate form. When you have completed this chapter, you should

- know the meaning of the argument of a complex number
- be able to multiply and divide complex numbers in modulus-argument form
- know how to represent multiplication and division geometrically
- be able to solve geometrical problems involving angles using complex numbers
- be able to write square roots in modulus-argument form
- know that complex numbers can be written as exponentials.

11.1 Modulus and argument

If s and t are complex numbers, the sum $s+t$ can be shown geometrically by the triangle rule for adding translations, or by the parallelogram rule in an Argand diagram. But you do not yet have a way of representing multiplication.

Replace x and y in the complex number $z = x + yi$ by $r\cos\theta$ and $r\sin\theta$, where (r,θ) are the polar coordinates of the point which represents z in an Argand diagram. Then

$$z = r\cos\theta + ir\sin\theta = r(\cos\theta + i\sin\theta).$$

To make the definitions precise, you need conventions restricting the values of r and θ. In an Argand diagram the radius vector is always taken to be positive (or zero if $z = 0$). This means that r is the same as the modulus $|z|$, as defined in Section 10.5.

The angle θ then has to be restricted within an interval of width 2π, and this is taken to be $-\pi < \theta \leqslant \pi$. This angle is called the **argument** of z, and denoted by $\arg z$. (The argument is not defined if $z = 0$.)

> The complex number $z \ (\neq 0)$ can be written in **modulus-argument form** as $z = r(\cos\theta + i\sin\theta)$, where $r = |z| > 0$ is the modulus and $\theta = \arg z$, with $-\pi < \theta \leqslant \pi$, is the argument.

Example 11.1.1
If $\arg z = \frac{1}{4}\pi$ and $\arg(z-3) = \frac{1}{2}\pi$, find $\arg(z-6i)$.

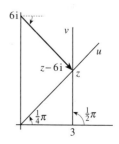

Fig. 11.1

This is best done with an Argand diagram (Fig. 11.1). Since $\arg z = \frac{1}{4}\pi$, the point z lies on the half-line u starting at O at an angle $\frac{1}{4}\pi$ to the real axis. (Points on the other half of the line, in the third quadrant, have $\arg z = -\frac{3}{4}\pi$.)

As $\arg(z-3) = \frac{1}{2}\pi$, the translation from 3 to z makes an angle $\frac{1}{2}\pi$ with the real axis, so the point z lies on the half-line v in the direction of the imaginary axis.

These two half-lines meet at $z = 3+3i$, so $\arg(z-6i) = \arg(3-3i)$. The translation $3-3i$ is at an angle $\frac{1}{4}\pi$ with the real axis in the clockwise sense, so that $\arg(z-6i) = -\frac{1}{4}\pi$.

Exercise 11A

1 Show these numbers on an Argand diagram, and write them in the form $a+bi$. Where appropriate leave surds in your answers, or give answers correct to 2 decimal places.

   (a) $2\left(\cos\frac{1}{3}\pi + i\sin\frac{1}{3}\pi\right)$ (b) $10\left(\cos\frac{3}{4}\pi + i\sin\frac{3}{4}\pi\right)$ (c) $5\left(\cos\left(-\frac{1}{2}\pi\right) + i\sin\left(-\frac{1}{2}\pi\right)\right)$

   (d) $3(\cos\pi + i\sin\pi)$ (e) $10(\cos 2 + i\sin 2)$ (f) $\cos(-3) + i\sin(-3)$

2 Write these complex numbers in modulus-argument form. Where appropriate express the argument as a rational multiple of π, otherwise give the modulus and argument correct to 2 decimal places.

   (a) $1+2i$ (b) $3-4i$ (c) $-5+6i$ (d) $-7-8i$

   (e) 1 (f) $2i$ (g) -3 (h) $-4i$

   (i) $\sqrt{2}-\sqrt{2}i$ (j) $-1+\sqrt{3}i$

3 Show in an Argand diagram the sets of points satisfying the following equations.

   (a) $\arg z = \frac{1}{5}\pi$ (b) $\arg z = -\frac{2}{3}\pi$ (c) $\arg z = \pi$

   (d) $\arg(z-2) = \frac{1}{2}\pi$ (e) $\arg(2z-1) = 0$ (f) $\arg(z+i) = \pi$

   (g) $\arg(z-1-2i) = \frac{3}{4}\pi$ (h) $\arg(z+1-i) = -\frac{2}{5}\pi$

4 Show in an Argand diagram the sets of points satisfying the following inequalities. Use a solid line to show boundary points which are included, and a dotted line for boundary points which are not included.

   (a) $0 < \arg z < \frac{1}{6}\pi$ (b) $\frac{1}{2}\pi \leqslant \arg z \leqslant \pi$

   (c) $\frac{1}{3}\pi < \arg(z-1) \leqslant \frac{2}{3}\pi$ (d) $-\frac{1}{4}\pi < \arg(z+1-i) < \frac{1}{4}\pi$

5 Use an Argand diagram to find, in the form $a+bi$, the complex number which satisfies the following pairs of equations.

   (a) $\arg(z+2) = \frac{1}{2}\pi$, $\arg z = \frac{2}{3}\pi$ (b) $\arg(z+1) = \frac{1}{4}\pi$, $\arg(z-3) = \frac{3}{4}\pi$

   (c) $\arg(z-3) = -\frac{3}{4}\pi$, $\arg(z+3) = -\frac{1}{2}\pi$ (d) $\arg(z+2i) = \frac{1}{6}\pi$, $\arg(z-2i) = -\frac{1}{3}\pi$

   (e) $\arg(z-2-3i) = -\frac{5}{6}\pi$, $\arg(z-2+i) = \frac{5}{6}\pi$ (f) $\arg z = \frac{7}{12}\pi$, $\arg(z-2-2i) = \frac{11}{12}\pi$

6 Use an Argand diagram to find, in the form $a+bi$, the complex number(s) satisfying the following pairs of equations.

   (a) $\arg z = \frac{1}{6}\pi$, $|z| = 2$ (b) $\arg(z-3) = \frac{1}{2}\pi$, $|z| = 5$

   (c) $\arg(z-4i) = \pi$, $|z+6| = 5$ (d) $\arg(z-2) = \frac{3}{4}\pi$, $|z+2| = 3$

7 If $\arg\left(z-\frac{1}{2}\right) = \frac{1}{5}\pi$, what is $\arg(2z-1)$?

8 If $\arg\left(\frac{1}{3}-z\right) = \frac{1}{6}\pi$, what is $\arg(3z-1)$?

9 If $\arg(z-1) = \frac{1}{3}\pi$ and $\arg(z-i) = \frac{1}{6}\pi$, what is $\arg z$?

10 If $\arg(z+1) = \frac{1}{6}\pi$ and $\arg(z-1) = \frac{2}{3}\pi$, what is $\arg z$?

11 If $\arg(z+\mathrm{i}) = 0$ and $\arg(z-\mathrm{i}) = -\frac{1}{4}\pi$, what is $|z|$?

12 If $\arg(z-2) = \frac{2}{3}\pi$ and $|z| = 2$, what is $\arg z$?

11.2 Multiplication and division

Suppose that s has modulus p and argument α, and t has modulus q and argument β. Then

$$st = p(\cos\alpha + \mathrm{i}\sin\alpha) \times q(\cos\beta + \mathrm{i}\sin\beta)$$
$$= pq(\cos\alpha\cos\beta + \mathrm{i}\sin\alpha\cos\beta + \mathrm{i}\cos\alpha\sin\beta + \mathrm{i}^2\sin\alpha\sin\beta)$$
$$= pq((\cos\alpha\cos\beta - \sin\alpha\sin\beta) + \mathrm{i}(\sin\alpha\cos\beta + \cos\alpha\sin\beta)).$$

The expressions inside the brackets are $\cos(\alpha+\beta)$ and $\sin(\alpha+\beta)$. Therefore

$$st = pq(\cos(\alpha+\beta) + \mathrm{i}\sin(\alpha+\beta)).$$

Therefore pq (which is positive, since $p > 0$ and $q > 0$) is the modulus of st. It may also be true that $\alpha+\beta$ is the argument of st; but if addition takes $\alpha+\beta$ outside the interval $-\pi < \theta \leqslant \pi$, then you must adjust $\alpha+\beta$ by 2π to bring it inside the interval.

Example 11.2.1

Show $s = -\sqrt{3} + \mathrm{i}$ and $t = \sqrt{2} + \sqrt{2}\,\mathrm{i}$ as points in an Argand diagram. Find st and $\dfrac{s}{t}$ in modulus-argument form, and put them into the diagram.

You will recognise in Fig. 11.2 triangles with angles of $\frac{1}{6}\pi$ and $\frac{1}{4}\pi$, so that

s has modulus $p = 2$ and argument $\alpha = \frac{5}{6}\pi$,

t has modulus $q = 2$ and argument $\beta = \frac{1}{4}\pi$.

It follows that st has modulus $pq = 4$.

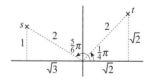

Fig. 11.2

Since $\alpha + \beta = \frac{5}{6}\pi + \frac{1}{4}\pi = \frac{13}{12}\pi > \pi$, the argument of st must be adjusted to $\frac{13}{12}\pi - 2\pi = -\frac{11}{12}\pi$.

Let $w = \dfrac{s}{t}$ have modulus m and argument γ. Since $tw = s$, equating moduli gives $qm = p$, so that $m = \dfrac{p}{q} = \dfrac{2}{2} = 1$. The argument of tw is $\beta + \gamma = \frac{1}{4}\pi + \gamma$, which (adjusted by 2π if necessary) must equal $\frac{5}{6}\pi$. In this case no adjustment is needed, since $\frac{5}{6}\pi - \frac{1}{4}\pi = \frac{7}{12}\pi$ lies inside the interval $-\pi < \theta \leqslant \pi$.

Therefore

$$st = 4\left(\cos\left(-\tfrac{11}{12}\pi\right) + i\sin\left(-\tfrac{11}{12}\pi\right)\right) \quad \text{and} \quad \frac{s}{t} = \cos\tfrac{7}{12}\pi + i\sin\tfrac{7}{12}\pi.$$

The corresponding points are shown on an Argand diagram in Fig. 11.3.

You will notice that, since complex numbers are multiplied by multiplying the moduli and adding the arguments, they are divided by dividing the moduli and subtracting the arguments.

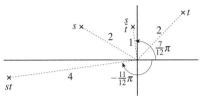

Fig. 11.3

The rules for multiplication and division in modulus-argument form are

$$|st| = |s||t|, \quad \arg(st) = \arg s + \arg t + k(2\pi),$$

$$\left|\frac{s}{t}\right| = \frac{|s|}{|t|}, \quad \arg\left(\frac{s}{t}\right) = \arg s - \arg t + k(2\pi),$$

where in each case the number k $(= -1, 0 \text{ or } 1)$ is chosen to ensure that the argument lies in the interval $-\pi < \theta \leqslant \pi$.

It would be a good idea to get used to these rules by working some of the earlier questions in Exercise 11B before going on to the next example.

Example 11.2.2
If z has modulus 1 and argument θ, where $0 < \theta < \pi$, find the modulus and argument
of   (a) $z+1$,   (b) $z-1$,   (c) $\dfrac{z-1}{z+1}$.

Since $z = \cos\theta + i\sin\theta$,

$$z+1 = \cos\theta + i\sin\theta + 1 = (1+\cos\theta) + i\sin\theta$$

and $z-1 = \cos\theta + i\sin\theta - 1 = -(1-\cos\theta) + i\sin\theta$.

These expressions can be simplified by using the identities $1 + \cos 2A \equiv 2\cos^2 A$ and $1 - \cos 2A \equiv 2\sin^2 A$ with θ in place of $2A$, that is $A = \tfrac{1}{2}\theta$. You will then also need to express $\sin\theta$ in terms of $\tfrac{1}{2}\theta$, using $\sin 2A = 2\sin A\cos A$.

(a) $z+1 = (1+\cos\theta) + i\sin\theta = 2\cos^2\tfrac{1}{2}\theta + 2i\sin\tfrac{1}{2}\theta\cos\tfrac{1}{2}\theta$

$$= 2\cos\tfrac{1}{2}\theta\left(\cos\tfrac{1}{2}\theta + i\sin\tfrac{1}{2}\theta\right).$$

This suggests that $|z+1| = 2\cos\tfrac{1}{2}\theta$ and $\arg(z+1) = \tfrac{1}{2}\theta$.

To be sure, you need to check that $2\cos\tfrac{1}{2}\theta > 0$ and that $-\pi < \tfrac{1}{2}\theta \leqslant \pi$. Since you are given that $0 < \theta < \pi$, so that $0 < \tfrac{1}{2}\theta < \tfrac{1}{2}\pi$, these inequalities are satisfied.

(b) $z - 1 = -(1 - \cos\theta) + i\sin\theta = -2\sin^2\frac{1}{2}\theta + 2i\sin\frac{1}{2}\theta\cos\frac{1}{2}\theta$

$\qquad = 2\sin\frac{1}{2}\theta\left(-\sin\frac{1}{2}\theta + i\cos\frac{1}{2}\theta\right).$

To get this into the standard modulus-argument form, notice that
$-\sin\frac{1}{2}\theta + i\cos\frac{1}{2}\theta$ can be written as $\left(\cos\frac{1}{2}\theta + i\sin\frac{1}{2}\theta\right) \times i.$

Since i has modulus 1 and argument $\frac{1}{2}\pi$, this expression is

$$\left(\cos\frac{1}{2}\theta + i\sin\frac{1}{2}\theta\right)\left(\cos\frac{1}{2}\pi + i\sin\frac{1}{2}\pi\right) = \left(\cos\left(\frac{1}{2}\theta + \frac{1}{2}\pi\right) + i\sin\left(\frac{1}{2}\theta + \frac{1}{2}\pi\right)\right)$$

so that

$$z - 1 = 2\sin\frac{1}{2}\theta\left(\cos\left(\frac{1}{2}\theta + \frac{1}{2}\pi\right) + i\sin\left(\frac{1}{2}\theta + \frac{1}{2}\pi\right)\right).$$

You again need to check that $2\sin\frac{1}{2}\theta > 0$ and that $-\pi < \frac{1}{2}\theta + \frac{1}{2}\pi \leq \pi$. Since
$0 < \theta < \pi$, these inequalities are certainly satisfied. It follows that

$$|z - 1| = 2\sin\frac{1}{2}\theta \quad \text{and} \quad \arg(z - 1) = \frac{1}{2}\pi + \frac{1}{2}\theta.$$

(c) The rules for division give

$$\left|\frac{z-1}{z+1}\right| = \frac{|z-1|}{|z+1|} = \frac{2\sin\frac{1}{2}\theta}{2\cos\frac{1}{2}\theta} = \tan\frac{1}{2}\theta$$

and $\arg\left(\dfrac{z-1}{z+1}\right) = \arg(z-1) - \arg(z+1) = \left(\frac{1}{2}\theta + \frac{1}{2}\pi\right) - \frac{1}{2}\theta = \frac{1}{2}\pi.$

This is shown in an Argand diagram in
Fig. 11.4. Since the modulus of z is 1
and $0 < \theta < \pi$, the point z lies on the
upper half of the unit circle, with centre
O and radius 1.

The points A, B and P represent the
complex numbers -1, 1 and z
respectively.

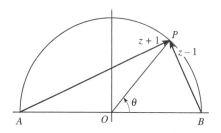

Fig. 11.4

The translation $\overrightarrow{BP}$ then represents $z - 1$;
and, writing $z + 1$ as $z - (-1)$, the translation $\overrightarrow{AP}$ represents $z + 1$. Since the
triangles OAP and OBP are isosceles, it is easy to see that the arguments of $z + 1$
and $z - 1$ are $\frac{1}{2}\theta$ and $\frac{1}{2}\pi + \frac{1}{2}\theta$ respectively. The argument of $\dfrac{z-1}{z+1}$ is the angle
you have to turn through to get from $\overrightarrow{AP}$ to $\overrightarrow{BP}$, that is $\frac{1}{2}\pi$ anticlockwise, or $+\frac{1}{2}\pi$.

Also the moduli of $z + 1$ and $z - 1$ are the lengths AP and BP. From the triangle
ABP, in which $AB = 2$ and angle $BAP = \frac{1}{2}\theta$,

$$AP = 2\cos\frac{1}{2}\theta \quad \text{and} \quad BP = 2\sin\frac{1}{2}\theta.$$

Exercise 11B

1 If $s = 2\left(\cos\frac{1}{3}\pi + i\sin\frac{1}{3}\pi\right)$, $t = \cos\frac{1}{4}\pi + i\sin\frac{1}{4}\pi$ and $u = 4\left(\cos\left(-\frac{5}{6}\pi\right) + i\sin\left(-\frac{5}{6}\pi\right)\right)$, write
the following in modulus-argument form.

   (a) st (b) $\dfrac{s}{t}$ (c) $\dfrac{t}{s}$ (d) su

   (e) $\dfrac{u}{s}$ (f) $\dfrac{t}{u}$ (g) s^2 (h) u^2

   (i) st^2u (j) $\dfrac{2s}{tu}$ (k) s^* (l) st^*

   (m) ts^* (n) $\dfrac{u^*}{t^2}$ (o) $\dfrac{1}{t}$ (p) $\dfrac{2}{s}$

   (q) $\dfrac{4i}{u^*}$ (r) $\dfrac{s^3}{u}$

2 If $s = 3\left(\cos\frac{1}{5}\pi + i\sin\frac{1}{5}\pi\right)$ and if $s^2t = 18\left(\cos\left(-\frac{4}{5}\pi\right) + i\sin\left(-\frac{4}{5}\pi\right)\right)$, express t in modulus-
argument form.

3 If $s = \cos\frac{2}{3}\pi + i\sin\frac{2}{3}\pi$ and $t = \cos\frac{1}{4}\pi + i\sin\frac{1}{4}\pi$, show in an Argand diagram

   (a) s,   (b) st,   (c) st^2,

   (d) st^3,   (e) $\dfrac{s}{t}$,   (f) $\dfrac{s}{t^2}$.

4 Repeat Question 3 with $s = 4\left(\cos\frac{2}{3}\pi + i\sin\frac{2}{3}\pi\right)$ and $t = 2\left(\cos\frac{1}{4}\pi + i\sin\frac{1}{4}\pi\right)$.

5 Give the answers to the following questions in modulus-argument form.

   (a) If $s = \cos\theta + i\sin\theta$, express s^* in terms of θ.

   (b) If $s = \cos\theta + i\sin\theta$, express $\dfrac{1}{s}$ in terms of θ.

   (c) If $t = r(\cos\theta + i\sin\theta)$, express t^* in terms of r and θ.

   (d) If $t = r(\cos\theta + i\sin\theta)$, express $\dfrac{1}{t}$ in terms of r and θ.

6 Write $1 + \sqrt{3}\,i$ and $1 - i$ in modulus-argument form. Hence express $\dfrac{\left(1 + \sqrt{3}\,i\right)^4}{(1 - i)^6}$ in the form
$a + bi$.

7 By converting into and out of modulus-argument form, evaluate the following with the aid
of a calculator. Use the binomial theorem to check your answers.

   (a) $(1 + 2i)^7$ (b) $(3i - 2)^5$ (c) $(3 - i)^{-8}$

8 Show in an Argand diagram the points representing the complex numbers i, $-i$ and $\sqrt{3}$.
Hence write down the values of

   (a) $\arg\left(\sqrt{3} - i\right)$,   (b) $\arg\left(\sqrt{3} + i\right)$,   (c) $\arg\dfrac{\sqrt{3} + i}{\sqrt{3} - i}$,   (d) $\arg\dfrac{2i}{\sqrt{3} + i}$.

9 A and B are points in an Argand diagram representing the complex numbers 1 and i.
P is a point on the circle having AB as a diameter. If P represents the complex number z,
find the value of $\arg \dfrac{z-1}{z-i}$ if P is in

    (a) the first quadrant,   (b) the second quadrant,   (c) the fourth quadrant.

10 Identify the set of points in an Argand diagram for which $\arg \dfrac{z-3}{z-4i} = \tfrac{1}{2}\pi$.

11 If A and B represent complex numbers a and b in an Argand diagram, identify the set of
points for which $\arg \dfrac{z-a}{z-b} = \pi$.

12 Identify the set of points in an Argand diagram for which $\arg \dfrac{z-i}{z+i} = \tfrac{1}{4}\pi$.

13 Find the modulus and argument of $1 + i\tan\theta$ in the cases

    (a) $0 < \theta < \tfrac{1}{2}\pi$,   (b) $\tfrac{1}{2}\pi < \theta < \pi$,   (c) $\pi < \theta < \tfrac{3}{2}\pi$,   (d) $\tfrac{3}{2}\pi < \theta < 2\pi$.

14 If $z = \cos 2\theta + i\sin 2\theta$, find the modulus and argument of $1 - z$ in the cases

    (a) $0 < \theta < \pi$,   (b) $-\pi < \theta < 0$.

Illustrate your answer using an Argand diagram.

11.3 Spiral enlargement

Suppose that a number $t = q(\cos\beta + i\sin\beta)$ is
represented by a translation $\overrightarrow{AT}$ (see Fig. 11.5). How
would you represent the number $w = st$, where
$s = p(\cos\alpha + i\sin\alpha)$?

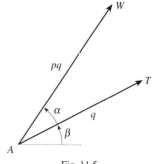

Fig. 11.5

Since multiplication by s multiplies the modulus by
p, and increases the angle with the real axis by α,
w could be represented by a translation $\overrightarrow{AW}$ whose
length is p times the length of $\overrightarrow{AT}$ and whose
direction makes an angle α with the direction of $\overrightarrow{AT}$
in the anticlockwise sense.

A transformation of a plane which multiplies lengths
of vectors by a scale factor of p and rotates them
through an angle α is called a **spiral enlargement**.

> If complex numbers are represented by translations of a plane,
> multiplication by a complex number s has the effect of a spiral
> enlargement of scale factor $|s|$ and angle $\arg s$.

Example 11.3.1

Fig. 11.6 shows an Argand diagram in which A and T are the points $1+i$ and $4-i$. W is a point such that $AW = 2AT$ and angle $TAW = \frac{1}{3}\pi$. Find the number represented by W.

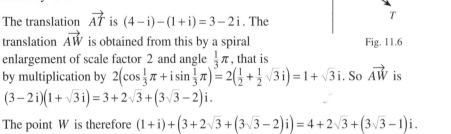

> The translation $\overrightarrow{AT}$ is $(4-i)-(1+i) = 3-2i$. The translation $\overrightarrow{AW}$ is obtained from this by a spiral enlargement of scale factor 2 and angle $\frac{1}{3}\pi$, that is by multiplication by $2\left(\cos\frac{1}{3}\pi + i\sin\frac{1}{3}\pi\right) = 2\left(\frac{1}{2} + \frac{1}{2}\sqrt{3}\,i\right) = 1+\sqrt{3}\,i$. So $\overrightarrow{AW}$ is $(3-2i)(1+\sqrt{3}\,i) = 3+2\sqrt{3}+\left(3\sqrt{3}-2\right)i$.
>
> The point W is therefore $(1+i)+\left(3+2\sqrt{3}+\left(3\sqrt{3}-2\right)i\right) = 4+2\sqrt{3}+\left(3\sqrt{3}-1\right)i$.

Fig. 11.6

Example 11.3.2*

ABC is a triangle. Fig. 11.7 shows three similar triangles BUC, CVA and AWB drawn external to ABC. Prove that the centroids of the triangles ABC and UVW coincide.

> The centroid of a triangle, the point where the medians intersect, was defined in P3 Example 5.5.2. There it was given as the point with position vector $\frac{1}{3}(\mathbf{a}+\mathbf{b}+\mathbf{c})$, where $\mathbf{a}$, $\mathbf{b}$ and $\mathbf{c}$ are the position vectors of the vertices of the triangle. But since complex numbers under addition behave exactly like two-dimensional vectors, the result carries straight over to an Argand diagram. If A, B and C correspond to complex numbers a, b and c then the centroid of the triangle corresponds to $\frac{1}{3}(a+b+c)$. Try writing out the proof for yourself using complex numbers instead of position vectors.

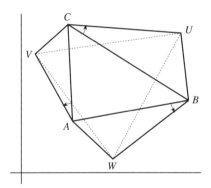

Fig. 11.7

What is new in the Argand diagram is that you now have a way of dealing with the similar triangles. Suppose that multiplication by a number s gives the spiral enlargement that transforms $\overrightarrow{CB}$ into $\overrightarrow{CU}$. Then the same spiral enlargement transforms $\overrightarrow{AC}$ into $\overrightarrow{AV}$, and $\overrightarrow{BA}$ into $\overrightarrow{BW}$. So, if U, V and W correspond to complex numbers u, v and w, you can write

$$u-c = s(b-c), \quad v-a = s(c-a) \quad \text{and} \quad w-b = s(a-b).$$

If you add these three equations, you get

$$(u-c)+(v-a)+(w-b) = s((b-c)+(c-a)+(a-b)) = 0,$$

so

$$u+v+w = a+b+c.$$

Therefore $\frac{1}{3}(u+v+w) = \frac{1}{3}(a+b+c)$. That is, ABC and UVW have the same centroid.

At the beginning of this section spiral
enlargements were described in terms of
general translations, and this is how they are
used in these examples. But if you take the
point A as the origin, you can also use them in
an Argand diagram. Fig. 11.8 shows s, t and
$w = st$ represented by points S, T and W.
Also shown is the point U representing the
number 1. Then multiplication by s gives a
spiral enlargement which transforms $\overrightarrow{OT}$ to
$\overrightarrow{OW}$; it also transforms $\overrightarrow{OU}$ to $\overrightarrow{OS}$, since
$s = s \times 1$. Therefore the triangles OTW and
OUS are similar.

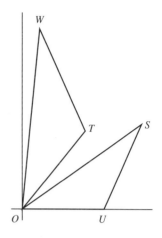

Fig. 11.8

> In an Argand diagram, the triangles formed by the
> points representing 0, t, st and 0, 1, s are similar.

This gives you a geometrical method of drawing the point st on an Argand diagram
when you know the points s and t.

Exercise 11C

1   A is the point in an Argand diagram representing $1 + 3i$. Find the complex numbers
    represented by the two points B such that $OB = \sqrt{2} \times OA$ and angle $AOB = \frac{1}{4}\pi$.

2   A is the point in an Argand diagram representing $3 - 2i$. Find the complex numbers
    represented by the two points B such that $OB = 2OA$ and angle $AOB = \frac{1}{3}\pi$.

3   Points A and B represent $1 + i$ and $2 - i$ in an Argand diagram. C is a point such that
    $AC = 2AB$ and angle $BAC = \frac{2}{3}\pi$. Find two possibilities for the complex number
    represented by C.

4   Points A, B and C represent i, $3 - i$ and $4 + 2i$ in an Argand diagram. D is the
    reflection of C in the line AB. Find the complex number which is represented by D.

5   A point S represents the complex number s in an Argand diagram. Draw diagrams to
    show how to construct the points which represent

    (a) s^2,   (b) s^3,   (c) $\dfrac{1}{s}$.

6   Points S and T represent the complex numbers s and t in an Argand diagram. Draw a
    diagram to show how to construct the point which represents $\dfrac{s}{t}$.

7   A snail starts at the origin of an Argand diagram and walks along the real axis for an hour,
    covering a distance of 8 metres. At the end of each hour it changes its direction by $\frac{1}{2}\pi$
    anticlockwise; and in each hour it walks half as far as it did in the previous hour. Find
    where it is

    (a) after 4 hours,   (b) after 8 hours,   (c) eventually.

8 Repeat Question 7 if the change of direction is through $\frac{1}{4}\pi$ and it walks $\dfrac{1}{\sqrt{2}}$ times as far as in the previous hour.

9 A and B are two points on a computer screen. A program produces a trace on the screen to execute the following algorithm.

   Step 1 Start at any point P on the screen.

   Step 2 From the current position describe a quarter circle about A.

   Step 3 From the current position describe a quarter circle about B.

   Step 4 Repeat Step 2.

   Step 5 Repeat Step 3, and stop.

   Show that the trace ends where it began.

10 A, B, C and D are four points on a computer screen. A program selects a point P on the screen at random and then produces a trace by rotating successively through a right angle about A, B, C and D. Show that, if the trace ends where it began, the line segments AC and BD are equal in length and perpendicular to each other.

11 ABC is a triangle such that the order A, B, C takes you anticlockwise round the triangle. Squares $ACPQ$, $BCRS$ are drawn outside the triangle ABC. If A, B and C represent complex numbers a, b and c in an Argand diagram, find the complex numbers represented by Q, S and the mid-point M of QS. Show that the position of M doesn't depend on the position of C, and find how it is related to the points A and B.

12 Points in an Argand diagram representing the complex numbers $-2\mathrm{i}$, 4, $2+4\mathrm{i}$ and $2\mathrm{i}$ form a convex quadrilateral. Squares are drawn outside the quadrilateral on each of the four sides. Find the numbers represented by the centres P, Q, R and S of the four squares. Hence prove that

   (a) $PR = QS$,   (b) PR is perpendicular to QS.

   Show that the same conclusion follows for any four points forming a convex quadrilateral.

13 In an Argand diagram points A, B, C, U, V and W represent complex numbers a, b, c, u, v and w. Prove that, if the triangles ABC and UVW are directly similar, then $aw + bu + cv = av + bw + cu$. ('Directly similar' means that, if you go round the triangles in the order A, B, C and U, V, W, then you go round both triangles in the same sense.) Prove that the converse result is also true. Hence show that a necessary and sufficient condition for a triangle to be equilateral is that $a^2 + b^2 + c^2 = bc + ca + ab$.

11.4 Square roots of complex numbers

Section 10.6 gave a method of finding square roots of complex numbers in the form $a + b\mathrm{i}$. You can also use a method based on modulus-argument form.

A special case of the rule for multiplying two complex numbers is that, if $s = p(\cos\alpha + \mathrm{i}\sin\alpha)$, then $s^2 = p^2(\cos 2\alpha + \mathrm{i}\sin 2\alpha)$. That is, to square a complex number, you square the modulus and double the argument (adjusting by 2π if necessary).

It follows that, to find a square root, you take the square root of the modulus and halve the argument. That is,

$$\sqrt{s} = \sqrt{p}\left(\cos\tfrac{1}{2}\alpha + i\sin\tfrac{1}{2}\alpha\right).$$

This is illustrated on an Argand diagram in Fig. 11.9.

This gives only one of the two square roots. Since the two square roots of s are of the form $\pm\sqrt{s}$, the two square roots are symmetrically placed around the origin in the Argand diagram. So the other root also has modulus $\sqrt{p}$, and has argument $\tfrac{1}{2}\alpha \pm \pi$, where the + or − sign is chosen so that the argument is between $-\pi$ and π.

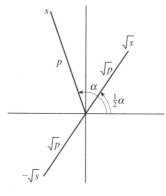

Fig. 11.9

> The square roots of a complex number s have modulus $\sqrt{|s|}$ and arguments $\tfrac{1}{2}\arg s$ and $\tfrac{1}{2}\arg s \pm \pi$ where the sign is + if $\arg s < 0$ and − if $\arg s > 0$.

Example 11.4.1
Find the square roots of   (a) $8i$,   (b) $3-4i$ (see Example 10.6.1).

(a) $8i$ has modulus 8 and argument $\tfrac{1}{2}\pi$. So its square roots have modulus $\sqrt{8} = 2\sqrt{2}$ and arguments $\tfrac{1}{4}\pi$ and $\tfrac{1}{4}\pi - \pi = -\tfrac{3}{4}\pi$. In cartesian form, these are

$$2\sqrt{2}\left(\frac{1}{\sqrt{2}} + \frac{1}{\sqrt{2}}i\right) \quad \text{and} \quad 2\sqrt{2}\left(\frac{1}{\sqrt{2}} - \frac{1}{\sqrt{2}}i\right),$$

that is $2+2i$ and $-2-2i$.

(b) $3-4i$ has modulus $\sqrt{3^2 + (-4)^2} = 5$ and argument $-\tan^{-1}\tfrac{4}{3} = -0.927\,295\,2\dots$. The square roots therefore have modulus $\sqrt{5}$ and arguments $-0.463\,647\,6\dots$ and $-0.463\,647\,6\dots + \pi$. In cartesian form, these are $2-i$ and $-2+i$.

11.5 The exponential form
The rule that, when you multiply two numbers, you add the arguments may have reminded you of a similar rule for logarithms, that $\log mn = \log m + \log n$. There is a reason for this; the arguments of complex numbers and logarithms can both be thought of as indices.

Even more extraordinary, the link between the two comes from Maclaurin expansions. You know the expansions

$$\cos y = 1 - \frac{y^2}{2!} + \frac{y^4}{4!} - \dots \quad \text{and} \quad \sin y = y - \frac{y^3}{3!} + \frac{y^5}{5!} - \dots.$$

(See Section 7.3. You will see later in this section the reason for choosing y rather than x or θ as the variable.) You can put these together in the form

$$\cos y + i \sin y = \left(1 - \frac{y^2}{2!} + \frac{y^4}{4!} - \ldots\right) + i\left(y - \frac{y^3}{3!} + \frac{y^5}{5!} - \ldots\right)$$

$$= 1 + \frac{y\,i}{1!} - \frac{y^2}{2!} - \frac{y^3\,i}{3!} + \frac{y^4}{4!} + \frac{y^5\,i}{5!} - \ldots.$$

Now since $i^2 = -1$, you can write $-y^2$ as $(y\,i)^2$. Similarly, $-y^3\,i = (y\,i)^3$, $y^4 = (y\,i)^4$, and so on. So

$$\cos y + i \sin y = 1 + \frac{y\,i}{1!} + \frac{(y\,i)^2}{2!} + \frac{(y\,i)^3}{3!} + \frac{(y\,i)^4}{4!} + \frac{(y\,i)^5}{5!} + \ldots.$$

You will recognise the right side of this equation as the expansion

$$e^x = 1 + \frac{x}{1!} + \frac{x^2}{2!} + \frac{x^3}{3!} + \ldots$$

with $y\,i$ in place of x. So this suggests that

$\cos y + i \sin y$ can be written as $e^{y\,i}$.

Is this a 'proof'? Not strictly, since e^x has so far only been defined when x is real. But notice that, if $e^{y\,i}$ is written as $\cos y + i \sin y$, then

$$e^{\alpha\,i} \times e^{\beta\,i} = (\cos\alpha + i\sin\alpha)(\cos\beta + i\sin\beta)$$

$$= \cos(\alpha + \beta) + i\sin(\alpha + \beta)$$

$$= e^{(\alpha+\beta)i} = e^{\alpha\,i+\beta\,i},$$

which is the usual multiplication rule for indices. This suggests that it would be a good idea to *define* $e^{y\,i}$ as $\cos y + i \sin y$. Then many of the properties of the exponential function that you know already, such as the multiplication rule and the Maclaurin expansion, would still hold.

Most people who use complex numbers in practice use the compact notation $e^{y\,i}$ in preference to the rather clumsy form $\cos y + i \sin y$ that you have used so far in this chapter. For instance, in Example 11.2.2 you could write z as $e^{\theta\,i}$ and $z+1$ as $2\cos\frac{1}{2}\theta\,e^{\frac{1}{2}\theta\,i}$.

Before stating this as a definition, it is worthwhile going one stage further, and defining $e^{x+y\,i}$ as $e^x \times e^{y\,i}$. You then have:

If $z = x + y\,i$, the **exponential function** e^z is defined by

$$e^z = e^x(\cos y + i \sin y).$$

Thus $|e^z| = e^x$, and $\arg e^z = y + k(2\pi)$, where k is chosen so that $-\pi < \arg e^z \leqslant \pi$.

A special case of this, with $x = 0$ and $y = \pi$, leads to a famous equation which connects five of the most important numbers in mathematics:

$$e^{\pi i} + 1 = 0.$$

Exercise 11D

1 Use the modulus-argument method to find the square roots of the following complex numbers.

(a) $4\left(\cos \frac{2}{5}\pi + i \sin \frac{2}{5}\pi\right)$ (b) $9\left(\cos \frac{4}{7}\pi - i \sin \frac{4}{7}\pi\right)$ (c) $-2i$

(d) $20i - 21$ (e) $1 + i$ (f) $5 - 12i$

2 Find

(a) the square roots of $8\sqrt{3}\,i - 8$,   (b) the fourth roots of $8\sqrt{3}\,i - 8$.

3 Prove that, if z is a complex number, then $e^z + e^{z^*}$ and $e^z \times e^{z^*}$ are both real. What can you say about $e^z - e^{z^*}$ and $e^z \div e^{z^*}$?

4 In an Argand diagram, plot the complex numbers

(a) $e^{\pi i}$,   (b) $e^{\frac{1}{2}\pi i}$,   (c) $2e^{-i}$,   (d) e^{4i},

(e) e^{1+i},   (f) e^{-1+i},   (g) e^{1-i}.

5 Find the square roots of

(a) $e^{\frac{2}{3}\pi i}$,   (b) e^{1+2i}.

6 If y is real, simplify $\dfrac{e^{yi} - e^{-yi}}{e^{yi} + e^{-yi}}$.

7 Prove that, if $s = a + bi$, then

(a) $\left(e^s\right)^2 = e^{2s}$,   (b) $\left(e^s\right)^3 = e^{3s}$,   (c) $\left(e^s\right)^{-1} = e^{-s}$.

8 Use the definition of e^z to prove that, if $s = a + bi$ and $t = c + di$, then $e^s \times e^t = e^{s+t}$.

9 Use the definition of e^z to prove that, if $s = a + bi$, then $\dfrac{d}{dx} e^{sx} = s e^{sx}$.

10 If $z = \cos\theta + i \sin\theta$, find the modulus and argument of e^z in terms of θ.

11 If $z = e^{\theta i}$, show that $z + 1 = e^{\frac{1}{2}\theta i}\left(e^{\frac{1}{2}\theta i} - e^{-\frac{1}{2}\theta i}\right)$. Deduce the result of Example 11.2.2(a).

Use a similar method to prove the result of Example 11.2.2(b).

Miscellaneous exercise 11

1 Given that $z = \tan\alpha + i$, where $0 < \alpha < \frac{1}{2}\pi$, and $w = 4\left(\cos\frac{1}{10}\pi + i \sin\frac{1}{10}\pi\right)$, find in their simplest forms

(a) $|z|$,   (b) $|zw|$,   (c) $\arg z$,   (d) $\arg\dfrac{z}{w}$.   (OCR)

2 Given that $(5+12\,\mathrm{i})z = 63+16\,\mathrm{i}$, find $|z|$ and $\arg z$, giving this answer in radians correct to 3 significant figures. Given also that $w = 3\!\left(\cos\frac{1}{3}\pi + \mathrm{i}\sin\frac{1}{3}\pi\right)$, find

(a) $\left|\dfrac{z}{w}\right|$,   (b) $\arg(zw)$.   (OCR)

3 In an Argand diagram, the point P represents the complex number z. On a single diagram, illustrate the set of possible positions of P for each of the cases

(a) $|z-3\,\mathrm{i}| \leqslant 3$,   (b) $\arg(z+3-3\,\mathrm{i}) = \frac{1}{4}\pi$.

Given that z satisfies both (a) and (b), find the greatest possible value of $|z|$.   (OCR)

4 A complex number z satisfies $|z-3-4\,\mathrm{i}| = 2$. Describe in geometrical terms, with the aid of a sketch, the locus of the point which represents z in an Argand diagram. Find

(a) the greatest value of $|z|$,

(b) the difference between the greatest and least values of $\arg z$.   (OCR)

5 Given that $|z-5| = |z-2-3\,\mathrm{i}|$, show on an Argand diagram the locus of the point which represents z. Using your diagram, show that there is no value of z satisfying both $|z-5| = |z-2-3\,\mathrm{i}|$ and $\arg z = \frac{1}{4}\pi$.   (OCR)

6 A complex number z satisfies the inequality $\left|z+2-2\sqrt{3}\,\mathrm{i}\right| \leqslant 2$. Describe, in geometrical terms, with the aid of a sketch, the corresponding region in an Argand diagram. Find

(a) the least possible value of $|z|$,   (b) the greatest possible value of $\arg z$.

                                                                     (OCR)

7 The quadratic equation $z^2 + 6z + 34 = 0$ has complex roots α and β.

(a) Find the roots, in the form $a+b\,\mathrm{i}$.

(b) Find the modulus and argument of each root, and illustrate the two roots on an Argand diagram.

(c) Find $|\alpha - \beta|$.   (MEI)

8 The complex numbers α and β are given by $\dfrac{\alpha+4}{\alpha} = 2-\mathrm{i}$ and $\beta = -\sqrt{6} + \sqrt{2}\,\mathrm{i}$.

(a) Show that $\alpha = 2+2\,\mathrm{i}$ and that $|\alpha| = |\beta|$. Find $\arg\alpha$ and $\arg\beta$.

(b) Find the modulus and argument of $\alpha\beta$. Illustrate the complex numbers α, β and $\alpha\beta$ on an Argand diagram.

(c) Describe the locus of points in the Argand diagram representing complex numbers z for which $|z-\alpha| = |z-\beta|$. Draw this locus on your diagram.

(d) Show that $z = \alpha + \beta$ satisfies $|z-\alpha| = |z-\beta|$. Mark the point representing $\alpha+\beta$ on your diagram, and find the exact value of $\arg(\alpha+\beta)$.   (MEI)

9 (a) Given that $\alpha = -1+2\,\mathrm{i}$, express α^2 and α^3 in the form $a+b\,\mathrm{i}$. Hence show that α is a root of the cubic equation $z^3 + 7z^2 + 15z + 25 = 0$. Find the other two roots.

(b) Illustrate the three roots of the cubic equation on an Argand diagram, and find the modulus and argument of each root.

(c) L is the locus of points in the Argand diagram representing complex numbers z for which $\left|z+\frac{5}{2}\right| = \frac{5}{2}$. Show that all three roots of the cubic equation lie on L and draw the locus L on your diagram.   (MEI)

10 Complex numbers α and β are given by $\alpha = 2\left(\cos\frac{1}{8}\pi + i\sin\frac{1}{8}\pi\right)$ and
    $\beta = 4\sqrt{2}\left(\cos\frac{5}{8}\pi + i\sin\frac{5}{8}\pi\right)$.

   (a) Write down the modulus and argument of each of the complex numbers α, β, $\alpha\beta$

        and $\dfrac{\alpha}{\beta}$. Illustrate these four complex numbers on an Argand diagram.

   (b) Express $\alpha\beta$ in the form $a + bi$, giving a and b in their simplest forms.

   (c) Indicate a length on your diagram which is equal to $|\beta - \alpha|$, and show that
        $|\beta - \alpha| = 6$.

   (d) On your diagram, draw

        (i) the locus L of points representing complex numbers z such that $|z - \alpha| = 6$,

        (ii) the locus M of points representing complex numbers z such that
              $\arg(z - \alpha) = \frac{5}{8}\pi$.   (MEI)

11 You are given that $\alpha = 1 + \sqrt{3}\,i$ is a root of the cubic equation $3z^3 - 4z^2 + 8z + 8 = 0$.

   (a) Write down another complex root β, and hence solve the cubic equation.

   (b) Find the modulus and argument of each of the complex numbers α, β, $\alpha\beta$ and $\dfrac{\alpha}{\beta}$.
        Illustrate these four complex numbers on an Argand diagram.

   (c) Describe the locus of points in the Argand diagram representing the complex numbers
        z for which $|z - \alpha| = \sqrt{3}$. Sketch this locus on your diagram.

   (d) Express $\dfrac{6 + \alpha}{2\alpha - i}$ in the form $a + bi$, where a and b are real numbers.   (MEI)

12* The fixed points A and B represent the complex numbers a and b in an Argand diagram
     with origin O.

   (a) The variable point P represents the complex number z, and λ is a real variable.
        Describe the locus of P in relation to A and B in the following cases, illustrating
        your loci in separate diagrams.

        (i) $z - a = \lambda b$ (ii) $z - a = \lambda(z - b)$ (iii) $z - a = i\lambda(z - b)$

   (b) By writing $a = |a|e^{i\alpha}$ and $b = |b|e^{i\beta}$, show that $|\operatorname{Im}(ab)| = 2\Delta$, where Δ is the area
        of triangle OAB.

13* A function f has the set of complex numbers for its domain and range. It has the property
     that, for any two complex numbers z and w, $|f(z) - f(w)| = |z - w|$. Explain why
     $f(1) - f(0)$ must be non-zero.
     The function g is defined by $g(z) = \dfrac{f(z) - f(0)}{f(1) - f(0)}$. Show that g has the same property as f,
     plus the additional properties $g(0) = 0$ and $g(1) = 1$. Prove, by making two suitable choices
     for w, that $|g(z)| = |z|$ and $|g(z) - 1| = |z - 1|$. By writing $z = x + yi$ and $g(z) = u + vi$,
     show that, for each z, $g(z)$ must equal either z or z^*.

     If z and w have non-zero imaginary parts, why is it impossible for $g(z)$ to equal z and
     $g(w)$ to equal w^*? Use your answer to write down the most general form for the function
     g. What is the most general form for the function f? Interpret your answer geometrically.
     (OCR)

Revision exercise 2

1 Find

(a) $\displaystyle\int_{\frac{1}{4}\pi}^{\frac{1}{3}\pi}\cot^4 x\,dx$, (b) $\displaystyle\int_0^{\frac{1}{2}\pi}\frac{\cos x}{\sqrt{1+\sin x}}\,dx$, (c) $\displaystyle\int_0^{\frac{1}{4}\pi}x\tan^2 x\,dx$, (d) $\displaystyle\int_0^{\frac{1}{2}\pi}e^{3x}\cos 4x\,dx$.

2 Describe the curve whose polar equation is $r=\sin\theta+\sqrt{3}\cos\theta$. Find the greatest value of r, the tangent at the origin and the equation of the line of symmetry.

Find also the polar equation of the tangent to the curve at the point where $\theta=\frac{1}{2}\pi$.

3 Find approximations to the value of $\displaystyle\int_0^{\frac{1}{6}\pi}\ln(1+\sin x)\,dx$

(a) by using the trapezium rule with 6 intervals,

(b) by approximating to the integrand by its Maclaurin polynomial of degree 3.

Give both of your answers to 4 significant figures.

4 Find the equation of the curve C which passes through the origin and satisfies the

differential equation $\dfrac{dy}{dx}+2xy=x^3$.

Find the equation of a polynomial function of degree 4 whose graph P approximates to C for small values of x. Draw sketches to show the relationship between P and C over the full range of values of x.

5 Find the complex numbers which satisfy the following equations.

(a) $(1+i)z=1+3i$

(b) $z^2+4z+13=0$

(c) $(1-i)z^2-4z+(1+3i)=0$

(d) $\begin{cases}(1-i)z+(1+i)w=2,\\(1+3i)z-(4+i)w=3i\end{cases}$

6 If $z=\cos\theta+i\sin\theta$, where $-\pi<\theta\leqslant\pi$, find the modulus and argument of
(a) z^2 and (b) $1+z^2$, distinguishing the cases

(i) $\theta=0$,

(ii) $\theta=\frac{1}{2}\pi$,

(iii) $\theta=\pi$,

(iv) $\theta=-\frac{1}{2}\pi$,

(v) $0<\theta<\frac{1}{2}\pi$,

(vi) $\frac{1}{2}\pi<\theta<\pi$,

(vii) $-\frac{1}{2}\pi<\theta<0$,

(viii) $-\pi<\theta<-\frac{1}{2}\pi$.

7 (a) Find the derivative of $f(x)=\sin^{-1}\dfrac{x}{\sqrt{a^2+x^2}}$ with respect to x, where a is a positive constant. Hence write $f(x)$ in a simpler form.

(b) Find $\displaystyle\int_0^a f(x)\,dx$.

8 (a) If $z=x+yi$, sketch in an Argand diagram the curves given by $\operatorname{Re}z^2=a$ and $\operatorname{Im}z^2=b$, where a and b are positive constants. Show that, where the two curves intersect, their tangents are in perpendicular directions.

(b) Repeat part (a) for the curves given by $\operatorname{Re}\dfrac{1}{z}=a$ and $\operatorname{Im}\dfrac{1}{z}=b$.

9 (a) Write $x^3 - 1$ and $x^3 + 1$ as products of real factors.

(b) Write $z^3 - 1$ and $z^3 + 1$ as products of complex factors.

(c) Solve the equations $x^6 - 1 = 0$, $x^6 + 1 = 0$ and $x^{12} - 1 = 0$ in real numbers, and illustrate your answers with graphs of $y = x^6 - 1$, $y = x^6 + 1$ and $y = x^{12} - 1$.

(d) Solve the equations $z^6 - 1 = 0$, $z^6 + 1 = 0$ and $z^{12} - 1 = 0$ in complex numbers, and illustrate your answers using Argand diagrams.

10 State the natural domain of the function defined by $f(x) = \cos^{-1} x + \tan^{-1} \sqrt{x}$. Find, correct to 4 significant figures, the maximum value of $f(x)$. Sketch the graph of $y = f(x)$.

11 Find numbers a, b, c and d such that the expansions of $\left(1 + ax^2\right)^b$ and $\dfrac{1 + cx^2}{1 + dx^2}$ agree with the expansion of $\cos x$ as far as the terms in x^4.

For these values of a, b, c and d, continue the expansions of the two expressions as far as the terms in x^6, and hence suggest which of them seems likely to provide the better approximation to the value of $\cos x$ for small values of x.

Verify your answer by comparing the values of the two expressions when $x = 0.1$ with the value of $\cos 0.1$.

12 This question is about the differential equation $x^2 \dfrac{dy}{dx} = 2xy - y^2$.

(a) Show that there are two solutions of the form $y = ax + b$, where a and b are constants.

(b) This is a Riccati equation, which can be solved by using the substitution $y = F(x) + \dfrac{1}{z}$, where $y = F(x)$ is a known solution and z is a function of x. By taking $y = F(x)$ to be the solution in part (a) for which $a \neq 0$, use this substitution to find the general solution of the differential equation.

(c) The differential equation can also be solved using the substitution $y = \dfrac{1}{w}$, where w is a function of x. Show that this converts the equation into a first order linear differential equation, and complete the solution by using the standard algorithm. Do your solutions to parts (b) and (c) agree with each other?

(d) By writing the solution in divided out form, sketch a few typical solution curves, giving particular attention to any asymptotes, stationary points and the form near $x = 0$.

(e) Explain why any stationary points of a solution curve must lie on one or other of the lines $y = 0$ and $y = 2x$. Does your answer to part (d) bear this out?

(f) By differentiating the differential equation, show that on any solution curve $\dfrac{d^2y}{dx^2} = \dfrac{2y(x - y)^2}{x^4}$. What does this tell you about the direction of bending of the solution curves?

13 (a) Sketch the curve whose polar equation is $r = \dfrac{9}{5 + 4\cos\theta}$, $-\pi < \theta \le \pi$.

(b) Write as an integral the area enclosed by this curve. Show that its value may be found

by using the substitution $t = \tan\frac{1}{2}\theta$ as $\displaystyle\int_{-\infty}^{\infty} \dfrac{81\left(1 + t^2\right)}{\left(9 + t^2\right)^2}\, dt$. Use the substitution

$t = 3\tan u$ to evaluate this integral.

(c) Show that the cartesian equation of the curve can be written as $y^2 = \frac{9}{25}\left(25 - (x + 4)^2\right)$.

(d) State the area enclosed by the curve with equation $y^2 = 25 - (x + 4)^2$. Hence find the area enclosed by the curve whose equation is given in part (c). Compare your answer with that found in part (b).

14 A, B and C are points in an Argand diagram representing the complex numbers $-1 + 0\,\mathrm{i}$, $1 + 0\,\mathrm{i}$ and $0 + \mathrm{i}$ respectively, and P is the point representing the complex number z. The displacements $\overrightarrow{AP}$ and $\overrightarrow{BP}$ make angles α and β with the x-axis, and the angle $APB = \frac{1}{4}\pi$.

(a) Show that $\arg(z - 1) - \arg(z + 1) = \frac{1}{4}\pi$.

(b) Show that $\dfrac{z + 1}{z^* + 1} = \cos 2\alpha + \mathrm{i}\sin 2\alpha$ and write down a similar expression for $\dfrac{z - 1}{z^* - 1}$.

(c) Show that $\dfrac{(z - 1)(z^* + 1)}{(z^* - 1)(z + 1)} = \mathrm{i}$ and deduce that $zz^* + \mathrm{i}(z - z^*) = 1$.

(d) Show that the equation in part (c) can be written as $(z - \mathrm{i})(z^* + \mathrm{i}) = 1$ and deduce that $|z - \mathrm{i}| = 2$.

(e) State in words what geometrical property is established by combining the results of parts (a) to (d).

15 Here is a 'spoof proof' of the obviously false proposition that all candidates who take the P4 module examination get the same number of marks. Your task is to find the error in the proof.

Proposition   Let $P(n)$ be 'all sets of n candidates get the same mark'.

Basis case   The theorem is clearly true for $n = 1$ as any candidate gets the same mark as him or herself.

Inductive step   Suppose that $P(k)$ is true. Then all sets of k candidates get the same mark as each other. Let $\{c_1, c_2, \ldots, c_k\}$ be one such set of k candidates. Now add candidate c_{k+1} and consider the set $\{c_2, \ldots, c_k, c_{k+1}\}$ where c_{k+1} replaces c_1. This is also a set of k candidates, so they all get the same mark, so c_{k+1} gets the same mark as $c_1, c_2, \ldots, c_k$. Therefore, if $P(k)$ is true, then $P(k + 1)$ is true.

Completion   Using the principle of mathematical induction, $P(n)$ is true for all positive integers, so all sets of n candidates get the same mark.

Mock examination 1

Time 1 hour 20 minutes

Answer all the questions.
You are permitted to use a graphic calculator in this paper.

1   Given that $y = \sin^{-1} x$, show that $(1 - x^2)\dfrac{d^2 y}{dx^2} = x\dfrac{dy}{dx}$. [4]

2

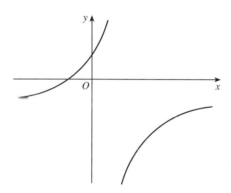

The diagram shows a sketch of the graph of $y = \dfrac{1 + x}{1 - x}$.

(i)   State the equations of the asymptotes. [2]

(ii) Sketch the graph of $y^2 = \dfrac{1 + x}{1 - x}$. [3]

3   By expanding the terms on the left-hand side, prove that
$$\sin(r\theta + \theta) - \sin(r\theta - \theta) = 2\cos r\theta \sin \theta.$$ [2]

Hence show that
$$2\sin\theta(\cos\theta + \cos 3\theta + \cos 5\theta + \ldots + \cos(2n - 1)\theta) = \sin 2n\theta.$$ [3]

4   Show, by using the substitution $u = x + y$, that the differential equation
$$\frac{dy}{dx} = \frac{x + y}{1 - x - y}$$

may be reduced to the form
$$\frac{du}{dx} = \frac{1}{1 - u}.$$ [3]

Hence find the solution of $\dfrac{dy}{dx} = \dfrac{x + y}{1 - x - y}$ for which $y = 0$ when $x = 0$. [4]

5   The polar equation of a curve is $r\cos\frac{1}{2}\theta = a$, for $-\pi < \theta < \pi$, where a is a positive constant.

  (i)   Show that $r\sin\theta$ may be expressed as $2a\sin\frac{1}{2}\theta$. Deduce that as $\theta \to \pm\pi$, the curve approaches the lines with cartesian equations $y = \pm 2a$.   [3]

  (ii) Sketch the curve.   [2]

  (iii) Calculate the area of the sector of the curve between $\theta = \pm\frac{1}{2}\pi$.   [3]

6   Express $\dfrac{5x^2}{\left(x^2 - 4\right)\left(x^2 + 1\right)}$ in partial fractions.   [5]

  Hence find the exact value of $\displaystyle\int_0^1 \frac{5x^2}{\left(x^2 - 4\right)\left(x^2 + 1\right)}\,dx$.   [4]

7   Prove by induction that

$$\sum_{r=1}^{n} \frac{r}{3^r} = \frac{1}{4}\left(3 - \frac{2n+3}{3^n}\right).$$ [5]

  Prove also, by induction or by a graphical argument, that $2n + 3 < 2^n$ for all integers $n \geqslant 4$.   [3]

  Hence show that $\displaystyle\sum_{r=1}^{\infty} \frac{r}{3^r}$ is convergent, and state the value of the sum to infinity.   [2]

8   One root of the cubic equation $z^3 + az + 10 = 0$ is $1 + 2\,i$.

  (i)   Find the value of the real constant a.   [4]

  (ii) Show all three roots of the equation on an Argand diagram.   [4]

  (iii) Show that all three roots satisfy the equation $|6z - 1| = 13$, and show the locus represented by this equation on your diagram.   [4]

Mock examination 2

Time 1 hour 20 minutes

Answer all the questions.
You are permitted to use a graphic calculator in this paper.

1 Find an expression in terms of n for the sum

$$\sum_{r=1}^{n} r(r-6)(r+6),$$

factorising your answer fully. [4]

2 A sequence of numbers $u_1, u_2, u_3, \ldots$ is defined by

$$u_1 = 1 \quad \text{and} \quad u_{n+1} = 2u_n + 1 \quad \text{for } n \geqslant 1.$$

Evaluate u_2, u_3, u_4 and u_5. Hence conjecture a formula for u_n in terms of n, and prove your conjecture by induction. [5]

3 Given that $y = \tan^{-1}(1+x)$, find $\dfrac{dy}{dx}$ and $\dfrac{d^2y}{dx^2}$. [3]

Hence find the Maclaurin series for $\tan^{-1}(1+x)$, up to and including the term in x^2.
[3]

4 The complex number z has modulus r and is such that both its real and imaginary parts are positive. In an Argand diagram, z is represented by the point P, and the complex numbers z^* and iz are represented by the points Q and R respectively.

(i) Draw a diagram showing P, Q and R, making clear the geometrical relation between them. [3]

(ii) State the equation of a simple locus on which P, Q and R all lie. [1]

(iii) State the equation of the locus of P given that the origin is the mid-point of QR.
[2]

5   Show that an integrating factor for the differential equation

$$\frac{dy}{dx} + \frac{x}{1-x^2}y = 1$$

is $\dfrac{1}{\sqrt{1-x^2}}$.   [3]

Solve the differential equation, given that $y = \frac{1}{4}\pi$ when $x = 0$, and find the exact value of x (between -1 and 1) for which $y = 0$.   [6]

6   The equation of a curve, in polar coordinates, is $r = a(\sin\theta + \cos\theta)$, where a is a positive constant.

   (i)   Find the area bounded by the lines $\theta = 0$, $\theta = \frac{1}{2}\pi$ and the part of the curve for which $0 \leqslant \theta \leqslant \frac{1}{2}\pi$.   [4]

   (ii) Express the equation of the curve in cartesian coordinates, and hence show that the curve is a circle.   [3]

   (iii) Sketch the curve, and state a set of values of θ corresponding to the complete curve.   [2]

7   (i)   Find the modulus and argument of the complex number $2 + 2\sqrt{3}\,i$.   [2]

   (ii) Hence, or otherwise, find the two square roots of $2 + 2\sqrt{3}\,i$, giving your answers in the form $a + ib$.   [3]

   (iii) Find the exact solutions of the equation

$$i z^2 - 2\sqrt{2}\,z - 2\sqrt{3} = 0,$$

giving your answers in the form $a + ib$.   [4]

8   The equation of a curve is $y = \dfrac{x^2}{x-a}$, where a is a positive constant.

   (i)   Find the equations of the asymptotes of the curve.   [3]

   (ii) Show that there are no points of the curve for which $0 < y < 4a$.   [4]

   (iii) Find the coordinates of the stationary points of the curve.   [3]

   (iv) Sketch the curve.   [2]

Answers

1 Rational functions

Exercise 1A (page 4)

1 (a) $\dfrac{1}{x-1} + \dfrac{1}{x^2+1}$

(b) $\dfrac{x+3}{x^2+2x+2} - \dfrac{1}{x+1}$

(c) $\dfrac{1}{x+3} + \dfrac{x-2}{x^2+3}$

(d) $\dfrac{4}{2x-3} + \dfrac{4-x}{x^2+x+3}$

(e) $\dfrac{1}{2+3x} - \dfrac{1}{3+3x+2x^2}$

(f) $\dfrac{8}{1+4x} + \dfrac{1-2x}{2+x+x^2}$

(g) $\dfrac{2}{x-2} - \dfrac{2x+1}{x^2+3x+1}$

(h) $\dfrac{-1}{2x-3} + \dfrac{x+2}{2x^2-3}$

(i) $\dfrac{3}{3x-2} - \dfrac{4x-3}{4x^2+3}$

(j) $\dfrac{3x-1}{x^2-x+2} - \dfrac{6}{2x+1}$

(k) $\dfrac{8}{5x-7} + \dfrac{4-3x}{2x^2-2x+5}$

(l) $\dfrac{5x-11}{4x^2-6x+9} - \dfrac{3}{2x+3}$

2 (a) $\dfrac{1}{2x-1} + \dfrac{2x+1}{x^2+3x-2}$

(b) $\dfrac{3}{4x-3} + \dfrac{5x+3}{2x^2+x-2}$

(c) $\dfrac{2}{x-1} + \dfrac{2x-1}{x^2+x+1}$

(d) $\dfrac{2}{3x-2} + \dfrac{2x-3}{3x^2-x+2}$

(e) $\dfrac{1}{2-x} + \dfrac{4x-5}{4x^2+3x+1}$

(f) $\dfrac{2}{1+x} + \dfrac{1-3x}{x^2-x+1}$

3 (a) 0 (b) $2\ln 2$

(c) $\ln\dfrac{50}{7}$ (d) $\ln 10$

Exercise 1B (page 10)

1 (a) $2 - \dfrac{1}{x+1} + \dfrac{2}{x-1}$ (b) $1 - \dfrac{2}{x+3} + \dfrac{1}{x-2}$

(c) $1 - \dfrac{2}{3-x} + \dfrac{2}{1-2x}$ (d) $3 - \dfrac{1}{x+2} + \dfrac{4}{2x-1}$

(e) $2x - 1 + \dfrac{3}{x+1} + \dfrac{3}{2x-1}$

(f) $3x + \dfrac{3}{3+x} - \dfrac{1}{1+3x}$

(g) $x^2 - 1 + \dfrac{2}{x+2} - \dfrac{1}{2x+1}$

(h) $2x^2 + x + 2 + \dfrac{3}{x+3} - \dfrac{3}{2x-3}$

(i) $3x + \dfrac{1}{x+1} - \dfrac{x+1}{x^2-x+1}$

2 (a) $1 + 2\ln\tfrac{3}{2}$ (b) $2 + \ln\tfrac{3}{2}$

(c) $3 + \ln 6$ (d) $4 - 4\ln 2$

Miscellaneous exercise 1 (page 11)

1 (a) $\dfrac{1}{x^2} + \dfrac{2}{x} + \dfrac{2}{1-x}$

(b) $2 - x - \dfrac{2}{x+2} + \dfrac{1}{x^2+2}$

2 (a) $A = -1, B = 1, C = 1$ (b) $a = \tfrac{1}{2}, b = -\tfrac{1}{2}$

3 (a) $A = 1, B = 4, C = 2$

4 (a) $\dfrac{1}{x-3} - \dfrac{1}{x-1}$,

$\dfrac{1}{(x-3)^2} - \dfrac{1}{x-3} + \dfrac{1}{(x-1)^2} + \dfrac{1}{x-1}$

(c) $\left(\dfrac{25}{48} - \ln\tfrac{3}{2}\right)\pi$

5 $\tfrac{1}{2}\ln\tfrac{2}{3}$

6 $3\tfrac{1}{2} - 3\ln 2$

7 $\tfrac{3}{2}\ln 3 - \ln 2 - \tfrac{1}{2}$

8 (a) $a = 2$ (b) $\tfrac{5}{8} + \ln 2$

2 Summing series

Exercise 2A (page 16)

1 (a) $8 + 27$ (b) $2 + 2 + 2$

(c) $1 + \tfrac{1}{2} + \tfrac{1}{3} + \tfrac{1}{4}$ (d) $1 + 4 + 9 + 16$

(e) $5 + 7 + 9 + 11$ (f) $u_0 + u_1 + u_2$

2 (a) $\displaystyle\sum_{r=2}^{4} r$ (b) $\displaystyle\sum_{r=1}^{4} r^2$ (c) $\displaystyle\sum_{r=1}^{5} 2r$

(d) $\displaystyle\sum_{r=1}^{3} \dfrac{1}{2r}$ (e) $\displaystyle\sum_{r=1}^{4}(2r+1)$ (f) $\displaystyle\sum_{r=1}^{5}(3r-1)$

3 (a) $0+1+2+\ldots+n$

   (b) $2^2+3^2+4^2+\ldots+(n-1)^2$

   (c) $\overbrace{3+3+3+\ldots+3}^{n-7\text{ of these}}$

   (d) $\frac{1}{1}+\frac{1}{2}+\frac{1}{3}+\ldots+1/(2n)$

   (e) $0^3+1^3+2^3+\ldots+(2n-1)^3$

   (f) $u_1+u_2+u_3+\ldots+u_{n-1}$

4 (a) True   (b) False   (c) False

   (d) True   (d) False   (f) True

5 (a) 1   (b) -1 (c) -1

   (d) 21   (e) $\frac{17}{60}$ (f) -1

6 (a) $\displaystyle\sum_{r=1}^{101}(-1)^{r+1}r$ (b) $\displaystyle\sum_{r=1}^{25}(-1)^r(2r)^2$

   (c) $\displaystyle\sum_{r=1}^{49}(-1)^{r+1}\frac{1}{r}$

7 (a) $\displaystyle\sum_{r=1}^{100}\left(r+\frac{1}{r}\right)$ (b) $\displaystyle\sum_{r=0}^{n}\binom{n}{r}x^r$

   (c) $\displaystyle\sum_{r=0}^{n}(r+1)x^r$ (d) $\displaystyle\sum_{r=0}^{2n}(-1)^r rx^{r-1}$

Exercise 2B (page 23)

1 (a) 338 350   (b) 333 298

   (c) 3080   (d) 24 497 550

2 (a) $\frac{1}{2}(n+1)(n+2)$ (b) $n(n+2)$

   (c) $\frac{1}{12}(n-1)n(n+1)(3n+2)$ (d) $4n^2$

3 n, $\frac{1}{2}n(n+1)$; $\frac{1}{2}n(2a+(n-1)d)$

4 (a) 112 761   (b) 215 589

5 $\frac{1}{12}n(n+1)(n+2)(3n+5)$

6 $np^2-\frac{1}{6}n(n+1)(2n+1)$

7 (a) $\frac{1}{6}n(n+1)(n+2)$ (b) $\frac{1}{12}n(n+1)^2(n+2)$

8 (a) 27 225 550

   (b) 25 497 450

   (c) 28 638 550

9 $-\frac{1}{4}\left(3n^2+2n^3\right)$, if n is even;

   $\frac{1}{4}(n+1)^2(2n-1)$, if n is odd

10 $-\frac{1}{2}n(n+1)\left(n^2+n-1\right)$, if n is even;

   $\frac{1}{2}n(n+1)\left(n^2+n-1\right)$, if n is odd

Exercise 2C (page 28)

1 (a) $\dfrac{2}{(2r-1)(2r+1)}$, $\dfrac{1}{2n-1}-\dfrac{1}{2n+1}$

   (b) $\dfrac{n}{2n+1}$

2 $\dfrac{1}{2(r-2)}-\dfrac{1}{2r}$, $\dfrac{3}{2}\dfrac{11}{24}$

3 (b) $(n+1)!-1$

4 $r(r+1)(r+2)$, $\frac{1}{4}n(n+1)(n+2)(n+3)$

5 $2\left(1+40r^2+80r^4\right)$,

   $\frac{1}{30}n(n+1)(2n+1)\left(3n^2+3n-1\right)$

6 $\dfrac{1}{2(r+1)}+\dfrac{1}{2(r-1)}$, $\dfrac{2n+1+(-1)^n}{2(2n+1)}$, $\frac{1}{2}$

Miscellaneous exercise 2 (page 28)

1 $\dfrac{1}{2(r+1)}-\dfrac{1}{2(r-1)}$

2 (a) $\frac{1}{3}$ (b) 1166 650

3 $4r+1$, $(n+1)(6n+1)$

4 $\frac{1}{3}n(n+1)(n+2)$; $\frac{1}{2}n\left(6n^2+15n+11\right)$

8 25 512 600

9 (a) $\dfrac{1}{2(n-1)}-\dfrac{1}{n}+\dfrac{1}{2(n+1)}$

   (b) $\dfrac{(N-1)(N+2)}{4N(N+1)}$ (c) $\frac{1}{4}$

10 $64r^3+16r$

3 Mathematical induction

Exercise 3A (page 36)

1 (a) The sum of the first n even numbers is n^2+n.

7 $\dfrac{d^n}{dx^n}\cos x=\cos\left(x+\frac{1}{2}n\pi\right)$

10 $4,9,16; n^2$

12 $\displaystyle\sum_{r=1}^{n}\frac{1}{\sqrt{r}}\leqslant\sqrt{n}+1$

Exercise 3B (page 40)

1 $\displaystyle\sum_{r=1}^{n}(3r(r+1)+1)=(n+1)^3-1$

2 $\displaystyle\sum_{r=1}^{n}r\times r!=(n+1)!-1$

3 The sum of three consecutive cubes is divisible by 9.

4 $3^{2n+1}+2^{4n+2}$ is divisible by 7.

5 (a) 2, 4, 7, 10, 16   (b) $\frac{1}{2}\left(n^2+n+2\right)$

Miscellaneous exercise 3 (page 40)

12 (a) $6, 3$ (b) $\frac{1}{3}, 2$

4 Graphs of rational functions

Exercise 4A (page 45)

1 (a) $x = 0, y = 0$ (b) $x = 1, y = 0$
  (c) $x = -2, y = 0$ (d) $x = \frac{1}{2}, y = 0$
  (e) $x = 0, y = 1$ (f) $x = -1, y = 3$
  (g) $x = -2, y = 4$ (h) $x = \frac{1}{2}, y = 3$
  (i) $x = 0, y = 1$ (j) $x = 0, y = 1$
  (k) $x = 1, y = 1$ (l) $x = -2, y = 3$

2 (a) $x = 0, y = x$ (b) $x = 0, y = x + 1$
  (c) $x = 1, y = 3x - 2$ (d) $x = 2, y = x - 3$
  (e) $x = 0, y = x$ (f) $x = 1, y = x - 1$
  (g) $x = -2, y = x + 1$ (h) $x = -1, y = 2x - 1$
  (i) $x = -\frac{1}{2}, y = 1 - x$

3 (a) $(-2, -4)$ maximum, $(2, 4)$ minimum
  (b) $(-2, 2)$ maximum, $(0, 2)$ minimum
  (c) $\left(-\frac{3}{4}, -5\right)$ maximum, $\left(-\frac{1}{4}, 3\right)$ minimum

4 (a) $x = 0, y = x$; $(-1, 0), (1, 0)$; no maxima or minima
  (b) $x = 0, y = x$;
    $(-1, -2)$ maximum, $(1, 2)$ minimum
  (c) $x = 0, y = 2x + 3$; $\left(\frac{1}{4}(-3 \pm \sqrt{5}), 0\right)$;
    $\left(-\frac{1}{2}, 1\right)$ maximum, $\left(\frac{1}{2}, 5\right)$ minimum
  (d) $x = \frac{1}{2}, y = x - 1$; $(0, 0), \left(\frac{3}{2}, 0\right)$;
    no maxima or minima
  (e) $x = 1, y = 9x + 4$; $(0, 3), \left(\frac{1}{18}(5 \pm \sqrt{133}), 0\right)$;
    $\left(\frac{2}{3}, 7\right)$ maximum, $\left(\frac{4}{3}, 19\right)$ minimum
  (f) $x = \frac{1}{2}, y = x + \frac{1}{2}$; $(0, 0)$; $(1, 2)$ minimum,
    $(0, 0)$ maximum

Exercise 4B (page 51)

1 (a) $x = 0, x = 2, y = 0$; $(1, -1)$ maximum
  (b) $x = 0, x = 2, y = 0$; no maxima or minima
  (c) $x = 0, x = 2, y = 1$; $(1, 0)$ maximum
  (d) $x = 1, y = x$; $(0, -1)$ maximum,
    $(2, 3)$ minimum
  (e) $x = -2, x = 2, y = 1$; $(0, 0)$ maximum
  (f) $x = -2, x = 2, y = 0$; no maxima or minima
  (g) $x = -2, x = 2, y = 0$; no maxima or minima
  (h) $x = -2, x = 2, y = 0$; $\left(0, -\frac{1}{4}\right)$ maximum

2 (a) $x = 0, y = 0$; no maxima or minima
  (b) $x = 0, y = 0$; $\left(2, \frac{1}{4}\right)$ maximum
  (c) $x = 1, y = 0$; no maxima or minima
  (d) $x = 1, y = 0$; $\left(-1, -\frac{1}{4}\right)$ minimum

3 (a) $y = 0$; $(0, 1)$ maximum
  (b) $y = 0$;
    $\left(-2, -\frac{1}{2}\right)$ minimum, $\left(0, \frac{1}{2}\right)$ maximum
  (c) $y = 0$;
    $\left(-1, \frac{1}{2}\right)$ maximum, $\left(1, -\frac{1}{2}\right)$ minimum
  (d) $y = 0$;
    $\left(-2, -\frac{1}{3}\right)$ minimum, $(0, 1)$ maximum

4 (a) $y = 1$; $\left(0, \frac{2}{3}\right)$; $(-2, 2)$ maximum,
    $\left(1, \frac{1}{2}\right)$ minimum
  (b) $x = 1, y = 1$; $(0, 0)$; $(0, 0)$ minimum
  (c) $x = 1, y = 1$; $(0, -1), (-1, 0)$;
    no maxima or minima
  (d) $y = 1$; $(0, -1), (-1, 0), (1, 0)$;
    $(0, -1)$ minimum

Exercise 4C (page 54)

3 (a) $y \geqslant -\frac{1}{8}$ (b) No restrictions
  (c) No restrictions

5 $0 < k < 3$

Miscellaneous exercise 4 (page 54)

1 $x = -1, y = x + 1$

2 $x < -2$ or $x > 2$; $x = -2, x = 2, y = 0$

3 $-\frac{1}{4}, \frac{1}{4}$; $y = 0$

4 No stationary values; $x = -2, x = 2, y = 0$

5 -1 minimum, $\frac{1}{7}$ maximum

6 $p < -1$

7 For example,
  (a) $y = -\dfrac{1}{x + 2}$ (b) $y = 4 - \dfrac{1}{x + 3}$
  (c) $y = 1 + \dfrac{x}{x^2 - 1}$ (d) $y = \dfrac{2x^2}{x^2 - 1}$

8 (a) $\left(-\sqrt{2}, 0\right), \left(\sqrt{2}, 0\right), \left(0, -\frac{1}{2}\right)$
  (b) $x = 2, y = 1$
  (c) $(1, -1)$

10 (a) $\left(-\frac{1}{2}, 0\right), x = 1$ (b) $(-2, -1)$

11 (a) $(4 - k)^2 \geqslant 4(4 - k)$ (b) $(-2, 0), (0, 4)$

12 (c) $(-a, 0)$

5 Graphs of functions involving square roots

Exercise 5 (page 63)

6 $(0,0)$, $(4,32)$; $\left(4,4\sqrt{2}\right)$, $\left(4,-4\sqrt{2}\right)$, $\pm\sqrt{6}$

7 10, $(-1,0)$

8 (e)

9 (c)

10 $(2,1)$, $(3,0)$, $(4,1)$

13

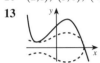

$(-3,1)$, $(-3,-1)$, $\left(2,\sqrt{5}\right)$, $\left(2,-\sqrt{5}\right)$;

17 There are two branches at the origin, with gradients $\pm\frac{1}{3}\sqrt{3}$.

Miscellaneous exercise 5 (page 64)

2 (a)   (b)

3 (a) has $y=0$ at $(0,0)$ and $(-b,0)$; gradients at these points are 0 and b^2.

    (b) has $y=0$ at the same points; gradients at these points are $\pm\sqrt{b}$ and '∞'.

5 (a)

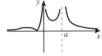

    (b)

7 (a) $x=\pm a$, $y=0$; $\left(0,-\dfrac{1}{a^2}\right)$

    (b) $x=\pm a$, $y=0$; $\left(0,\dfrac{1}{a^2}\right)$

    (c) $x=\pm a$, $y=0$

8 $\left(1,\pm\frac{1}{2}\sqrt{2}\right)$

9 (a)   (b)

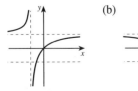

Revision exercise 1

(page 66)

2 $(x+2)\left(x^2-2x+4\right)$, $\dfrac{2x-2}{x^2-2x+4}-\dfrac{2}{x+2}$; $a=-1$, $b=3$

3 (a) $\dfrac{4\left(20-8x-x^2\right)}{(x+4)^2}$, $(-10,100)$, $(2,4)$

    (b) $x=-4$, $y=36-4x-\dfrac{144}{x+4}$, $y=36-4x$

    (d) $(-10,10)$, $(-10,-10)$, $(2,2)$, $(2,-2)$; $(0,0)$, $(5,0)$

4 (a) $-2\frac{1}{2}<x<-2$ or $0<x<\frac{1}{2}$

    (b) $\dfrac{\frac{1}{2}}{r}-\dfrac{\frac{1}{2}}{r+2}$, $\dfrac{3}{4}-\dfrac{2n+3}{2(n+1)(n+2)}$

5 (a) $A=-1$, $B=1$

6 $\frac{1}{2}n^2(n+1)$

7 (a) $x=-1$, $y=1$

10 (b) $\ln 2+3\tan^{-1}2-3\tan^{-1}3$

12 $n(n-r)(1+r)$; no difference

14 (a) $(r+1)(r+2)\ldots(r+k)$

    (b) $\frac{1}{5}n(n+1)(n+2)(n+3)(n+4)$

6 Trigonometric functions

Exercise 6A (page 68)

2 For example, in part (e)

$$\int \cot x\,dx$$
$$= \begin{cases} \ln(\sin x) & \text{if } 2n\pi<x<(2n+1)\pi, \\ \ln(-\sin x) & \text{if } (2n+1)\pi<x<(2n+2)\pi. \end{cases}$$

Exercise 6B (page 74)

1 (a) $-\cot x-x+k$

    (b) $\frac{1}{2}\tan^2 x+\ln|\cos x|+k$

    (c) $\frac{1}{3}\tan^3 x-\tan x+x+k$

2 (a) $\frac{2}{3}(\sin x)^{\frac{3}{2}}+k$

    (b) $\frac{1}{3}\sin^3 x-\frac{1}{5}\sin^5 x+k$

    (c) $-\cos x+\frac{2}{3}\cos^3 x-\frac{1}{5}\cos^5 x+k$

    (d) $-\operatorname{cosec}\theta-\sin\theta+k$

    (e) $-\ln|\cos\theta|-\sin\theta+k$

    (f) $\ln|1+\tan t|+k$

3 $1, \cos^2\theta, 1+\sin 2\theta$

  (a) $2\tan\theta - 2\sec\theta - \theta + k$

  (b) $\tan\theta + \sec\theta + k$

  (c) $\sin\theta - \cos\theta - \frac{2}{3}\cos^3\theta + \frac{2}{3}\sin^3\theta + k$

4 (a) $-x\cot x + \ln|\sin x| + k$

  (b) $-\cos x \ln(\sin x) + \ln(\tan\frac{1}{2}x) + \cos x + k$

  (c) $\tan x \ln(\sec x) - \tan x + x + k$

5 (a) $\frac{1}{2}e^\theta(\cos\theta + \sin\theta) + k$

  (b) $\frac{1}{5}e^\theta(\sin 2\theta - 2\cos 2\theta) + k$

  (c) $e^{\theta\cos\alpha}\cos(\theta\sin\alpha - \alpha) + k$

6 $x, \ln|\cos x + \sin x|;$

  $\frac{1}{2}(x + \ln|\cos x + \sin x|) + k,$

  $\frac{1}{2}(x - \ln|\cos x + \sin x|) + k$

  (a) $\frac{1}{4}\pi$ (b) $\frac{1}{2}\ln 2$

7 $0.8, 0.6$

8 $\frac{1}{3}$ or 3

9 (a) 0.6435 or 2.2143   (b) −2.2143 or 1.1760

  (c) −1.1760 or 0.9273

10 (a), (b) 61.9, 180   (c) 61.9

  Because $t = \tan\frac{1}{2}x°$ is undefined when $x = 180$.

11 (a) $\ln\left|\dfrac{1 + 2\tan\frac{1}{2}x}{2 - \tan\frac{1}{2}x}\right| + k$ (b) $\ln\left|\dfrac{1 + \tan\frac{1}{2}x}{1 - \tan\frac{1}{2}x}\right| + k$

  (c) $\frac{1}{5}\ln\left|\dfrac{3 + \tan\frac{1}{2}x}{2 - \tan\frac{1}{2}x}\right| + k$

12 In some of these questions more than one method is possible, and you may get answers which look different from those printed. As a check, plot the graph of your answer minus the printed answer; this should be constant.

  (a) $-x\cot x + \ln|\sin x| - \frac{1}{2}x^2 + k$

  (b) $-\cot\frac{1}{2}t - t + k$

  (c) $\ln|\tan\theta| + \ln|\sec\theta + \tan\theta| + k$

  (d) $\sin x(\ln(\sin x) - 1) + k$

  (e) $-\frac{1}{2}\ln|\cos\theta - \sin\theta| - \frac{1}{2}\theta + k$

  (f) $-\frac{1}{3}\cot^3 x + \cot x + x + k$

  (g) $-\ln|1 + \cos t| + k$

  (h) $\frac{1}{13}\left(\ln\left|5\tan\frac{1}{2}\theta - 1\right| - \ln\left|\tan\frac{1}{2}\theta + 5\right|\right) + k$

  (i) $\frac{1}{2}(\ln(\sec u))^2 + k$

  (j) $\frac{1}{2}x - \frac{1}{2}\ln|\sin x + \cos x| + k$

13 (b) $x\tan x + \ln|\cos x| - \frac{1}{2}x^2 + k$

Exercise 6C (page 80)

1 (a) $\frac{2}{3}\pi$ (b) $\frac{1}{3}\pi$ (c) $\frac{1}{4}\pi$ (d) $-\frac{1}{3}\pi$

2 (a) $\frac{1}{2}\pi - a$ (b) b

3 (a) $x^2 + y^2 = x^2y^2$ (b) $xy = 1$

  (c) $x^2y^2 + 1 = y^2$

4 (a) $\tan^{-1}\frac{5}{12}$ (b) $\tan^{-1}\frac{120}{119}$ (c) $\tan^{-1}\frac{1}{239}$

5 (a) $yz + zx + xy = 1$

  (b) $x^2 + y^2 + z^2 = 1 + 2xyz$

6 (a) $\dfrac{-1}{|x|\sqrt{x^2-1}}$ (b) $\dfrac{2}{1+4x^2}$

  (c) $\dfrac{1}{\sqrt{9-x^2}}$ (d) $\dfrac{1}{|x|\sqrt{9x^2-1}}$

  (e) $\tan^{-1}x + \dfrac{x}{1+x^2}$ (f) $\dfrac{2\sin^{-1}x}{\sqrt{1-x^2}}$

  (g) $\dfrac{1}{2\sqrt{x(1-x)}}$ (h) $\dfrac{3\sqrt{x}}{2(1+x^3)}$

  (i) $\dfrac{1}{x^2 - 2x + 2}$

  (j) $\dfrac{-1}{\sqrt{1-x^2}}$ if $x > 0$, $\dfrac{1}{\sqrt{1-x^2}}$ if $x < 0$

7 (a) $\frac{1}{2}(1+x^2)\tan^{-1}x - \frac{1}{2}x + k$

  (b) $x\sin^{-1}x + \sqrt{1-x^2} + k$

  (c) $\frac{1}{4}(2x^2 - 1)\sin^{-1}x + \frac{1}{4}x\sqrt{1-x^2} + k$

8 $\frac{1}{54}\pi^3$

9 $\frac{2}{3}\pi - \ln(2+\sqrt{3})$

10 $\pi(\pi - 2)$

Exercise 6D (page 83)

1 (a) $\frac{1}{4}\pi$ (b) $\frac{1}{3}\pi$ (c) $\dfrac{1}{6\sqrt{3}}\pi$

  (d) $\frac{1}{24}\pi$ (e) $\frac{3}{16}\pi$ (f) $\frac{2}{3}\sqrt{3} - 1$

  (g) $\ln(2+\sqrt{3})$ (h) $\frac{1}{6}\pi$ (i) $\frac{1}{2}\pi - 1$

  (j) $(1 - \frac{1}{2}\sqrt{2})\ln(\sqrt{2} + 1)$

2 (a) $\frac{1}{2}\sin^{-1}\frac{2}{3}x + k$ (b) $\frac{1}{6}\tan^{-1}\frac{2}{3}x + k$

  (c) $\dfrac{1}{ab}\tan^{-1}\left(\dfrac{bx}{a}\right) + k$

  (d) $\frac{1}{3}\sec^{-1}\frac{1}{3}x + k$ if $x > 0$,

      $-\frac{1}{3}\sec^{-1}\frac{1}{3}x + k$ if $x < 0$

  (e) $\sqrt{x^2 - 9} + k$ (f) $\tan^{-1}(x+2) + k$

  (g) $\frac{1}{4}\tan^{-1}(x - \frac{1}{2}) + k$ (h) $\sin^{-1}(x-1) + k$

  (i) $\frac{1}{3}\sin^{-1}(\frac{1}{2}x + \frac{2}{3}) + k$

3 (a) 0.19% too small   (b) 0.12% too large

4 $\frac{1}{2}(\sec u \tan u - \ln(\sec u + \tan u)) + k$;

$\frac{1}{2}\left(x\sqrt{1+x^2} + \ln\left(x + \sqrt{1+x^2}\right)\right) + k$,

$\frac{1}{2}\left(x\sqrt{x^2-1} - \ln\left(x + \sqrt{x^2-1}\right)\right) + k$,

$\sqrt{x(1+x)} - \ln\left(\sqrt{x} + \sqrt{1+x}\right) + k$,

$\sqrt{x(x-1)} + \ln\left(\sqrt{x} + \sqrt{x-1}\right) + k$

Miscellaneous exercise 6 (page 84)

1 $\frac{2}{5}\sin^5 x + k$

3 $\frac{4}{3}\pi + \frac{1}{2}\sqrt{3}$

4 $2\sqrt{2}\left(\cos\frac{1}{2}x - \frac{2}{3}\cos^3\frac{1}{2}x\right) + k$

5 $\frac{1}{2}\ln\frac{3}{2}$

6 $\sin^{-1}\frac{1}{5}(x+3) + k$

7 $\tan^{-1}(x-3) + k$

9 $\frac{1}{64}x^2 - \frac{1}{36}y^2 = 1$;

$x = 4\left(\frac{1}{t} + t\right),\ y = 3\left(\frac{1}{t} - t\right)$;

$4(1-p^2)y = 3(1+p^2)x - 48p;\ \left(10, 4\frac{1}{2}\right)$

10 $y^2 = 4x^2 + 4x\sin 2x + 2\cos 2x + 1$

12 0.185; minimum

14 $\frac{1}{4}\sqrt{3} - \frac{1}{12}\pi$

17   (a) $\frac{1}{2}\sqrt{2}\ln\left(\sec\left(X + \frac{1}{4}\pi\right) + \tan\left(X + \frac{1}{4}\pi\right)\right)$

$\qquad\qquad\qquad -\frac{1}{2}\sqrt{2}\ln\left(1 + \sqrt{2}\right)$;

$\qquad \int_0^{\frac{1}{4}\pi}$ does not exist

  (b) $\frac{1}{2}\tan\left(X + \frac{1}{4}\pi\right) - \frac{1}{2}$

  (c) $A = 2 - 2\sqrt{1 - \frac{1}{4}\pi} = 1.073\ldots$,

$\qquad B = \frac{1}{2}\pi = 1.570\ldots$

7 Maclaurin expansions

Exercise 7A (page 91)

1   (a) $1 + \frac{3}{2}x + \frac{3}{8}x^2 - \frac{1}{16}x^3$

  (b) $1 + \frac{3}{2}x + \frac{15}{8}x^2 + \frac{35}{16}x^3$

  (c) $1 - 6x + 24x^2 - 80x^3$

  (d) $1 + \frac{1}{2}x^2$

2   (a) $x - \frac{1}{6}x^3 + \frac{1}{120}x^5$

  (b) $2x - \frac{4}{3}x^3 + \frac{4}{15}x^5$

  (c) $1 + x + \frac{1}{2}x^2 + \frac{1}{6}x^3 + \frac{1}{24}x^4$

  (d) $1 - 3x + \frac{9}{2}x^2 - \frac{9}{2}x^3 + \frac{27}{8}x^4$

  (e) x^2

  (f) $1 - x^2$

  (g) $-x - \frac{1}{2}x^2 - \frac{1}{3}x^3 - \frac{1}{4}x^4$

  (h) $1 + x + \frac{3}{2}x^2 + \frac{5}{2}x^3$

  (i) $1 - \frac{1}{2}x^2 + \frac{1}{8}x^4$

  (j) $x^2 - \frac{1}{2}x^4$

3 $1, \frac{1}{2}$

4 $1, \frac{1}{2}$

5 $\frac{1}{2}, -\frac{1}{24}$

6 $1 + mx + \dfrac{m(m-1)}{2}x^2 + \dfrac{m(m-1)(m-2)}{6}x^3$

$\qquad + \dfrac{m(m-1)(m-2)(m-3)}{24}x^4$

Exercise 7B (page 94)

1   (a) 1.6487 (b) 0.8415 (c) 0.9655

  (d) 0.9397 (e) -0.0513 (f) 0.8109

  (g) -0.9900

2 $2x + \frac{2}{3}x^3 + \frac{2}{5}x^5 + \ldots + \dfrac{2}{2r+1}x^{2r+1} + \ldots,$

$\qquad -1 < x < 1$; 1.099; $x = 2$ is outside interval of validity

3 $-\frac{1}{3}x^3 + \frac{1}{30}x^5$; $-\frac{1}{3}$

4   (a) 2 (b) $\frac{1}{2}$ (c) 1 (d) $-\frac{1}{2}$

6 $1, 2$; the second, which uses a value of x closer to 0

7 4×10^{-4}, 7×10^{-10}. For any value of x, the error in using $p_n(x)$ for $\cos x$ becomes very small if n is large, suggesting that the expansion is valid for all real numbers.

Exercise 7C (page 97)

1   (a) $1 + 3x + \frac{3}{2}x^2 - \frac{1}{2}x^3 + \frac{3}{8}x^4$

  (b) $1 - 2x + 2x^2 - \frac{4}{3}x^3 + \frac{2}{3}x^4$

  (c) x^3

  (d) x^3

2 (a) $1+3x+\frac{9}{2}x^2+\ldots+\frac{3^r}{r!}x^r+\ldots,$ $\mathbb{R}$

(b) $1-\frac{1}{8}x^2+\frac{1}{384}x^4-\ldots+\frac{(-1)^r}{2^{2r}(2r)!}x^{2r}+\ldots,$ $\mathbb{R}$

(c) $x-\frac{1}{6}x^2+\frac{1}{120}x^3-\ldots+\frac{(-1)^{r-1}}{(2r-1)!}x^r+\ldots,$

positive $\mathbb{R}$

(d) $-x-\frac{1}{2}x^2-\frac{1}{3}x^3-\ldots-\frac{1}{r}x^r-\ldots,$

$-1\leqslant x<1$

(e) $2x-2x^2+\frac{8}{3}x^3-\ldots+\frac{(-1)^{r-1}2^r}{r}x^r+\ldots,$

$-\frac{1}{2}<x\leqslant\frac{1}{2}$

(f) $e+ex+\frac{1}{2}ex^2+\ldots+\frac{e}{r!}x^r+\ldots,$ $\mathbb{R}$

(g) $1-x^2+\frac{1}{3}x^4+\ldots+\frac{(-1)^r2^{2r-1}}{(2r)!}x^{2r}+\ldots,$ $\mathbb{R}$

(h) $1+\frac{1}{e}x-\frac{1}{2e^2}x^2+\ldots+\frac{(-1)^{r-1}x^r}{re^r}+\ldots,$

$-e<x\leqslant e$

(i) $\cos1-(\sin1)x-\left(\frac{1}{2}\cos1\right)x^2+\ldots$

$+\frac{(-1)^r\cos1}{(2r)!}x^{2r}$

$+\frac{(-1)^{r+1}\sin1}{(2r+1)!}x^{2r+1}+\ldots,$ $\mathbb{R}$

3 (a) $e+2ex+3ex^2+\frac{10}{3}ex^3+\frac{19}{6}ex^4$

(b) $e+\frac{1}{2}ex+\frac{1}{48}ex^3-\frac{5}{384}ex^4$

(c) $1-\frac{1}{2}x^2+\frac{5}{24}x^4$

(d) $\sin1-\left(\frac{1}{2}\cos1\right)x^2+\frac{1}{24}(\cos1-3\sin1)x^4$

(e) $1+\frac{1}{2}x^2-\frac{1}{12}x^4$

(f) $1+\frac{1}{2}x^2+\frac{5}{24}x^4$

(g) $x+\frac{1}{3}x^3$

(h) $\ln2+\frac{1}{2}x+\frac{1}{8}x^2-\frac{1}{192}x^4$

(i) $1+x+\frac{1}{2}x^2+\frac{1}{2}x^3+\frac{3}{8}x^4$

4 (a) e^{x^2} (b) $\frac{1}{2}(e^x+e^{-x})$

(c) $\begin{cases}\frac{1}{2}\left(e^{\sqrt{x}}+e^{-\sqrt{x}}\right) & \text{if } x\geqslant0, \\ \cos\left(\sqrt{-x}\right) & \text{if } x<0.\end{cases}$

Exercise 7D (page 100)

1 $x+\frac{1}{6}x^3+\frac{3}{40}x^5+\ldots$

$+\frac{3\times5\times7\times\ldots\times(2r-1)}{(2r+1)r!2^r}x^{2r+1}+\ldots,$

$\frac{1}{2}\pi-x-\frac{1}{6}x^3-\frac{3}{40}x^5-\ldots;$ 3.1416

2 3.14159

3 $x-\frac{1}{18}x^3+\frac{1}{600}x^5-\ldots$

$+\frac{(-1)^r}{(2r+1)(2r+1)!}x^{2r+1}+\ldots$

4 $x+\frac{1}{4}x^2+\frac{1}{18}x^3+\ldots+\frac{1}{r(r)!}x^r+\ldots;$ 0.570

5 $\frac{1}{3}\theta+\frac{2}{81}\theta^3;$ 0.82 radians

6 $(-1)^n\int_0^x\frac{u^n}{1+u}\,du$ (a positive error means that the

approximation is too small)

7 6

Miscellaneous exercise 7 (page 101)

1 $\ln3+\frac{1}{3}x-\frac{1}{18}x^2$

2 $-\frac{1}{4}$

3 $\frac{1}{2},\frac{1}{2}$

4 10

5 $3,2,-1$

6 $\frac{1}{9};$ 0.223137

7 $1+x+\frac{1}{2}x^2$

8 $r\left(\theta-\frac{1}{24}\theta^3+\frac{1}{1920}\theta^5\right),$ $r\left(2\theta-\frac{1}{3}\theta^3+\frac{1}{60}\theta^5\right);$

$2r\theta-\frac{1}{240}r\theta^5,$ error $\frac{1}{240}r\theta^5;$ 0.016%;

$\frac{1}{6}r(8a-b)$

9 $2x+\frac{4}{3}x^3+\frac{12}{5}x^5+\frac{40}{7}x^7$

10 e is an irrational number.

8 Polar coordinates

Exercise 8A (page 105)

2 (a) $(0,10)$ (b) $\left(-\sqrt{3},1\right)$

(c) $\left(-2\sqrt{2},-2\sqrt{2}\right)$ (d) $\left(-3,-3\sqrt{3}\right)$

(e) $(-5,0)$ (f) $(-1.248\ldots,2.727\ldots)$

3 (a) $(3,\pi)$

(b) $(13,0.394\ldots)$

(c) (i) $\left(2\sqrt{2},1\frac{3}{4}\pi\right)$ (ii) $\left(2\sqrt{2},-\frac{1}{4}\pi\right)$

(d) (i) $\left(4,1\frac{1}{2}\pi\right)$ (ii) $\left(4,-\frac{1}{2}\pi\right)$

(e) (i) $(5,4.068\ldots)$ (ii) $(5,-2.214\ldots)$

(f) $\left(2,\frac{2}{3}\pi\right)$

4 $\sqrt{19}$

5 (a) $\left(r\cos\frac{1}{2}(\beta-\alpha),\frac{1}{2}(\alpha+\beta)\right)$

　　(b) $\left(-r\cos\frac{1}{2}(\beta-\alpha),\frac{1}{2}(\alpha+\beta)\pm\pi\right)$

Exercise 8B (page 112)

2 (a) (ii) $0,\pi^2$　(iii) $\theta=0$　(iv) $\theta=0$ (or π)

　　(b) (ii) $0,2$　(iii) $\theta=-\frac{1}{4}\pi,\frac{3}{4}\pi$

　　　　(iv) $\theta=\pm\frac{1}{4}\pi$ (or $\pm\frac{3}{4}\pi$)

　　(c) (ii) $\frac{1}{3}$, no greatest

　　　　(iii) doesn't contain pole

　　　　(iv) $\theta=0$ (or π)

　　(d) (ii) $0,2$　(iii) $\theta=\frac{1}{2}\pi$

　　　　(iv) $\theta=\frac{1}{2}\pi$ (or $\frac{3}{2}\pi$)

3 (a) $x^2+y^2=2y$

　　(b) $\left(x^2+y^2\right)^3=a^2\left(x^2-y^2\right)^2$ for $x>0$

　　(c) $y=a$　(d) $8x^2+8x+9y^2=16$

4 (a) $r^2=2\mathrm{cosec}\,2\theta$ for $0<\theta<\frac{1}{2}\pi$

　　(b) $r=2$

　　(c) $r=2(\cos\theta+\sin\theta)$ for $-\frac{1}{4}\pi<\theta<\frac{3}{4}\pi$

　　(d) $r=a(\sec\theta+\mathrm{cosec}\,\theta)$ for $0<\theta<\frac{1}{2}\pi$

5 Through $(2a,0)$ perpendicular to the initial line

Exercise 8C (page 115)

1 (a) $\frac{1}{4}\left(e^{2\pi}-1\right)$　　　　　(b) $\frac{1}{5}\pi^5$

　　(c) $\pi a^2+2\pi^2 ab+\frac{4}{3}\pi^3 b^2$　(d) $\frac{1}{8}(\pi+2)a^2$

　　(e) $2ab+\frac{1}{4}\pi\left(2a^2+b^2\right)$

2 $\frac{1}{2}a^2$

3 $\frac{1}{2}\pi$

5 $\frac{1}{2}\pi a^2$

Exercise 8D (page 117)

4 Simple closed curve if $k\geqslant1$; convex if $k\geqslant2$, dented if $1<k<2$, cusp if $k=1$.
Integral represents area enclosed.
Closed curve with two loops if $0<k<1$. Integral represents sum of areas of loops.
Circle if $k=0$. Integral represents twice the area enclosed.

5 $\frac{1}{4}\pi$ if n is odd, $\frac{1}{2}\pi$ if n is even

6 (b) $\theta=\pi$　(c) $\theta=0$　(d) $\theta=\pm\frac{1}{3}\pi$;

　　for $k=-2$, area $=\sqrt{3}+\frac{4}{3}\pi-4\ln\left(2+\sqrt{3}\right)$

7 $\frac{1}{2}(4-\pi)a^2$

Miscellaneous exercise 8 (page 118)

1 (a) 7　(b) $10\sqrt{3}$

3 (a) $\left(x^2+y^2\right)^2=x^3$　(b) $y^2=x^2(x-1)$

---

4 $r=\sec^2\theta+\mathrm{cosec}^2\theta$

5 (a) $\frac{5}{8}\pi$　(b) $\left(\frac{3}{4}\sqrt{3},-\frac{1}{6}\pi\right)$

6 OCQ, CQP

7 $r=a(\cos\theta-\sin\theta)$;

　　$r=\sqrt{2}a\cos\theta$, $x^2+y^2=\sqrt{2}ax$

8 $r^2\cos2\theta=a^2$; $2xy=a^2$

9 $\dfrac{(x+4)^2}{25}+\dfrac{y^2}{9}=1$

10 $x^2+y^2=x^{\frac{4}{3}}$

11 $\frac{1}{3}\pi$, $\frac{1}{2}\pi$, $\frac{2}{3}\pi$; $\alpha=\frac{1}{3}\pi$,

　　$\mathrm{f}(\theta)=\frac{1}{2}(\cos3\theta+2\cos\theta)^2$; $\frac{5}{6}\pi+\frac{3}{4}\sqrt{3}$

12 $\frac{1}{2}(4-\pi)a^2$

13 $\frac{8}{3}\sqrt{2}$

14 $-\frac{1}{8}$, $\cos^{-1}\left(-\frac{1}{4}\right)$; $6\frac{3}{4}\pi$

9　First order differential equations

Exercise 9A (page 125)

1 (a) $y=\frac{1}{3}x^2+\dfrac{k}{x}$　(b) $x=(t+k)\mathrm{cosec}\,t$

　　(c) $y=-\dfrac{1}{2x}+kx$　(d) $u=(2x+k)e^{-x^2}$

2 (a) $y=\dfrac{x-1}{x^2}$　　(b) $y=\mathrm{cosec}\,x$

　　(c) $y=\dfrac{x^2+3}{4\sqrt{x}}$

3 (a) $u=\frac{1}{3}x+\dfrac{k}{x^2}$　(b) $y=k\sec x-\cos x$

　　(c) $x=ke^{4t}-\frac{1}{2}e^{2t}$　(d) $y=kx^3-x^2$

　　(e) $y=(t+k)\cos t$　(f) $y=\cos x+k\cot x$

4 (a) $y=3x-1+ke^{-3x}$ with $k=-1,0,1,2,3$

　　(b) $y=\frac{1}{4}x^2+\dfrac{k}{x^2}$ with $k=-\frac{1}{4},\frac{3}{4},\frac{7}{4},-4,0,4$

　　(c) $y=\sec x+k\cos x$ with $k=-3,-2,-1,0,1$

　　(d) $y=kx^3-x$ with $k=2,1,0,1,2,3$

5 $y=x(1-\ln x)$

6 $\dfrac{dx}{dt}=-0.1x$, $\dfrac{dy}{dt}=0.1x-0.2y$; $x=50e^{-0.1t}$,

　　$y=50\left(e^{-0.1t}-e^{-0.2t}\right)$; 12 litres, after 6.93 hours

7 $\dfrac{dx}{dt}=c(a+b\sin ct-x)$

9 $y = 2x + kx^2$; gradient positive within the acute angles between $y = x$ and the y-axis, negative within the obtuse angles.

10 $y = \dfrac{k}{x} - \dfrac{1}{x^2}$; solution curves bend upwards above $y = \dfrac{2}{x^2}$, bend downwards below.

Exercise 9B (page 132)

1 $y = ke^{\frac{x}{y}}$

2 $y^2 = x(x+k)$

3 $y = \dfrac{x}{x^2 + k}$

4 $y = \dfrac{(x-1)^2}{4x}$

5 $q = -\frac{1}{2}$; $y = \dfrac{1}{\sqrt{x^2(1 + kx^2)}}$

6 $y = \sqrt[3]{16x^3 - \frac{3}{2}x}$

7 (a) $y = \dfrac{1}{\sqrt{\left(x^2 + x + \frac{1}{2} + ke^{2x}\right)}}$

(b) $y = \left(x - 2 + ke^{-\frac{1}{2}x}\right)^2$

8 $x^2 + y^2 = ky$; circle through O with centre on the y-axis

9 $y = x + \dfrac{1}{x^2 + k}$

10 $m = 2, a = 2; y = 2x^2 + \dfrac{1}{x + k}$

Miscellaneous exercise 9 (page 133)

1 $s = \left(\frac{1}{2}t^2 + k\right)e^{3t}$

2 $y = \frac{1}{5}x + \dfrac{k}{x^4}; \frac{1}{5}\left(x + \dfrac{4}{x^4}\right)$

3 $y = \left(\frac{1}{2}x^2 + k\right)e^{x^3}; y = \left(\frac{1}{2}x^2 + 1\right)e^{x^3}$

4 $y = 10(x + 2)e^{-x^2}$

5 $y = 1 - x\cot x + k\csc x$; $y = 1 - x\cot x - \csc x$

6 $y = \dfrac{1}{x}\left(1 + ke^{-x}\right); y = \dfrac{1}{x}\left(1 + e^{1-x}\right)$

7 $y = \dfrac{k - \sin^{-1}x}{\sqrt{1-x^2}}; y = \dfrac{\cos^{-1}x}{\sqrt{1-x^2}}$

8 $\ln x$; $y = \frac{1}{2}\left(\ln x + \dfrac{1}{\ln x}\right)$

9 $y = -x - \frac{1}{4} - \frac{3}{4}e^{4(x-1)}$

10 $V = 5t - 80 + 80e^{-0.05t}; t = 216$

11 $V = \dfrac{1}{\alpha + \beta}\left(e^{\beta t} - e^{-\alpha t}\right)$

12 (a) $y = x^2 - 2x + 2$

(b) $y = x^2 - 2x + 2 + (A - 2)e^{-x}$

13 (c) $P(x) = x - 1$

14 $y = \dfrac{\left(1+x^2\right)^{\frac{3}{2}}}{3x^2} + \dfrac{k}{x^2}; y = \dfrac{\left(1+x^2\right)^{\frac{3}{2}} + 3 - 2\sqrt{2}}{3x^2}$;

y becomes very large;

$y \approx \dfrac{c}{x^2} + \frac{1}{2} + \frac{1}{8}x^2$ (writing $c = \frac{1}{3} + k$);

$y = \dfrac{\left(1+x^2\right)^{\frac{3}{2}} - 1}{3x^2}$; other solutions exist for $x < 0$, but these do not cross over to $x > 0$.

15 $Y = -\dfrac{1}{X^2}\cos X + \dfrac{2}{X^3}\sin X + \dfrac{2}{X^4}\cos X + \dfrac{k}{X^4}$;

$Y \to \frac{1}{4}$ (with $k = -2$)

16 (b) (i) $y = \dfrac{1}{k}\left(2 - e^{-kx}\right)\sin x$

(ii) $y = -\dfrac{1}{k}e^{-kx}\sin x$;

(i) approximates to a periodic oscillation for large x, (ii) tends to zero

(c) $y = (x + k)\sin x$, oscillates unboundedly for large x

17 (a) $E = \dfrac{2G}{1 + 4k^2}(\cos\theta - 2k\sin\theta) + ce^{-2k\theta}$

(b) $\cos\alpha + 2k\sin\alpha = e^{2k(\alpha+\beta)}(\cos\beta - 2k\sin\beta)$

18 (a) $1, 2$ (b) $\dfrac{dy}{dx} = u + x\dfrac{du}{dx}$

(d) $y_0(y - x) = (y - 2x)^2$, solutions lie in half-plane $y - x > 0$

19 (a) $y = \dfrac{3}{x^3}$

(b) $z = \frac{1}{2}x^3 + kx$, $y = \dfrac{\frac{3}{2}x^2 + k}{x^3\left(\frac{1}{2}x^2 + k\right)}$

(c) $k = 0$ gives $y = \dfrac{3}{x^3}$, $k \to \infty$ gives $y = \dfrac{1}{x^3}$

(d) solutions with $k > 0$

20 $\displaystyle\int e^{x^2}\,dx$ can't be found algebraically;

$f'''(x) = -4f'(x) - 2xf''(x)$; $1 + x - x^2 - \frac{2}{3}x^3$

10 Complex numbers

Exercise 10A (page 140)

1 (a) 4   (b) $6i$ (c) 13 (d) $24i$
   (e) $24i$ (f) -10 (g) 16 (h) -36

2 (a) $4-i$ (b) $2+3i$ (c) $7+0i$
   (d) $5+2i$ (e) $5-5i$ (f) $8+6i$
   (g) $\frac{1}{5}(1+7i)$ (h) $\frac{1}{10}(1-7i)$ (i) $1-3i$
   (j) $2+4i$ (k) $\frac{1}{2}(-1-3i)$ (l) $\frac{1}{5}(3+i)$

3   $2x-y=1$, $x+2y=3$; $x=1$, $y=1$; $1+i$

4 (a) 3   (b) -3 (c) 3   (d) -6
   (e) $\frac{1}{2}$ (f) -1

5   (a), (b), (d)

Exercise 10B (page 144)

1 (a) $-2-5i$ (b) $\frac{1}{3}(7-2i)$
  (c) $\frac{1}{2}(-5+i)$ (d) $\frac{1}{25}(7+24i)$

2 (a) $z=2, w=i$ (b) $z=1+i, w=2i$

3 (a) $\pm3i$ (b) $-2\pm i$
  (c) $3\pm4i$ (d) $\frac{1}{2}(-1\pm5i)$

4 (a) $1-7i$ (i) 2   (ii) $14i$ (iii) 50
     (iv) $\frac{1}{25}(-24+7i)$
  (b) $-2-i$ (i) -4 (ii) $2i$ (iii) 5
     (iv) $\frac{1}{5}(3-4i)$
  (c) 5   (i) 10   (ii) 0   (iii) 25
     (iv) 1
  (d) $-3i$ (i) 0   (ii) $6i$ (iii) 9
     (iv) -1

5 (a) $(z-5i)(z+5i)$
  (b) $(3z-1-2i)(3z-1+2i)$
  (c) $(2z+3-2i)(2z+3+2i)$
  (d) $(z-2)(z+2)(z-2i)(z+2i)$
  (e) $(z-3)(z+3)(z-i)(z+i)$
  (f) $(z-2)(z+1-2i)(z+1+2i)$
  (g) $(z+1)(z-2-i)(z-2+i)$
  (h) $(z-1)^2(z+1-i)(z+1+i)$

6   $1-i$, $-1+2i$, $-1-2i$

7   $-2, 1$, $2+\sqrt{11}i$, $2-\sqrt{11}i$

10   $a^5-10a^3b^2+5ab^4$, $5a^4b-10a^2b^3+b^5$;
   $a^5-10a^3b^2+5ab^4$, $-5a^4b+10a^2b^3-b^5$

Exercise 10C (page 149)

3 (a) $\pm1, \pm i$ (b) $-1, \frac{1}{2}(1\pm\sqrt{3}i)$
  (c) $-2, 1\pm3i$ (d) $-3, 1, -1\pm\sqrt{2}i$
  (e) $\pm2i, \frac{1}{2}(-1\pm\sqrt{3}i)$

4   $-1, 1, \frac{1}{2}(1\pm\sqrt{3}i)$

5 (a) Circle centre O radius 5, $x^2+y^2=25$
  (b) Line $x=3$ (c) Line $x=3$
  (d) Line $y=1$
  (e) Circle centre $2+0i$ radius 2,
     $x^2+y^2-4x=0$
  (f) Line $x=2$ (g) Line $y=2x+3$
  (h) Circle centre $\frac{1}{2}+0i$ radius $1\frac{1}{2}$,
     $x^2+y^2-x=2$
  (i) Parabola $y^2=4x$

6 (a) Exterior of circle centre O radius 2,
     $x^2+y^2>4$
  (b) Interior and boundary of circle centre $0+3i$
     radius 1, $x^2+y^2-6y+8\leqslant0$
  (c) Half-plane including boundary, $x+y\leqslant0$
  (d) Interior of circle centre $-1+0i$ radius 2,
     $x^2+y^2+2x-3<0$

11   If in a triangle ABC, O is the mid-point of BC,
   then $AB^2+AC^2=2OA^2+2OC^2$ (this is
   Apollonius's theorem).

Exercise 10D (page 153)

1 (a) $1-i$, $-1+i$ (b) $1+2i$, $-1-2i$
  (c) $3+2i$, $-3-2i$ (d) $3-i$, $-3+i$

2 (a) $i, -1-i$ (b) $2, -3+i$
  (c) $-1-i$, $-3+i$ (d) $-2i, -1+i$
  (e) $1, -2-i$

3 (a) $2+2i$, $-2-2i$, $2-2i$, $-2+2i$
  (b) $\frac{1}{2}\sqrt{2}(3+i)$, $\frac{1}{2}\sqrt{2}(-3-i)$, $\frac{1}{2}\sqrt{2}(1-3i)$,
     $\frac{1}{2}\sqrt{2}(-1+3i)$

4   $-2i$, $\sqrt{3}+i$, $-\sqrt{3}+i$

5   $-1-i$; $z^2-(1+i)z+2i=0$;
   $\frac{1}{2}(1+\sqrt{3})+\frac{1}{2}(1-\sqrt{3})i$, $\frac{1}{2}(1-\sqrt{3})+\frac{1}{2}(1+\sqrt{3})i$

Miscellaneous exercise 10 (page 154)

1   $3-4i$

2   $-3i$, $\frac{5}{3}$

3   $1-3i$; $z^3-4z^2+14z-20=0$

4 (a) 3, 3   (b) $4i$

5   $5-2i$, $-5+2i$

6   $3-i$, $-3+3i$

7   $-2i$, $-2-2i$, -4;
  (a) $p=-4$, $q=2$ (b) $1-i$, $1+i$, -1, -4

8   2

10 (a) $kz^2+2iz-k=0$; $a=1$, $b=-1$, $c=0$,
     $d=1$
  (b) α is real and negative
  (c) $\beta-\frac{1}{2}ki=\dfrac{k}{2(k^2+1)}\left(2k+(1-k^2)i\right)$

11 Complex numbers in polar form

Exercise 11A (page 156)

1. (a) $1+\sqrt{3}i$ (b) $-5\sqrt{2}+5\sqrt{2}i$
   (c) $0-5i$ (d) $-3+0i$
   (e) $-4.16+9.09i$ (f) $-0.99-0.14i$

2. $r(\cos\theta + i\sin\theta)$ where

   (a) $r=2.24, \theta=1.11$ (b) $r=5, \theta=-0.93$
   (c) $r=7.81, \theta=2.27$
   (d) $r=10.63, \theta=-2.29$
   (e) $r=1, \theta=0$ (f) $r=2, \theta=\frac{1}{2}\pi$
   (g) $r=3, \theta=\pi$ (h) $r=4, \theta=-\frac{1}{2}\pi$
   (i) $r=2, \theta=-\frac{1}{4}\pi$ (j) $r=2, \theta=\frac{2}{3}\pi$

5. (a) $-2+2\sqrt{3}i$ (b) $1+2i$
   (c) $-3-6i$ (d) $1+\sqrt{3}i$
   (e) $2-2\sqrt{3}+i$ (f) $\left(1-\sqrt{3}\right)+\left(1+\sqrt{3}\right)i$

6. (a) $\sqrt{3}+i$ (b) $3+4i$
   (c) $-3+4i, -9+4i$
   (d) $\mp\frac{1}{2}\sqrt{2}+\left(2\pm\frac{1}{2}\sqrt{2}\right)i$

7. $\frac{1}{5}\pi$

8. $-\frac{5}{6}\pi$

9. $\frac{1}{4}\pi$

10. $\frac{1}{3}\pi$

11. $\sqrt{5}$

12. $\frac{1}{3}\pi$

Exercise 11B (page 160)

1. $r(\cos\theta + i\sin\theta)$, where

   (a) $r=2, \theta=\frac{7}{12}\pi$ (b) $r=2, \theta=\frac{1}{12}\pi$
   (c) $r=\frac{1}{2}, \theta=-\frac{1}{12}\pi$ (d) $r=8, \theta=-\frac{1}{2}\pi$
   (e) $r=2, \theta=\frac{5}{6}\pi$ (f) $r=\frac{1}{4}, \theta=-\frac{11}{12}\pi$
   (g) $r=4, \theta=\frac{2}{3}\pi$ (h) $r=16, \theta=\frac{1}{3}\pi$
   (i) $r=8, \theta=0$ (j) $r=1, \theta=\frac{11}{12}\pi$
   (k) $r=2, \theta=-\frac{1}{3}\pi$ (l) $r=2, \theta=\frac{1}{12}\pi$
   (m) $r=2, \theta=-\frac{1}{12}\pi$ (n) $r=4, \theta=\frac{1}{3}\pi$
   (o) $r=1, \theta=-\frac{1}{4}\pi$ (p) $r=1, \theta=-\frac{1}{3}\pi$
   (q) $r=1, \theta=-\frac{1}{3}\pi$ (r) $r=2, \theta=-\frac{1}{6}\pi$

2. $2\left(\cos\frac{4}{5}\pi + i\sin\frac{4}{5}\pi\right)$

5. (a) $\cos\theta - i\sin\theta$ (b) $\cos\theta - i\sin\theta$
   (c) $r(\cos\theta - i\sin\theta)$ (d) $\frac{1}{r}(\cos\theta - i\sin\theta)$

6. $2\left(\cos\frac{1}{3}\pi + i\sin\frac{1}{3}\pi\right)$,
   $\sqrt{2}\left(\cos\left(-\frac{1}{4}\pi\right) + i\sin\left(-\frac{1}{4}\pi\right)\right)$; $-\sqrt{3}+i$

7. (a) $29+278i$ (b) $-122-597i$
   (c) $(-8.432+5.376i)\times10^{-5}$

8. (a) $-\frac{1}{6}\pi$ (b) $\frac{1}{6}\pi$ (c) $\frac{1}{3}\pi$ (d) $\frac{1}{3}\pi$

9. (a) $\frac{1}{2}\pi$ (b) $-\frac{1}{2}\pi$ (c) $-\frac{1}{2}\pi$

10. The semicircle in the first quadrant of the circle with 3 and 4i at ends of a diameter

11. The line segment AB

12. The major arc of the circle with centre -1 passing through i and $-i$

13. (a) $\sec\theta, \theta$ (b) $-\sec\theta, \theta-\pi$
    (c) $-\sec\theta, \theta-\pi$ (d) $\sec\theta, \theta-2\pi$

14. (a) $2\sin\theta, \theta-\frac{1}{2}\pi$ (b) $-2\sin\theta, \theta+\frac{1}{2}\pi$

Exercise 11C (page 163)

1. $-2+4i, \ 4+2i$

2. $\left(3+2\sqrt{3}\right)+\left(3\sqrt{3}-2\right)i, \ -\left(2\sqrt{3}-3\right)-\left(3\sqrt{3}+2\right)i$

3. $\pm2\sqrt{3}+\left(3\pm\sqrt{3}\right)i$

4. $\frac{8}{13}(1-5i)$

7. (a) $6+3i$ (b) $\frac{17}{16}(6+3i)$ (c) $\frac{16}{15}(6+3i)$

8. (a) $10(1+i)$ (b) $\frac{15}{2}(1+i)$ (c) $8(1+1)$

11. $(1-i)a+ic, \ (1+i)b-ic, \ \frac{1}{2}(a+b)+\frac{1}{2}(b-a)i$;
    M is the third vertex of an isosceles right-angled triangle having AB as hypotenuse.

12. $3-3i, \ 5+3i, \ 4i, \ -2$

Exercise 11D (page 167)

1. (a) $\pm2\left(\cos\frac{1}{5}\pi + i\sin\frac{1}{5}\pi\right)$
   (b) $\pm3\left(\cos\frac{2}{7}\pi + i\sin\frac{2}{7}\pi\right)$ (c) $\pm(1-i)$
   (d) $\pm(2+5i)$ (e) $\pm(1.098...+0.455...i)$
   (f) $\pm(3-2i)$

2. (a) $\pm\left(2+2\sqrt{3}\right)i$ (b) $\pm\left(\sqrt{3}+i\right), \ \pm\left(1-\sqrt{3}i\right)$

3. $e^z - e^{z^*}$ is imaginary, $e^z \div e^{z^*}$ has modulus 1.

5. (a) $e^{\frac{1}{3}\pi i}, \ e^{\frac{4}{3}\pi i}$ (b) $\pm\sqrt{e}(\cos1 + i\sin1)$

6. $i\tan y$

10. $e^{\cos\theta}, \ \sin\theta$

Miscellaneous exercise 11 (page 167)

1. (a) $\sec\alpha$ (b) $4\sec\alpha$ (c) $\frac{1}{2}\pi - \alpha$
   (d) $\frac{2}{5}\pi - \alpha$

2. $5, -0.927$;   (a) $\frac{5}{3}$ (b) 0.120

3. 6

4. Circle with centre $3+4i$ and radius 2;
   (a) 7 (b) $2\sin^{-1}0.4 \approx 0.823$

6. Interior and boundary of the circle with centre $-2+2\sqrt{3}i$ and radius 2;   (a) 2 (b) $\frac{5}{6}\pi$

7. (a) $-3\pm5i$ (b) $\sqrt{34}, \ \pm2.11$ (c) 10

8 (a) $\frac{1}{4}\pi$, $\frac{5}{6}\pi$ (b) 8, $-\frac{11}{12}\pi$

(c) Perpendicular bisector of line segment joining points representing α and β

(d) $\frac{13}{24}\pi$

9 (a) $-3-4\mathrm{i}$, $11-2\mathrm{i}$; $-1-2\mathrm{i}$, -5

(b) $\sqrt{5}$, ±2.03; 5, π

10 (a) 2, $\frac{1}{8}\pi$; $4\sqrt{2}$, $\frac{5}{8}\pi$; $8\sqrt{2}$, $\frac{3}{4}\pi$;

$\frac{1}{4}\sqrt{2}$, $-\frac{1}{2}\pi$

(b) $-8+8\mathrm{i}$

11 (a) $1-\sqrt{3}\mathrm{i}$, $-\frac{2}{3}$

(b) 2, $\frac{1}{3}\pi$; 2, $-\frac{1}{3}\pi$; 4, 0; 1, $\frac{2}{3}\pi$

(c) Circle with centre $1+\sqrt{3}\mathrm{i}$ and radius $\sqrt{3}$

(d) $1-\sqrt{3}\mathrm{i}$

12 (a) (i) Line through A parallel to OB
(ii) Line AB
(iii) Circle having AB as a diameter

13 $|f(1)-f(0)|=1$
$(g(z)=z$ and $g(w)=w^{*})\Rightarrow|z-w|=|z-w^{*}|$
$\Rightarrow \mathrm{Im}\,z\times\mathrm{Im}\,w=0\Rightarrow \mathrm{Im}\,z=0$ or $\mathrm{Im}\,w=0$;
$g(z)=z$ or $g(z)=z^{*}$
$f(z)=\alpha+\beta z$ with $|\beta|=1$ (rotation then translation) or $f(z)=\alpha+\beta z^{*}$ with $|\beta|=1$ (reflection in real axis then rotation then translation)

Revision exercise 2
(page 170)

1 (a) $\frac{8}{27}\sqrt{3}-\frac{2}{3}+\frac{1}{12}\pi$ (b) $2(\sqrt{2}-1)$

(c) $\frac{1}{4}\pi-\frac{1}{32}\pi^{2}-\frac{1}{2}\ln 2$ (d) $\frac{3}{25}\left(e^{\frac{3}{2}\pi}-1\right)$

2 Circle, centre at $r=1$, $\theta=\frac{1}{6}\pi$; 2, $\theta=-\frac{1}{3}\pi$

(or $\frac{2}{3}\pi$), $\theta=\frac{1}{6}\pi$; $r(\sin\theta-\sqrt{3}\cos\theta)=1$

3 (a) 0.1155 (b) 0.1163

4 $y=\frac{1}{7}\left(x^{2}-1+e^{-x^{2}}\right)$; $y=\frac{1}{4}x^{4}$

5 (a) $2+\mathrm{i}$ (b) $-2\pm3\mathrm{i}$ (c) i, $2+\mathrm{i}$

(d) $z=2+\mathrm{i}$, $w=\mathrm{i}$

6 (a) (i) 1, 0 (ii) 1, π (iii) 1, 0
(iv) 1, π (v) 1, 2θ (vi) 1, $2\theta-2\pi$
(vii) 1, 2θ (viii) 1, $2\theta+2\pi$

(b) (i) 2, 0 (ii) 0, undefined   (iii) 2, 0
(iv) 0, undefined   (v) $2\cos\theta$, θ
(vi) $-2\cos\theta$, $\theta-\pi$ (vii) $2\cos\theta$, θ
(viii) $-2\cos\theta$, $\theta+\pi$

7 (a) $\dfrac{a}{a^{2}+x^{2}}$, $\tan^{-1}\dfrac{x}{a}$ (b) $\left(\frac{1}{4}\pi-\frac{1}{2}\ln 2\right)a$

9 (a) $(x-1)(x^{2}+x+1)$, $(x+1)(x^{2}-x+1)$

(b) $(z-1)\left(z+\frac{1}{2}+\frac{1}{2}\sqrt{3}\mathrm{i}\right)\left(z+\frac{1}{2}-\frac{1}{2}\sqrt{3}\mathrm{i}\right)$,
$(z+1)\left(z-\frac{1}{2}+\frac{1}{2}\sqrt{3}\mathrm{i}\right)\left(z-\frac{1}{2}-\frac{1}{2}\sqrt{3}\mathrm{i}\right)$

(c) -1, 1; no roots; -1, 1

(d) ±1, $\pm\frac{1}{2}\pm\frac{1}{2}\sqrt{3}\mathrm{i}$; $\pm\mathrm{i}$, $\pm\frac{1}{2}\sqrt{3}\pm\frac{1}{2}\mathrm{i}$;
±1, $\pm\mathrm{i}$, $\pm\frac{1}{2}\pm\frac{1}{2}\sqrt{3}\mathrm{i}$, $\pm\frac{1}{2}\sqrt{3}\pm\frac{1}{2}\mathrm{i}$ (where the $\pm$ signs are independent of each other)

10 $0\leqslant x\leqslant1$; 1.791

11 $-\frac{1}{3}$, $\frac{3}{2}$, $-\frac{5}{12}$, $\frac{1}{12}$; $\ldots+\frac{1}{432}x^{6}$, $\ldots-\frac{1}{288}x^{6}$, second is better; $0.995\,004\,169$, $0.995\,004\,163$, $0.995\,004\,165$

12 (a) $y=0$, $y=x$ (b) $y=\dfrac{cx^{2}}{cx-1}$

(c) $y=\dfrac{x^{2}}{x+k}$, equivalent by taking $k=-\dfrac{1}{c}$

(d) $y=x-k+\dfrac{k^{2}}{x+k}$ has asymptotes $x=-k$ and $y=x-k$, stationary points at $(0,0)$ and $(-2k,-4k)$, approximates to $y=\dfrac{1}{k}x^{2}$ near $x=0$.

(e) From the differential equation, $\dfrac{\mathrm{d}y}{\mathrm{d}x}=0$ when $y(2x-y)=0$

(f) Bends upwards when $y>0$, downwards when $y<0$

13 (b) $\displaystyle\int_{-\pi}^{\pi}\dfrac{81}{2(5+4\cos\theta)^{2}}\,\mathrm{d}\theta$, 15π

(d) 25π, 15π

14 (b) $\cos 2\beta+\mathrm{i}\sin 2\beta$

(e) If angle $APB=\frac{1}{4}\pi$, P lies on a circle centre C, radius $\sqrt{2}$.

15 Examine the argument from 2 people to 3 people.

Mock examinations

Mock examination 1 (page 173)

2 (i) $x=1$, $y=-1$

(ii)

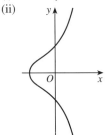

4 $y = \frac{1}{2}(x+y)^2$

5 (ii)

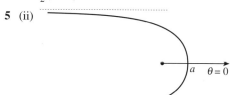

(iii) $2a^2$

6 $\dfrac{1}{x-2} - \dfrac{1}{x+2} + \dfrac{1}{x^2+1}$, $\ln\frac{1}{3} + \frac{1}{4}\pi$

7 $\frac{3}{4}$

8 (i) 1

(ii) and (iii)

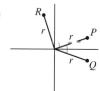

Mock examination 2 (page 175)

1 $\frac{1}{4}n(n+1)(n-8)(n+9)$

2 3, 7, 15, 31; $u_n = 2^n - 1$

3 $\dfrac{1}{1+(1+x)^2}$, $\dfrac{-2(1+x)}{\left(1+(1+x)^2\right)^2}$; $\frac{1}{4}\pi + \frac{1}{2}x - \frac{1}{4}x^2$

4 (i)

(ii) $|z| = r$

(iii) $\arg z = \frac{1}{4}\pi$

5 $y = \left(\frac{1}{4}\pi + \sin^{-1}x\right)\sqrt{1-x^2}$, $-\frac{1}{2}\sqrt{2}$

6 (i) $\frac{1}{4}a^2(\pi+2)$

(ii) $x^2 + y^2 = a(x+y)$;

centre is $\left(\frac{1}{2}a, \frac{1}{2}a\right)$ and radius is $\frac{1}{2}a\sqrt{2}$

(iii)

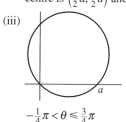

$-\frac{1}{4}\pi < \theta \leqslant \frac{3}{4}\pi$

7 (i) 4, $\frac{1}{3}\pi$

(ii) $\pm\left(\sqrt{3}+i\right)$

(iii) $1 - i\left(\sqrt{3}+\sqrt{2}\right), -1 + i\left(\sqrt{3}-\sqrt{2}\right)$

8 (i) $x = a$, $y = x + a$

(iii) $(0,0)$, $(2a,4a)$

(iv)

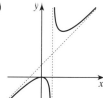

Index

The page numbers refer to the first mention of each term, or the shaded box if there is one.